MANAGERIAL ACCOUNTING AND CONTROL TECHNIQUES FOR THE NON-ACCOUNTANT

MANAGERIAL ACCOUNTING AND CONTROL TECHNIQUES FOR THE NON-ACCOUNTANT

Mary M. K. Fleming, DBA, CMA, CPA

Professor of Accounting
California State University, Fullerton

VNR VAN NOSTRAND REINHOLD COMPANY
NEW YORK   CINCINNATI   TORONTO   LONDON   MELBOURNE

Copyright © 1984 by Van Nostrand Reinhold Company Inc.

Library of Congress Catalog Card Number: 83-12412
ISBN: 0-442-22573-3

Manufactured in the United States of America

Published by Van Nostrand Reinhold Company Inc.
135 West 50th Street
New York, New York 10020

Van Nostrand Reinhold Company Limited
Molly Millars Lane
Wokingham, Berkshire RG11 2PY, England

Van Nostrand Reinhold
480 Latrobe Street
Melbourne, Victoria 3000, Australia

Macmillan of Canada
Division of Gage Publishing Limited
164 Commander Boulevard
Agincourt, Ontario M1S 3C7, Canada

15 14 13 12 11 10 9 8 7 6 5 4 3 2 1

Library of Congress Cataloging in Publication Data

Fleming, Mary M. K.
   Managerial accounting and control techniques for the
non-accountant.

   Includes index.
   1. Managerial accounting.   I. Title.
HF5635.F565   1984   658.1'511   83-12412
ISBN 0-442-22573-3

To
The John J. Katzer family

Preface

The purpose of this book is to present a comprehensive summary of the most important managerial accounting techniques and models useful for decision making by non-accountants. Accounting data serves as the basis for most business decisions. Whether managers operate in service, manufacturing, marketing, or nonprofit environments, rarely can they perform satisfactorily without extensive knowledge of accounting. To master the idiosyncrasies of accounting as taught through formal university accounting courses is tedious and time consuming. Knowledge of the technical aspects of accounting systems is not needed by non-accountants; hence we place little emphasis on the mechanical aspects of a basic financial/managerial accounting system.

This book is intended for:

1. Non-accounting managers, eg., engineering, sales, production, and purchasing. It is suitable for all levels of management including lower, middle and top executives. We expect readers' educational backgrounds to range from no university to beyond a graduate degree. Similarly, we expect management experience to vary from an entry level position to many years of experience, and size of the business from sole proprietorships to large multinational corporations.

2. Candidates aspiring to pass any one of the three professional *examinations:* (1) Certified Public Accountant (CPA), (2) Certified Internal Auditor (CIA), and especially (3) Certified Management Accountant (CMA). The CMA examination is a comprehensive examination covering decision models, and managerial and financial accounting. Most of the material in this book has been tested on the CMA examination during the last ten years; hence, the book can be very beneficial to individuals preparing for professional certification.

3. *University students.* Undergraduate and graduate students will find the book useful as supplementary material for managerial accounting and many other business courses. A combination of this book with one of the excellent case books currently available in the area of managerial accounting would constitute excellent study material for a graduate course in managerial accounting and control.

To aid clarity, understanding, and readability, the writing has been deliberately left simple and straightforward. Knowledge of business and accounting terms is essential for communication; consequently, general business terms are used and explained when appropriate. We attempt to define accounting terms in lay person's language rather than from a rigid technical viewpoint essential only to professional accountants.

This book assumes no previous knowledge of accounting, although a basic understanding of financial accounting is helpful. Therefore, after the introductory chapter we devote the next chapter to the three basic financial statements and Chapter 3 to those ratios helpful in assessing the significance of information contained in financial statements. Throughout the book we integrate financial accounting with managerial accounting because non-accounting managers have no reason to treat them as separate disciplines.

Because this book is not meant to be a text on general business theory and practice, readers are expected to have some knowledge of business practices. For example, we assume that readers generally understand the goal of profitability, how products are manufactured and marketed, the use of credit, and the substantial impact that human behavior has on decisions. Our purpose is to satisfy the information needs of managers already working in the business world, rather than introduce readers to an entirely new discipline.

We also assume limited mathematical capability. The engineer or mathematician may be frustrated by our efforts to keep the arithmetic simple, and the professional accountant will note the lack of sophistication in explaining accounting theory. It is hoped the nonmathematician and non-accountant will appreciate our efforts. Our goal is not to educate managers to be professional accountants, mathematicians, or computer experts, but to provide them with sufficient information so that they will know when to consult experts in other disciplines.

Emphasizing only the relevant, the practical, and the useful, we present few proofs, no scientific support of theory, limited philosophical discussion, and minimal quoting of research. The exceptions to normal situations are rarely expounded. We present the advantages and disadvantages of models as well as their limitations because this knowledge is essential for decision makers to ascertain if they are selecting the best decision model given the circumstances.

Although we expended extensive effort to keep the sequencing of chapters flexible, most readers will probably find it beneficial to study the first ten chapters in the order presented; thereafter, the remaining chapters may be selected for study in any order desired.

Most of the material in this book is based on lecture notes used for videotaping a 21-module course in management accounting and control by The American Graduate University. This course is designed as a broad-based survey course to provide students with an understanding of the conceptual framework of accounting, the role of reporting, and the analytical environment in which accountants function. Its objective is to educate managers in the intelligent use of accounting concepts that underlie corporate decisions, planning, and control. Therefore, it emphasizes the close relationship between accounting and financial management and the role of accounting in controlling current and future operations.

These videotapes, ranging from one half to one hour in length, are suitable for independent private study or group seminars. For further information contact:

The American Graduate University
733 North Dodsworth Avenue
Covina, California 91724
213 966-4576

Acknowledgment

We are indebted to all individuals who over the centuries have contributed to accounting thought. Specifically, we acknowledge the National Association of Accountants, The Institute of Management Accounting, the Financial Accounting Standards Board, and the American Institute of Certified Public Accountants. Special thanks to the staff of the American Graduate University, especially Mr. Paul McDonald, Sr., President, and Ms. Marie Sirney, Director of Research. Our colleagues and the accounting students at California State University, Fullerton, were very supportive of this project. Cynthia Fleming was most diligent in her proofreading efforts; all errors are our own.

Contents

MANAGERIAL ACCOUNTING AND CONTROL TECHNIQUES FOR THE NON-ACCOUNTANT

1. Introduction to Managerial Accounting

Three top executives of a small residential construction company were discussing their latest crisis.

"We are short of cash again; we just borrowed $20,000 last week, and already there is not enough cash to cover this month's bills."

"But we sold six houses during the month. Where did all that cash go?"

"We paid several subcontractors, and then there was the note due the 1st National Bank."

"I just don't understand why we aren't making more money; we're building a lot of houses and are having no trouble selling them."

"Our costs are quite high."

"Maybe the selling prices are too low."

"They include a 20% markup on total costs."

"Perhaps it's time to call in an accountant to look over the numbers."

The accountant found no budgets, inadequate cost-accounting records, and no control system. Costs per house were accumulated in memo form only. There was no attempt to reconcile the memo records with the formal financial accounting records. There were many errors and omissions. The majority of common costs such as street paving and utilities installation were never allocated to the houses sold. In reality, the firm's selling prices did not cover full costs, much less allow for a profit.

A major cause of business failure in the U.S. is inadequate knowledge of financial information. Managers must have pertinent data to make intelligent decisions. This book is concerned with the financial aspects of decision making. We will discuss how decisions are made and implemented and the nature of financial data inserted into decision models.

All organizations need information to operate effectively. The primary purpose of managerial accounting is to supply financial information required by managers to carry out their duties. All firms keep some sort of financial records, commonly referred to as the financial accounting system. Yet the financial and managerial accounting systems should not be mutually exclusive of each other. Rather, the managerial accounting system should be a subset of the financial accounting system; that is, it should supplement and complement financial accounting.

DIFFERENCES BETWEEN FINANCIAL AND MANAGERIAL ACCOUNTING

Let us start out by explaining a few of the fundamental differences between financial and managerial accounting. Most people have some knowledge of the functions of financial accounting. For example, they may know that financial accountants record economic transactions in accounting records, classify data, summarize data into meaningful classifications, and report the firm's current status and results of operations in financial statements to interested readers.

Independent financial accountants, called Certified Public Accountants (CPAs), are responsible for such activities as auditing, tax return preparation, tax consulting, and management services. In addition, some CPAs, notably in smaller firms, assist in record keeping and reporting, even to the point of maintaining a client's entire set of books.

Managerial accountants are a great deal more interested in providing financial data to users within the firm. These data can be and usually are reported in a very different format than published financial statements. Managerial accountants focus their interest on the direct needs of users, whom many times managerial accountants are personally acquainted with and whose information needs, therefore, they often have first-hand knowledge of.

Throughout this book, we shall assume that the goal of the firm is profits and that internal users of financial data are attempting to maximize profits. Many of the principles we will be discussing are equally applicable to nonprofit organizations, whose goals may be the optimal rendering of goods and services to their constituents.

Although each organization may be unique, all have similar characteristics. For example, each will have:

1. Established objectives
2. Strategies designed to assist in achieving these objectives
3. Individuals performing the functions of managers
4. Responsibility relationships among managers
5. Need for accounting information

What are some of the important differences between financial and managerial accounting?

1. First, as to users, we repeat, financial accountants tend to serve interested groups outside the firm. Among the more noteworthy are investors and potential investors (commonly called stockholders), creditors, consumer groups, labor, financial institutions, and governmental agencies. Managerial accountants focus on the needs of management personnel working within the firm; hence the users are internal rather than external.

2. Financial reporting takes three basic formats:

Balance sheet—reports the properties owned by the firm, its liabilities, and ownership as of a given point in time.

Income statement—reflects revenue earned and expenses incurred by the organization during a specified period of time. The difference between revenue and expenses is a residual amount called profit or loss.

Statement of changes in financial position—explains the sources of funds during a specified period and how these funds were utilized.

The financial statements report in part how well managers are performing their stewardship function.

The report formats used internally are not as well structured as the three basic financial statements. Internal reports can have any appearance, style, and content.

3. Financial reports are published periodically, at least once a year, but most firms desire quarterly or monthly reporting. It should be pointed out that the more frequent the reporting, the less accurate. Theoretically, we cannot precisely measure the total profit or loss of a firm until the firm ceases to exist, but we can approximate measurements that are good enough for reporting and evaluation purposes.

Managerial reports are disseminated when needed as determined by management. Many managerial reports are compiled periodically, such as weekly payroll or daily spoilage reports. Others, such as the cost of a labor strike, are issued on an exception basis only.

4. Financial reports tend to focus on the past, whereas managerial reports emphasize the future. This is because the users of the latter are making decisions affecting the future rather than the past.

5. Since financial reports reflect past events, the basis of measurement is primarily historical. There has been a growing departure from this tradition in recent years. Internal reports may encompass many valuation methods, such as constant dollars, replacement cost, present value of future earnings, or reproduction costs. Many of these models are not as precise or objective as historical costs. Still, sometimes, historical data can be very relevant in serving as a guide to future expectations. If not, another measurement base may be more appropriate.

6. Various government agencies require financial accounting. The Internal Revenue Service specifies that sufficiently detailed accounting records be maintained in order to determine taxable income in accordance with its code and regulations. Large firms must comply with the extensive reporting require-

ments of the Securities and Exchange Commission. Today, the extent of governmental reporting requirements is vast.

Internal reports are prepared strictly at the option of management. Their optional rather than mandatory character leads to some interesting results. Many managers are so overloaded with paperwork that they spend most of their time preparing reports rather than utilizing them. On the opposite end is the firm, usually those of a smaller size, where no formal reporting is done. Management may not know what information is available, what they need for decisions, or what to do with it, if furnished. Managers may even pride themselves on the ability to keep all relevant data in their heads. It is little wonder that the majority of smaller firms do not enjoy longevity in the United States.

7. Financial accountants record, measure, and report transactions according to generally accepted accounting principles. There is no one comprehensive set of accounting principles, but standards issued by the Financial Accounting Standards Board and its predecessor, the Accounting Principles Board, are considered to be authoritative. This basically means that the burden of justification for departures rests with the individual advocating superior methods.

There are no generally accepted accounting principles that managerial accountants must comply with. Any monetary or physical measurement can be appropriate. Keep in mind, however, what we said previously, that the managerial accounting system should be a subset of and reconcilable with the financial accounting system. Numerous fragmented sets of books, each with its own valuation methods, are costly and confusing. Hence, we can conclude that the emphasis in financial accounting is on adherence to generally accepted accounting principles, whereas relevance and flexibility of data are key attributes of internal reporting.

8. Financial reports cover the entire firm. Consolidated reports are usually prepared when one firm has a controllable interest in another. Intercompany transactions are eliminated in consolidated reports. To provide the reader with more details, frequently segment reporting by division, product line, customer, and so on, supplement the basic financial statements.

Internal reporting can cover the spectrum from extreme detail to highly aggregated data. For example, a shop foreman may want hourly spoilage for each machine, whereas the president may only desire an annual reporting of the total spoilage cost. Internal reports can focus on any part of the firm, any product, division, machine, department, service, or employee.

9. Financial reporting is a relatively independent discipline, whereas managerial accounting is very dependent on other disciplines. The decision-making function is closely related to psychology, learning theory, and management. Numerous mathematical models are helpful to solve problems, many of which require computer capability. Control of material and labor overlap in the fields of purchasing, production management, personnel, and engineering. Manage-

rial accounting is strongly rooted in economics, which is the study of the optimal utilization of scarce resources to satisfy human wants.

PROFESSIONAL CERTIFICATION

We have just finished discussing some of the characteristics that differentiate financial from managerial accounting. Turning our attention now to professional certification, we can distinguish two types of certified accountant: Certified Public Accountant (CPA) and Certified Management Accountant (CMA). The Certified Public Accountant audits the books and records supporting published financial statements. The Certified Management Accountant is a professional who has obtained managerial accounting competence. Both the CPA and CMA pass a rigorous two-and-a-half day examination given twice a year.

Certified Public Accountant

The Certified Public Accountant's examination is administered by the American Institute of Certified Public Accountants, and candidates are licensed by the state board of accountancy in the state where the candidate is a resident. The examination covers four areas—accounting problems, accounting theory, auditing, and business law. A college education, several years of experience, and high moral character are requirements for certification in most states.

Certified Management Accountant

The Certified Management Accountant's examination is given by the Institute of Management Accounting, which is associated with the National Association of Accountants. It is a broader examination in that in addition to accounting, it covers finance, economics, management, and decision models. The work experience requirement is two years. After certification, the CMA must comply with an education requirement of 120 hours every three years. More than one half of the states have similar continuing education requirements for practicing CPAs.

A prominent professional organization for CMAs and managerial accountants is the National Association of Accountants, an organization devoted to the development and dissemination of cost-accounting theory and practice. Its house organ is *Management Accounting*.

The American Institute of Certified Public Accountants (AICPA) is a national professional association of CPAs. Its monthly publication is the *Journal of Accountancy*. The AICPA is the recognized authority in areas of public accounting and auditors' reports.

FUNCTIONS OF MANAGERS

Since the purpose of managerial accounting is to aid managers, let us turn our attention to the functions of managers. We define the responsibilities of managers as:

1. Planning
2. Organizing
3. Directing
4. Controlling
5. Decision making

Planning

In planning, managers determine which steps are most advantageous to lead to desired goals. Note that establishment of goals is essential before valid plans can be made. An example of planning is budgeting, but first, a word or two of caution: Good planning does not mean a blind adherence to plans in the face of changes in the environment or evidence of a misreading of the strategic factors on which the original plans were based. Should subsequent events indicate that the original plan is no longer valid, the plan should be revised. Hence, a plan, such as a budget, should not be an inflexible dictator of performance. Changes in our economy are inevitable and even desirable in many situations. Good managers are constantly on the lookout for how changing conditions will affect the firm. They seek methods of capitalizing on change, to the advantage of the firm rather than to its detriment.

Organizing

Organizing consists of determining which combination of human and other resources will best carry out the firm's plans. It includes identifying a strategic fit between resources and the firm's environment.

Directing

Directing is the supervisory function and is more concerned with the overseeing of day-to-day activities.

Controlling

Controlling is taking whatever steps are essential to ensure that all parts of an organization are functioning efficiently and effectively. (1) Efficiency has to do with producing the largest possible outputs from a given quantity of inputs. (2)

Effectiveness is measured by how well the expected or intended results are achieved. In reality, control is exercised over people who incur costs rather than over the costs themselves. The emphasis in this book is on the planning, controlling, and decision-making functions of managers. The planning and controlling processes can be further defined as follows:

Strategic Planning. Strategic planning consists of broad strategies to help the organization obtain its goals. Strategic planning is long range, considers all variables that have an impact on the firm, cuts across all horizons of the firm, and results in policies and procedures.

Management Control. Management control ensures that the firm's strategies are carried out. Hence, it is result oriented and involves the whole organization. In addition, it tends to be periodic, for example, a monthly comparison of total orders obtained with orders shipped.

Operational Control. Operational control is task oriented and closely related to the interest of a particular department or operation. It consists of day-by-day surveillance. The foreman may establish a tolerance range in which a machine is assumed to be operating satisfactorily. The machine is out of control if it exceeds the range.

Decision Making

Decision making is concerned with selecting the best, most rational choice among alternatives. Good reliable information is essential for sound decisions. What are the steps in decision making?

1. *Defining the problem.* This is perhaps the most important step because errors in problem identification lead to errors of decision. It is also the most difficult step. In highly complex situations the problem is not always obvious.

2. *Identifying alternatives.* Many times it is necessary to limit the number of alternatives in the interest of cost and expediency. Imagine an investor attempting to analyze all stock listed on a national stock exchange. Such a task is humanly impossible and the passing of time and the changing environment would nullify much of the analysis completed.

3. *Accumulating relevant information.* As in identifying alternatives, boundaries must be placed on the amount of information accumulated. Individuals who seek unlimited data are unable to assimilate all the information they acquire. Thus, the information remains unprocessed in a condition called "information overload." The role of information in decision making is to increase knowledge to the point where the benefits of a rational decision exceed the costs. Usually, accumulating information is necessary to minimize or control risk.

4. *Making the decision.* The decision maker must utilize a decision model in making the decision. It may be a very simple one, such as rejecting all lots with two or more defective items, or a highly complex model such as many capital

acquisition models, which we discuss later. It is essential that the model be fitted to the problem. Solutions generated by models are only as good as the input data. Managers should be aware of the strengths and limitations of the model used. Irrational adherence to the output of models is hardly effective management. In this book we discuss many decision models, including their input, strengths, limitations, and uses.

Research shows that most individuals make decisions based on relatively few variables—seldom more than six. Individuals may not be cognizant of the variables involved, especially when they are psychological in nature. For example, a person may accept a job offer from a friend, rationalizing that the job is close to home. His "real" reason for accepting the position is that he is fearful of going on interviews.

Systems Approach. Many problems overlap several areas of responsibility. A systems approach may be useful for solving complex business problems. The systems approach is global in scope in that it considers all interrelationships and associated variables. A task force of representatives from the areas affected serves to study various facets of the problem and propose alternate solutions. For example, assume that the firm is considering introducing a major new product line. The task force might consist of representatives from marketing, engineering, production, and accounting. Each representative would contribute his or her expertise in identifying variables critical to the success or failure of the new product line. A systems approach requires that the problem be manageable in size and that all aspects be comprehensible by the participants.

MANAGERIAL ACCOUNTANTS' FUNCTION

We said that the managerial accountant's function is to supply data needed for the five responsibilities of managers: planning, organizing, directing, controlling, and decision making. This includes furnishing not only financial data, but information of a nonfinancial nature, like the number of employees in a department or the gross weight of daily shipments. The complexities of such a task can be overwhelming because the need for data is nearly unlimited and the cost of furnishing it is high. Balancing costs with benefits is essential. Additionally, useful data must possess the properties of relevance, timeliness, and accuracy.

DETERMINING DATA TO FURNISH

How do accountants know what data to furnish? Certainly data essential to monitoring key variables should be supplied. Every firm must identify several key variables useful in measuring progress and explaining success or failure. Larger firms may wish to establish key variables for each major activity. For example, the Marketing Department's key variables may be sales quantity, sales dollars, and number of new customers. Variables should be volatile in nature and serve as an early warning system should significant changes occur that require prompt management action.

Some theorists maintain that information should serve one or more of the following three functions:

1. Scorekeeping
2. Attention directing
3. Problem solving

Scorekeeping data demonstrate how well the company objectives are being met. For example, the budget is established as the formal plan for how the firm intends to meet its objective, say, a profit of one million dollars. Revenue and expenses are estimated. In the scorekeeping function, actual revenue and actual expenses are recorded in the accounting records.

Attention-directing data draw managers' attention to problems. In the above illustration, a comparison of budgeted with actual revenue can inform managers which products, divisions, salesmen, and so forth are performing better or worse than expected.

Finally, problem-solving data focus on the best solution to a problem or the best method of performing a task. Again, referring to our previous example, we might find that product A is not selling well. Problem-solving data might consist of an analysis of the pricing structure, competitors, markets, advertising, and selling techniques.

It is important to reemphasize that the amount of data furnished must be kept under control. Remember that all data is subject to the law of diminishing productivity; that is, as more and more data are furnished, each incremental piece is unlikely to have the same information content as the piece preceding it. Hence, a "data dump" on managers is not the best means of scorekeeping, attention directing, and problem solving. Much control should take the form of management-by-exception. This simply means drawing managers' attention to significant deviations from expected performance, rather than reporting all results.

INTERRELATIONSHIPS AMONG MANAGERS' FUNCTIONS

The interrelationship among the functions of managers can be seen in Exhibit 1-1. An organization must first define its goals, stating the direction in which the firm will operate. Goals should be stated in writing and ranked according to order of priority. The organizing function consists of gathering together the resources of the firm in the most effective combination. Of course, the optimal

Exhibit 1-1
Functions of Managers.

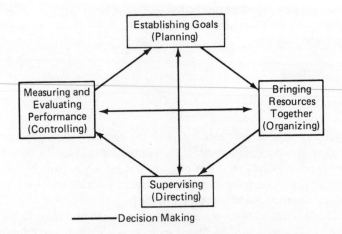

combination is never known with absolute certainty. The coordination of resources takes the form of directing activities. Motivation of employees is a key element. Finally, the firm must measure performance and compare it to a predetermined standard, a budget, for instance. Undesirable deviations can be corrected at this time and if needed, the goals may have to be revised.

Note that this model is a feedback model whose components have an impact on each other. Without feedback we cannot have a real control system. Obviously, a communication network serves as a means of transmitting information among the components. The components can be depicted in an organization chart.

ORGANIZATION CHART

The organization chart indicates the formal responsibilities of the company's major management positions. Firms also have an informal organization that may many times be more indicative of actual behavior than the formal organization.

A typical organization chart for a manufacturing firm would look like Exhibit 1-2. A person can view the organization chart by its functions, line or staff. If there is a direct line of authority from one position to another, a line function exists. The president has line authority over the vice president of manufacturing. If a function serves to support or advise another position, it serves in a staff capacity. Staff cannot issue orders or directives to correct deficiencies.

Exhibit 1-2
Organization Chart.

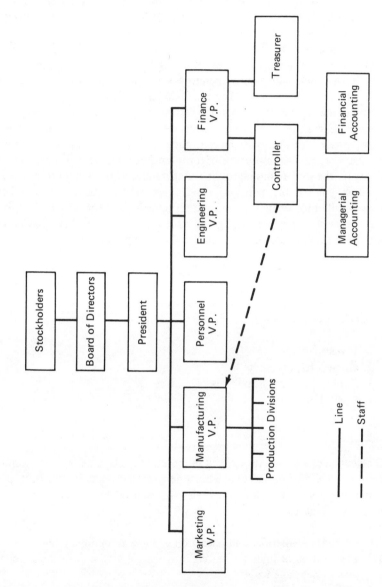

In this book, we are primarily interested in the positions of financial managers. The treasurer and the controller report to the vice president of finance, who in turn has line authority over them. Similarly, the treasurer and controller have line authority over employees reporting to them. But the controller does not have line authority over the vice president of manufacturing, managers of production divisions, or any employee reporting to these individuals. The controller serves in a staff capacity insofar as these individuals are concerned. Hence, the controller cannot dictate corrective action to a foreman, say, for unfavorable labor variance. The controller can only advise.

Sometimes we say that a position can have functional authority over another position. This simply means a very narrow range of line authority is given to a staff position. For example, the controller might have functional authority over the shop foreman as to the type of form the foreman uses to report labor hours.

Again, the understanding of line/staff relationships is important because as we already noted, the managerial accountant who is part of the controller staff is responsible for compiling accounting reports used for control. Yet, it is the line supervisors, not the managerial accountant or controller, who utilize the data for planning, corrective action, and decision making.

Treasurer

The treasurer is responsible for custody of the corporate funds. Typically, his or her duties include:

1. Investments
2. Capital requirements
3. Banking and credit policies
4. Cash flow

Controller

The controller's duties are defined in more detail since he or she is responsible for supplying information to line managers for decisions. Most aspects of managerial accounting are associated with the controller's functions. Some of the most important are:

1. Design, installation, and operation of the accounting system
2. Preparation of financial statements, tax returns, and financial reports to government agencies
3. Design, installation, and operation of programming and budgeting systems
4. Preparation and analysis of performance reports

5. Advice to managers on financial matters
6. Establishment of adequate safeguards against errors, theft, and defalcations

SUMMARY

We discussed the differences between managerial and financial accounting, the functions of managers, how decisions are made, and the role of managerial accounting in the decision-making process. The duties of the treasurer and controller were defined and their positions noted on the organization chart. In the next chapter we discuss financial statements and their significance.

2. Overview of Financial Statements

INTRODUCTION

In a short chapter we of course cannot teach you all there is to know about financial statements or make you into a financial accountant. Rather our intent is for you to become sufficiently familiar with financial statements to use them for decision making and to know how material discussed later in the book relates to financial statements. In order to utilize financial reports, you must have an understanding of the terms, the methods of measurement, and the interrelationships of the accounts reported.

A frequent misconception about financial statements is that they report precise information. This is not true. Many of the figures are estimated, and judgment plays an important role in reporting, as it does in the auditing of financial statements by independent accountants. The data on financial statements tend to be highly aggregated and condensed. The Financial Accounting Standards Board has narrowed the number of generally accepted accounting principles to account for an economic event and has extensively standardized the types and extent of information disclosure. Still, there is considerable room for variation from one reporting entity to another.

USERS OF FINANCIAL STATEMENTS

Financial statements are prepared by management and reviewed by independent auditors. Certified Public Accountants do not prepare audited financial statements, as is frequently assumed.

There are many individuals interested in the financial reports of a firm. The Financial Accounting Standards Board has taken the position that financial statements are primarily prepared for investors and potential investors. Some of the other publics who rely on financial reports are:

1. Creditors and suppliers
2. Employees and labor unions
3. Governmental agencies
4. Regulatory bodies
5. Financial analysis firms
6. General public

We could add managers, but managers generally need much more current information and in considerably more detail than the financial statements offer. Still, the statements provide them with a good summary of financial activities during the period as well as the current financial position of the firm.

TYPES OF FINANCIAL STATEMENTS

There are three basic financial statements:

1. *Balance sheet,* sometimes called *statement of financial position* or *statement of assets and equities*
2. *Income statement,* also called *profit and loss statement* or *revenue and expense statement*
3. *Statement of changes in financial position* or *funds statement*

Notes and accompanying schedules are part of financial statements, and information is presented several ways:

1. Parenthetically.

   Marketable Securities (lower of cost or market, market
   $10,000) $8,000

2. Short—no amount is added to other accounts.

   Contingent liability. Former employee has sued for $1 million
   for injury sustained during employment.

3. Footnotes. These may be quite lengthy and detailed.
4. Schedules. These are used primarily for lengthy disclosure of numerical data.

BALANCE SHEET

The balance sheet shows the financial status of the firm. It provides information concerning assets, liabilities, and ownership at a given instance of time, that is, the date of the balance sheet. Usually, more than one year of data is provided so the firm's current standing can be compared with preceding periods. A balance sheet for a typical small manufacturing firm is presented as Exhibit 2-1.

Note that the date of the balance sheet is December 31, 19X3. On the left-hand side we generally list the assets while the right hand side consists of lia-

Exhibit 2-1
ABC COMPANY
Balance Sheet
as of December 31, 19X3
(In Thousands of Dollars)

ASSETS

CURRENT ASSETS:

Cash		$ 490	
Marketable securities (at cost, market value $700)		600	
Notes receivable		350	
Accounts receivable	$1,000		
Less: Allowance for doubtful accounts	50	950	
Inventories (lower of cost or market, FIFO)		1,800	
Prepaid assets		50	
Total Current Assets			$ 4,240

INVESTMENTS:

Stock of affiliated companies (at cost—5% ownership)	$1,040	
Fund for retirement of bonds	300	
Land for future plant	600	
Cash surrender value of life insurance	100	
Total Investments		$ 2,040

PLANT ASSETS:

	Cost	Acc. Depc'n	Book Value	
Land	$1,000		$1,000	
Buildings	5,000	$2,500	2,500	
Equipment	1,000	500	500	
Total Plant and Equip.	$7,000	$3,000	$4,000	$ 4,000

INTANGIBLES:

Goodwill (net of amortization)	$ 100	
Patents (net of amortization)	50	
Trademarks	25	
Total Intangibles		$ 175
TOTAL ASSETS		$10,455

LIABILITIES AND STOCKHOLDERS' EQUITY
LIABILITIES

CURRENT LIABILITIES:

Trade accounts payable	$ 700	
Accrued liabilities	115	
Income tax payable	125	
Advances by employees	60	
Employees' retirement benefits, payable in current period	40	
Notes payable in current period	1,000	
Total Current Liabilities		$ 2,040

LONG TERM LIABILITIES:

7% Bonds payable, due December 31, 19X5	$ 2,000	
Less: Discount on bonds payable	150	
Net bonds payable	1,850	
Mortgage payable (secured by buildings)	1,200	
Employees' retirement benefits payable in future years	800	
Deferred income taxes	565	
Total Long-Term Liabilities		$ 4,415
TOTAL LIABILITIES:		$ 6,455

STOCKHOLDERS' EQUITY

Paid in capital

10% cumulative preferred stock $100 par (callable at $110 a share, authorized 1000 shares, outstanding 900 shares)	$ 90	
Common stock $10 par, (authorized 800,000 shares, outstanding 300,000 shares)	3,000	
Paid in capital in excess of par		
On preferred stock	15	
On common stock	100	
Total Paid in Capital	$ 3,205	

Retained Earnings

Balance, January 1, 19X3	$595	
Income for 19X3	609	
Less dividends declared during 19X3: Preferred stock (9)		
Common stock (400)		
Total Retained Earnings, December 31, 19x3	795	

TOTAL STOCKHOLDERS' EQUITY	$ 4,000
TOTAL LIABILITIES AND STOCKHOLDERS' EQUITY	$10,455

bilities and ownership. An alternate way is to put assets on the top of the page, followed by liabilities and ownership.

Assets

Assets are expected future economic benefits arising from current or past transactions. Hence, they are items of value owned by the firm, or items that the firm has economic rights to, such as leases. We usually detail assets by type: current, investments, plant, and intangibles. Such a classification enables the reader to grasp significant relationships, many of which can be expressed as a ratio.

Current Assets.   Current assets consist of cash and other assets that are expected to be converted into cash or consumed in operations within a relatively short period of time called the *current period*. The current period is abitrarily established at one year or the operating cycle if it exceeds one year. The operating cycle is the period of time it takes the firm to convert an activity from its initial state into cash. Study the diagram in Chart 2-1.

Some firms have very short operating cycles, such as bakeries; others have very long ones, such as shipbuilders. Obviously, if the firm operates on a cash basis in lieu of credit, the cycle is shorter. Similarly, shortening the period of holding inventory or receivables decreases the operating cycle accordingly.

Current assets are normally listed according to the order of liquidity, that is, how soon they will be converted into cash. Therefore, the most current asset is cash.

Cash.   Cash consists of cash on hand and all checking and saving accounts that are not subject to time or use restrictions. A bond sinking fund restricted solely to the redemption of long-term bonds payable would not be listed as a current asset. Rather it would be classified as an investment.

Marketable Securities.   In order for securities to be classified as current, they must meet two criteria:

1. Management must intend to liquidate them within the current period, and
2. They must be readily marketable.

Securities failing to meet both requirements are classified as investments. Marketable securities are shown on the balance sheet at lower of cost or market. If cost is below market, the presentation is:

Marketable securities, lower of cost or market (market $700) $600

Chart 2-1

If cost is higher than market, the firm retains the cost in its account, but uses a valuation account for balance sheet presentation. A valuation account (also called a contra account) reduces the basic account to a different valuation. Assume the cost is $800 and the market value is $700. The presentation would look like this:

Marketable securities, lower of cost or market		
At cost	$800	
Less: allowance to reduce account to lower of cost or market	100	
Net marketable securities, at market		$700

Remember that lower of cost or market is determined by a comparison of the aggregate cost of all marketable securities with their aggregate market, rather than by each security separately. The amount required each period to adjust the allowance account to lower of cost or market is reported on the income statement.

Receivables.   If material in amount, each type of receivable should be shown separately. Examples include short-term notes receivables, interest receivables, and receivables from officers and employees. A large dollar amount is likely to be accounts (trade) receivable. Since we are interested in liquidity, we normally report receivables at net realizable value. Hence, we again use a valuation account to reduce receivables from their historical-cost basis to expected cash inflow.

There are several popular methods for estimating the amount considered to be uncollectible:

1. A percentage of total sales or sales on account
2. A percentage of accounts receivable
3. An aging of accounts receivable, with higher estimates of uncollectibility for older accounts. An example of an aging schedule follows:

AGE OF RECEIVABLE	GROSS ACCOUNT RECEIVABLE	PERCENTAGE ESTIMATED TO BE UNCOLLECTIBLE	ALLOWANCE FOR UNCOLLECTIBLE ACCOUNTS
Under 30 days	$500,000	.024	$12,000
30–60 days	300,000	.050	15,000
61–90 days	180,000	.100	18,000
over 91 days	20,000	.250	5,000
	$1,000,000		$50,000

Hence, you can see that the older the receivable, the higher the probability of uncollectibility. The amount reported on the balance sheet as uncollectible is $50,000.

Percentages used in each of the above models are based on past experience, adjusted for future expectations. The amount required each period to adjust the *allowance for bad debts* is reported on the income statement as *bad debt expense.*

Inventories.   Inventories are items held for resale, which, for manufacturing firms, are usually detailed by type of inventory: raw material, work in process, and finished goods. Inventories are normally listed on the balance sheet at lower of cost or market, with the amount required each period to adjust the account to lower of cost or market being reported on the income statement. Determination of lower of cost or market can be calculated individually on each item of inventory, by major product classification, or by aggregated inventory. In addition, the method of cost flow is disclosed. We explain inventory cost flow methods in Chapter 16.

Prepaid Assets.   Prepaid assets are future expenses that have been paid in advance. For example, if year 4's rent of $5,000 was prepaid in year 3, the $5,000 would appear as a prepaid asset on year 3's balance sheet and rent expense on year 4's income statement. Other types of prepaid assets include interest, taxes, insurance, and supplies.

At this point we total the current assets. The total is a significant figure in assessing the liquidity of the firm, a point to be discussed more fully in the next chapter.

Investments.   Investments refer to holdings of a relatively permanent nature. Some of the more common ones are discussed below.

Stock of Affiliated Companies.   The parent company uses the cost method of recording its investment in common stock of another firm if the parent company does not exercise significant influence (i.e., control of the board of directors) over the subsidiary. Significant influence is assumed to be absent if the parent owns less than 20% of the outstanding voting stock of the subsidiary. Under the cost method, the investment is recorded at cost, and dividends are reported on the income statement as revenue when received. No entry is made on the parent company's books when the subsidiary earns a profit or loss.

When significant influence is present the parent company uses the equity method in accounting for its investment in a subsidiary. Under the equity method, the parent company records the investment at cost, increases the investment account for its portion of the subsidiary's income (or decreases it if the subsidiary reports a loss), and decreases the investment account when dividends are declared by the subsidiary.

On the parent company's income statement, the difference between the cost and equity method is that:

1. No income of the subsidiary is reported under the cost method, whereas the parent company's portion of the subsidiary's income is reported under the equity method.

2. Dividends declared by the subsidiary are reported as dividend revenue on the parent's books under the cost method, whereas no dividend income is included under the equity method.

If the parent owns more than 50% of a subsidiary voting stock, consolidated financial statements are usually prepared. This means that the financial statements of the parent and subsidiary are combined after eliminating intercompany transactions.

Unconsolidated investments in affiliated companies (cost or equity method) are reported on the balance sheet at lower of cost or market. Like marketable securities, a valuation account is used to reduce cost to market, but unlike marketable securities, the offsetting entry is a reduction of stockholders' equity, rather than an income statement account.

Investment in bonds is also shown at lower of cost or market, with cost being defined as book value. Book value is original cost adjusted for any unamortized premium or discount. The difference between cost and maturity amount is written off to interest income over the life of the bonds. Thus, a purchase in excess of maturity results in a premium, and the effective rate of interest is less than the face rate. On the other hand, bonds purchased at a discount (less than par) have a higher effective interest rate. When the discount is amortized to the income statement, it increases interest income.

Fund for Retirement of Bonds.   Sinking funds and special purpose funds that are not available for payment of current liabilities are classified as investments. These funds may be required by contract (i.e., bond indenture), by law, or by management prerogative. The nature of any restrictions on the funds should be disclosed.

Land for Future Plant.   Land acquired for a future plant site is not a current asset nor a plant asset. The same thing is true of assets not currently being used in production.

Cash Surrender Value of Life Insurance.   This account appears on the balance sheet only when the firm owns the policies and is the beneficiary should the insuree die.

Other kinds of investments include long-term notes receivables and advances to subsidiaries that are not expected to be converted into cash within the current period.

Plant Assets   Plant assets consist of long-lived items of a tangible nature used in the operation of business, rather than held for resale. They are usually recorded on the books at cost and reported on the balance sheet net of accumulated depreciation. Depreciation is an allocation of cost to expense using a systematic rational method. Hence, each period a portion of the cost of a plant asset is transferred to the income statement as an expense. The total amount written off from acquisition of the asset to the balance sheet date is *accumulated depreciation.* Cost less accumulated depreciation is called *book value,* and it is this figure that is added to other assets on the balance sheet. Since land generally does not wear out, no depreciation is deducted. Leasehold improvements are depreciated and capitalized leases (although technically intangible assets but treated as plant assets) are amortized to expense over their useful lives, which in both cases is usually the lease term.

Intangible Assets.   Intangibles represent amortizable operating assets that lack physical substance. They are written off to expense over their useful lives, not to exceed 40 years. Five years is a common write-off period since this period is sanctioned by the Internal Revenue Service for tax purposes. Intangibles usually are shown net of amortization; however, an accumulated amortization account (much like accumulated depreciation) is permissible. Amortization is in substance like the concept of depreciation. The current period's amortization write-off is an expense on the income statement.

Some examples of intangible assets include goodwill (only if purchased), patents, copyrights, trademarks, and secret recipes. Research and development expenses are not capitalized as intangible assets even if they possess future economic value.

Liabilities

Liabilities are economic obligations of the firm. The firm settles obligations through conveyance of assets or performance of services.

Current Liabilities   Current liabilities are expected to be satisfied with the use of current assets. Most current liabilities are paid for with cash. Deferred revenue accounts are liquidated by delivery of goods or services. Another way of satisfying current liabilities is through renegotiation of a long-term liability or equity. The Financial Accounting Standards Board has taken the position that a liability coming due within the current period should be classified as a current liability unless the firm:

1. Has the intent to renegotiate the liability and
2. Can demonstrate the ability to do so

Current liabilities may be listed on the balance sheet according to order of magnitude, due date, alphabetically, or by some other rational method.

Trade Accounts Payable.   Trade accounts payable arise from the purchase of inventory. It is usually a relatively high dollar account. If purchase discounts are material in amount, trade accounts payable should be shown net of discounts.

Accrued Liabilities.   Accrued liabilities include debt accrued because of the passage of time. Examples are rent, taxes, interest, bonuses, salaries, and wages.

Income Tax Payable.   This account includes income taxes currently payable to city, state, or federal governments.

Advances by Employees. Firms frequently owe officers and employees for travel, entertainment, and other reimbursable obligations when funds have not been adequately advanced. Loans from officers and employees would also be included in this category.

Employees' Retirement Benefits. Most employees' retirement benefits are likely to be of a long-term nature; however, the amount due within the current period should be classified as a current liability.

Notes Payable. The current portion of notes payable is a current liability. Many firms issue notes in lieu of open accounts. The value of notes over open accounts to the holder is that notes usually carry interest, are validated in writing, and are more legally enforceable since the maker has implicitly accepted the value and quality of goods or service received.

Long-Term Liabilities. These liabilities are not expected to be satisfied from current assets. They are debts in which liquidation is expected to occur after a relatively long period of time; hence they are reported on the balance sheet at present value.

Bonds Payable. Most bonds are issued in a denomination of $1,000 each, meaning that $1,000 is payable to the holder of the bond at maturity. If an 8% bond sells for more than $1,000, say $1,050, it sells at a premium. The premium of $50 is written off (amortized) against interest expense over the life of the bond; therefore, the effective rate of interest is less than 8%. Any unamortized premium is added to the maturity amount of the bond for balance sheet presentation.

Conversely, if a bond sells for less than par, it sells at a discount, and the effective rate of interest is higher than the face rate. Amortizing the discount increases interest expense. The bonds are shown on the balance sheet net of the unamortized discount. In our illustration, Exhibit 2-1, the maturity amount of the bonds is two million dollars; there is $150,000 unamortized discount remaining to be written off to interest expense on future income statements.

Other information commonly disclosed for bonds includes their face rates of interest, dates of interest payments, due dates, types of bonds, collateral, sinking fund requirements, and any restrictions on retained earnings.

Mortgage Payable. Mortgages generally are secured by collateral such as buildings, equipment, or inventories. Additional disclosures required include the interest rate, the life of mortgage, and the amount of periodic payments.

Employee Retirement Benefits. This account includes the long-term portion of pensions to former and current employees. It is one of the few long-term liabilities that is not reported at present value. The complexity of the measurement of the amount owed is beyond the scope of this book.

Deferred Income Taxes. Income taxes deferred because of timing differences, that is, the income tax effect on differences between book income and taxable income, can be current or long term. Since most firms attempt to postpone the payment of income taxes as long as possible, the magnitude of this account can be high. Further explanation concerning the nature and measurement of this account is deferred to Chapter 17.

Stockholders' Equity

Stockholders' equity is the net worth of the firm, or total assets less total liabilities. We usually break stockholders' equity into two parts: paid-in capital and retained earnings.

Paid-in Capital. Paid-in capital consists of the total amount originally paid in to the firm in exchange for stock. For each of the two classifications of stock, preferred or common, we show par and the amount the stock sold for in excess of par. This excess is called by many names such as paid-in capital in excess of par, premium on stock, or contributed capital in excess of par. Par, which is stated in the corporate charter, is the amount which must be retained in the firm. In other words, dividends cannot be paid out of par. In some states, dividends cannot be paid out of paid-in capital in excess of par either. If they are the stockholders must be notified accordingly because these dividends are in reality a return of capital instead of dividend income. The result to the recipient is a reduction of the amount recorded in the investment account (an asset on the stockholders' books).

Preferred Stock. Stock that is preferred as to income, liquidation, or other privilege is preferred stock. The dividend rate must be shown. A flat dollar amount per share, say $5, means that each share carries an annual dividend rate of $5. Another way of stating dividends is by percentage of par. An 8% preferred stock means that the annual dividend rate is 8% of par.

The nature of dividend privileges must be disclosed. For example, preferred stock dividends may be:

1. Cumulative: If dividends are bypassed in past years (called dividends in arrears), preferred stockholders are entitled to past dividends and current dividends before any dividends can be paid to common stockholders.

2. Noncumulative: If dividends are not declared during a particular year, preferred stockholders permanently forfeit their dividends for that particular year.

Preferred stock can also be participative or nonparticipative. Nonparticipative stock receives only the stated dividend rate, but participative preferred stock can share with common stock in any excess distributions after common stock has been paid a dividend rate comparable to the preferred stock basic dividend rate.

A callable stock can be paid off (called in) at the option of the firm for a call price; consequently, the call price indirectly serves as a ceiling for the market price.

The number of shares authorized (given in the corporate charter) and issued must be shown. The number of shares issued multiplied by par equals the dollar amount (see Exhibit 2-1, $90,000). If several series of preferred stock have been issued (each with its unique features) details of each series would be disclosed.

Common Stock. Stock that is not preferred is common stock. Details that must be disclosed include par and number of shares authorized (from the corporate chapter), issued, and outstanding. The latter would be the same number unless the firm reacquired some of its own stock (treasury stock). Treasury stock is shown as a reduction of stockholders' equity.

Paid-in Capital in Excess of Par. Frequently, stock originally is sold for a selling price in excess of par. If so, this difference is called paid-in capital in excess of par. Amounts applicable to preferred and common stock are shown separately.

Retained Earnings. This account consists of cumulative net profits (and losses) of the firm since inception (or date of reorganization, if any) minus dividends paid. Hence, net earnings from the income statement increase the account and dividends declared decrease it. Note that the amount of dividends paid to preferred stockholders lowers retained earnings by $9,000 (10% of $90,000).

If the number of transactions affecting retained earnings is large, a company would prepare a separate statement of retained earnings that would provide details of changes in the account for the period. The ending balance would be included in the balance sheet.

Retained earnings is added to total paid-in capital to arrive at total stockholders' equity. The stockholders' equity plus total liabilities equals total assets, in accordance with the fundamental accounting equation:

$$\text{Assets} = \text{liabilities} + \text{stockholders' equity}$$

Because liabilities and stockholders' equity represent total claims on the assets, they must agree with total assets.

INCOME STATEMENT

The income statement presents the results of operations for a period of time. It summarizes revenue and expenses. The final result is net income or net loss which, as we said before, increases or decreases retained earnings. Hence, the income statement is really an extension of the balance sheet.

Exhibit 2-2 shows the income statement for the year 19X3.

Revenue

The first item on the income statement is revenue. If a firm sells merchandise, revenue consists of receipts from sales, whereas for a CPA firm revenue is professional fees and for real estate firms revenue may consist of rental income and commissions. Sales returns and allowances, and sales discounts are usually deducted from sales to arrive at net sales.

Cost of Goods Sold

For merchandising and manufacturing firms, the largest expense on the income statement is likely to be the cost of the merchandise sold. We compute this amount by adding the beginning inventory with the merchandise acquisition cost (purchases for a merchandising firm and cost of manufacturing for a man-ufacturing firm) and deducting the end of the period's inventory. The cost of goods sold is a crucial figure for planning and control, as is gross profit on sales (the difference between net sales and the cost of goods sold). We will expand our discussion of this principle in later chapters.

Selling Expenses

Major classifications of selling expenses provide the reader with knowledge of the types and amounts of marketing expenses necessary to sell the products. Note that depreciation and occupancy expenses consist solely of facilities appli-cable to the selling department.

General and Administrative Expenses (G&A)

Expenses not directly applicable to purchasing, producing, or distributing prod-ucts are called general and administrative expenses. Examples include the com-pensation and occupancy cost of corporate executives and the accounting department. General and administrative expenses are reported on the income statement during the period they are applicable; hence they are called *period costs*. Selling expenses are also period costs.

Exhibit 2-2
ABC COMPANY
Income Statement
For The Year Ended December 31, 19X3
(In Thousands of Dollars)

Gross Sales	$14,000	
Less: Sales returns and allowances	100	
Sales discounts	50	
Net Sales		$13,850
Cost of goods sold:		
Finished goods inventory, January 1, 19X3	$ 500	
Cost of goods manufactured (schedule attached)	7,800	
Goods Available for Sale	8,300	
Less Finished goods, December 31, 19X3	300	
Cost of Goods Sold		8,000
Gross Profit on Sales		$ 5,850
Operating expenses:		
Selling expenses:		
Sales force expense	$ 1,800	
Advertising and promotion expense	200	
Delivery expense	150	
Depreciation on buildings and equipment	40	
Other occupancy expenses	160	
Travel and entertainment	100	
Miscellaneous selling expenses	50	
Total Selling Expenses		$ 2,500
General and Administrative Expenses:		
Administrative salaries	$ 1,400	
Employee fringe benefits	300	
Property taxes	300	
Depreciation	100	
Other general and administrative expenses	240	
Total General and Administrative Expenses		$ 2,340
		$ 1,010
Other Income and Expenses:		
Investment income	$ 84	
Gain on disposal of equipment	120	
Amortization of goodwill	(20)	
Interest expense	(14)	170
Income Before Income Taxes		$ 1,180
Income Taxes		571
Net Income After Taxes		609
Earnings per share on common stock (609-9/300 shares)		$ 2

Other Income and Expenses

Income and expenses not directly related to the normal operations of a firm are listed separately. Some of the more common items are shown in Exhibit 2-2. Many of these items are related to investing and financing operations.

Income Before Income Taxes

Since a high percentage of profit must be shared with the government, we conventionally provide the reader with details as to income before income tax expense and net income after taxes. (Note that in Exhibit 2-2 the $609,000 is transferred to retained earnings on the balance sheet.) A word of caution: Because of timing differences, the income tax expense of $571,000 is not necessarily the amount of taxes paid or owed for the year as computed on the tax returns. We explain timing differences in Chapter 17.

   Other items that might appear at the bottom of an income statement include extraordinary gains or losses (unusual and infrequent items), the cumulative effect of changing from one generally accepted accounting method to another generally accepted accounting method, and gains or losses on disposition of a segment of the business. Each of these would be shown net of applicable income tax, and an earning (loss) per share would be computed for each, as well as for net income after income taxes. An example of an extraordinary loss might look like this:

Extraordinary loss. Earthquake loss not covered by insurance	$1,000,000	
Less applicable income tax	480,000	
Net extraordinary loss		$520,000
EPS on extraordinary loss		$.02

Earnings Per Share (EPS)

The amount of earnings applicable to each share of common stock is included (calculation of this amount is discussed in Chapter 3).

   For the illustrated income statement, earnings per share is simply net income less preferred stock dividends divided by the number of shares of common stock outstanding.

$$\frac{\$609,000 - \$9,000}{300,000} = \$2.00$$

STATEMENT OF COST OF GOODS MANUFACTURED

This statement supports the income statement in that it provides information on the cost of manufacturing goods during an accounting period. To make an item, three kinds of cost are incurred:

1. Direct material—material that can be directly identified in the end product
2. Direct labor—labor costs directly incurred to manufacture the product
3. Manufacturing overhead—all indirect manufacturing costs

The statement of the cost of goods manufactured provides information about these three kinds of costs. Because direct material is the raw material physically used in production, we calculate its amount by taking the beginning raw material inventory and adding purchases of raw material, net of purchase discounts and purchase returns and allowances. Freight is part of the cost of purchases. Since raw material on hand at the end of the accounting period has not been used, we deduct ending raw material inventory to arrive at material directly used in production. To this amount, we add direct labor (taken from payroll distribution) and factory overhead. Factory overhead is detailed by major categories. Methods of allocating factory overhead to inventory are covered in Chapter 4, so you need not be concerned with the account *underapplied overhead* now. Study Exhibit 2-3 thoroughly.

The $7,750,000 is the manufacturing costs incurred during the period of Exhibit 2-3, but it is not the cost of goods manufactured (completed). To obtain the latter, we add our beginning work-in-process inventory and deduct the ending work-in-process inventory. The result, $7,800,000, is the cost of goods manufactured, that is, the cost of making items transferred to finished-goods inventory. Hence, it is this amount that appears on the income statement as the cost of manufacturing finished goods.

Your attention is drawn to the fact that all inventory on hand at the end of the accounting period is an asset; therefore, the inventory of $1,800,000 shown on the balance sheet consists of:

Raw material inventory (from the statement of the cost of goods manufactured)	$ 500,000
Work-in-process inventory (from the statement of the cost of goods manufactured)	1,000,000
Finished-goods inventory (from the income statement)	300,000
	$1,800,000

STATEMENT OF CHANGES IN FINANCIAL POSITION

The statement of changes in financial position summarizes the financing and investing activities of the firm. This statement is commonly called a funds statement. It is prepared one of two ways:

1. Working capital basis (current assets less current liabilities)
2. Cash basis

Exhibit 2-3
ABC COMPANY
Statement of Cost of Goods Manufactured
For the Year Ended December 31, 19X3
(In Thousands of Dollars)

Direct Materials:		
Raw materials inventory, January 1, 19X3	$ 310	
Purchases	2,770	
Less: Purchase discounts	(30)	
Add: Freight in	200	
Materials available for use	3,250	
Less: Raw material inventory, December 31, 19X3	(500)	
Direct materials used		$2,750
Direct Labor		3,000
Factory Overhead:		
Depreciation on buildings and equipment	$ 260	
Utilities	150	
Insurance	200	
Property taxes	500	
Indirect labor	125	
Indirect material	160	
Amortization of patents	5	
Rent on equipment	100	
Repairs and maintenance	150	
Employee fringe benefits	300	
Overtime premium	80	
Other factory overhead	70	
Total factory overhead incurred	$2,100	
Less: underapplied overhead	100	
Factory overhead applied		$2,000
Total manufacturing costs		$7,750
Add: Work in process inventory, January 1, 19X3		1,050
Less: Work in process inventory, December 31, 19X3		(1,000)
Cost of goods manufactured		$7,800

This statement helps answer questions such as:

1. What management decision created events that caused funds to change?
2. What amount of funds was generated through profit and loss statement activities?

3. How much of the changes in funds was the result of transactions related to long-term assets, long-term debt, and stockholders' equity?

Examples of types of transactions that increase working capital or cash are:

1. Net profit
2. Sale of noncurrent assets
3. Issuance of long-term debt
4. Issuance of capital

Examples of transactions that decrease funds or cash include:

1. Declaration of a cash dividend
2. Purchase of noncurrent assets
3. Redemption of long-term debt
4. Repurchase of capital stock

Cash Basis

Exhibit 2-4 is the funds statement for the ABC Company prepared on a cash basis.

We are trying to explain how the $190,000 increase (see bottom of statement in Exhibit 2-4) in cash came about. We know that some of it resulted from income statement activities. Therefore, under cash provided, we list first the cash resulting from profit and loss statement activities. We know that net income is not equal to cash inflow because some expenses are not paid in cash (i.e., depreciation) and some expenses are still unpaid at the end of the accounting period. These are current liabilities on the balance sheet. In addition, some sales are still uncollected and are shown as accounts receivable on the balance sheet. Therefore, we adjust the income from the profit and loss statement as follows:

Add: Debit accounts (subtractions) on the profit and loss statement
    that are not paid in cash (i.e., depreciation)
  Decreases in current assets
  Increases in current liabilities
Subtract: Credit accounts (additions) on the profit and loss statement
    that are not received in cash (i.e., amortization of bond premium)
  Increases in current assets
  Decreases in current liabilities

Exhibit 2-4
ABC COMPANY
Statement of Changes in Financial Position
(Cash Basis)
For the Year Ended December 31, 19X3
(In Thousands of Dollars)

Cash Provided:

Cash Provided from Operations:

Net Income	$609	
Add: Depreciation expense	400	
Amortization of patents	5	
Amortization of goodwill	20	
Decrease in accounts receivable (net)	21	
Decrease in inventories	60	
Decrease in prepayments	12	
Increase in trade accounts payable	10	
Increase in accrued liabilities	5	
Increase in advances by customers	2	$1,144
Less: Gain on disposal of equipment	$120	
Increase in marketable securities	80	
Increase in notes receivable	10	
Decrease in employee retirement benefits	50	
Decrease in short term notes payable	200	$ 460
Cash Provided From Operations		$ 684
Proceeds from sales of equipment		600
Issuance of common stock for equipment		200
Cash received from repayment of loan by affiliated company		65
Total Cash Received		$1,549
Cash Applied:		
Purchase of investments	$100	
Extinguishment of long term notes payable	50	
Purchase of land for future plant	600	
Purchase of equipment by common stock	200	
Payment of dividends	409	
Total Cash Applied		$1,359
Increase in Cash		$ 190
Change in Cash		
Cash balance, January 1, 19X3		$ 300
Cash balance, December 31, 19X3		490
Increase in Cash		$190

The result, called *cash provided from operations,* is a very important figure. It is the dollar increase in cash resulting from profit and loss statement activities. To cash provided from operations, we add cash received from noncurrent balance sheet transactions, such as sale of long-term assets or collection of long term debt. We deduct cash outflow resulting from such balance sheet activities as purchase of land or payment of dividends.

If a balance sheet transaction does not affect cash but is an economically significant transaction, we list it both as cash provided and cash applied. The result is zero effect on cash but the reader is made aware that an important transaction occurred. In Exhibit 2-4, equipment purchased by common stock is an example. This type of treatment is commonly known as the *all-inclusive concept.*

The increase in cash, $190,000 per the statement of changes in financial position, equals the change in cash during the accounting period. To prepare a funds statement, it is necessary to have the balance sheets for the end of the current period and the end of the preceding period. You cannot trace most of the figures in Exhibit 2-4 to their source because we did not furnish you with the December 31, 19X2 balance sheet.

Generally, the cash basis is more informative than the working capital basis. If the latter were prepared, the balance sheet current assets and current liabilities adjustments would not be made to net income.

Working Capital Basis

The working capital version looks like Exhibit 2-5.

Recall that working capital by definition is current assets less current liabilities. Therefore, on the bottom of the funds statement, we list the changes in current accounts according to their effects on working capital. The increase in working capital for the period is $420,000. On the top of the funds statement, we again start out with net income adjusted to remove the effect of any income statement transactions that did not affect working capital. The amount of $914,000 is the change in current assets and current liabilities (working capital) resulting from profit and loss statement activities. To this amount we add any balance sheet transactions increasing working capital to obtain net increase in working capital. From this we deduct the working capital applied from balance sheet activities to arrive at the net increase in working capital of $420,000. Note that the balance sheet transactions are identical to those listed on the cash basis statement of changes in financial position.

A word of caution concerning funds statements: A net profit on the income statement does not necessarily mean an increase in cash or working capital during the period. Similarly, a net loss does not always mean a decrease in cash or working capital.

Exhibit 2-5

ABC COMPANY

Statement of Changes in Financial Position

(Working Capital Concept)

For the Year Ended December 31, 19X3

(In Thousands of Dollars)

Working Capital Provided:

From Operations:

Net income	$ 609
Depreciation	400
Amortization of patents and goodwill	25
Gain on disposal of equipment	(120)
Working capital provided from operations	$ 914
Proceeds from sale of equipment	600
Issued common stock for equipment	200
Repayment of loan by affiliated company	65
Total Working Capital Provided	$1,779

Working Capital Applied:

Purchase of investments	$100	
Extinguishment of long term notes payable	50	
Purchase of land for future plant	600	
Purchase of equipment by common stock	200	
Payment of dividends	409	
Total Working Capital Applied		$1,359
Net Increase in Working Capital		$ 420

Change in Working Capital:

	Working Capital	
	Increase	Decrease
Increase in Cash	$190	
Decrease in accounts receivable		$ 21
Decrease in inventories		60
Decrease in prepayments		12
Increase in trade accounts payable		10
Increase in accrued liabilities		5
Increase in advances by customers		2
Increase in marketable securities	80	
Increase in notes receivable	10	
Decrease in employee retirement benefits	50	
Decrease in short term notes payable	200	
	$530	$110
	110	
Increase in Working Capital	$420	

Exhibit 2-6
ABC COMPANY
Balance Sheet
as of December 31, 19X3
(In Thousands of Dollars)

Current assets	$ 4,240
Investments	2,040
Plant assets	4,000
Intangibles	175
Total Assets	$10,455
Current liabilities	$ 2,040
Long-term liabilities	4,415
Total Liabilities	6,455
Paid in capital	3,205
Retained earnings	795
Total Liabilities and Stockholders' Equity	$10,455

SINGLE-STEP FORMATS

In lieu of the multistep balance sheet and income statement, sometimes it is desirable to condense them into single-step formats. Exhibit 2-6 is a condensed balance sheet.

Note that the items listed are the major classifications on the multistep balance sheet. A single-step income statement is shown as Exhibit 2-7.

Other than simplicity, the major difference between the single- and multistep income statements is that the former lists all revenue first and then deducts all expenses. A frequent criticism of the single-step income statement is that gross profit is not shown.

WEAKNESSES OF FINANCIAL STATEMENTS

Before leaving financial statements, let us talk a bit about their weaknesses. The complaints of many critics that financial statements are not relevant to the needs of users can be summarized as follows:

1. Many items in financial statements are rooted in historical costs, for example, plant assets and inventory. Consequently, cost write-offs to the income statement, such as depreciation, are also historical. The book value of

Exhibit 2-7
ABC COMPANY
Income Statement
For the Year Ended December 31, 19X3
(In Thousands of Dollars)

Revenue:		
Sales (Net)		$13,850
Other revenue		204
Total Revenue		$14,054
Expenses		
Cost of goods sold	$8,000	
Selling expenses	2,500	
General and administrative expense	2,340	
Other expenses	34	
Income tax expense	571	
Total Expenses		$13,445
Net Income after Taxes		$ 609

the assets and depreciation expense is not relevant to decision making where the decision maker is more interested in replacement cost, reproduction cost, fair market value, or historical cost adjusted for inflation.

2. Financial statements reflect mutiple generally accepted accounting principles. Various inventory and depreciation methods and differences in revenue recognition illustrate this situation. Statements lose their comparability among firms when multiple generally accepted accounting principles are allowed and when a firm is allowed to change from one generally accepted method of accounting to another. Although the Financial Accounting Standards Board has worked hard to resolve these issues, much remains to be done. It is important to remember that standardization at the expense of accuracy might be even less satisfactory.

3. Financial statements are too complex. How can the lay reader possibly be expected to understand accounting jargon and the multitude of accounting procedures? Footnotes are long, ambiguous, and meaningless. The complexities of leases or pensions are beyond the average reader's comprehension.

4. Financial statements do not predict the future; therefore, of what value are they? Their predictive ability is limited to the extent that the future will mirror the past, which is often not true for progressive, developing firms.

5. Financial statements are incomplete, which means that many items crucial to the success or failure of a firm are not included in them. Some cannot

be measured at all, and others can be measured with only limited accuracy. Examples of omitted or incomplete data include:

1. Caliber of management
2. Efficiency and morale of employees
3. Brand loyalty
4. Markets
5. New products, processes, and technology
6. Goodwill (other than purchased)
7. Condition of facilities
8. Value of human resources

HUMAN RESOURCE ACCOUNTING

This topic warrants extra attention because labor represents an important cost to most firms. During the 1970s substantial attention was directed toward the question of whether the value of human resources should be capitalized as an asset on the balance sheet. Advocates of human resource accounting criticized conventional accounting along the following lines:

1. Many human resource costs should be capitalized instead of expensed. Failure to do so understates assets, net income, and retained earnings.

2. Lack of adequate data: Since human resources are expensed, management does not know its investment in its employees. It has inadequate data for important decisions such as the cost of recruiting or developing an employee.

3. Failure to establish human resource objectives: Unless some effort is made to measure employee cost, managers cannot know what they are trying to achieve. Additionally, they have insufficient information for planning and control.

4. Lack of social responsibility: The maximization of profit is not the only goal of a firm. Social and environmental values must also be considered.

5. Ignoring employees' needs: Since workers contribute to the success or failure of a firm, it is incumbent on managers to recognize employees' abilities and skills. A data bank of employee talents can be immensely helpful in matching employees with jobs.

6. Human resources can be measured. Admittedly no perfect measurement has been agreed upon, but the same thing can be said for depreciation and warranty costs.

The main controversy is whether human resources should be reported on published financial statements. There is little controversy over the need for internal data on employees. Internal data can be detailed by:

1. Acquisition costs—recruitment, selection, hiring, and induction of employees

2. Development costs—orientation, on- and off-the-job training
3. Replacement costs—separation pay, low performance costs, and vacant position costs

SUMMARY

In this chapter we discussed the three primary financial statements published in annual reports:

1. Balance sheet
2. Income statement
3. Statement of changes in financial position

The balance sheet discloses the assets, liabilities, and capital as of a particular point in time. The income statement shows the revenue and expenses during a period of time. The statement of changes in financial position explains how balance sheets change from one period to another.

You should know the composition of each statement, generally how the data are measured, and how to interpret financial statements. To help you with the latter, in the next chapter we turn our attention to ratios.

3. Analysis of Financial Statements

INTRODUCTION

A company is judged to a large extent on the information revealed in its financial statements. This information is subjected to critical analysis by many interested parties. For managers this analysis is, in reality, a partial evaluation how well they have performed.

Statement analysis can be combined with other planning and control techniques. For example, inventory turnover ratio is related to inventory control. Accounts receivable turnover is a means of cash control.

By itself one ratio has very little meaning, but when it is interpreted with a series of ratios over a period of time, significant relationships can be detected. Before discussing individual ratios and their significance, let us impress upon you several limitations of ratios.

LIMITATIONS OF RATIOS

The first one we already mentioned.

1. One ratio has very limited meaning. One positive ratio does not define success, any more than one robin confirms the arrival of spring. Many ratios and their interrelationships must be studied.

2. Ratios should be compared with preceding periods. We are interested in trends. Keep in mind that changes in price levels over a period of years can cause serious distortion in trends.

3. Ratios should be compared with industry averages. Care must be taken to define an industry accurately. To the extent possible, ratios should be computed by segment of the enterprise.

4. Ratios are only as good as the data on which they are based; that is, variation in accounting methods and estimates can cause ratios to lose their comparability. Additionally, ratios may be computed on atypical financial statements. Balance sheets are prepared as of one moment in time. Short-term fluctuations in assets and equities are not reflected in balance sheets. Managers may deliberately "window dress" the statements to make the firm appear more prosperous than it really is. For example, managers may pay off current liabilities immediately before the balance sheet date. If a firm has $300,000 current assets and $200,000 current liabilities, its current ratio is 1.5 ($300,000/

$200,000). By paying off $50,000 current liabilities, its current ratio "improves" to 1.67 ($250,000/$150,000).

5. Ratios are based primarily on historical costs, not current values. Many unrealized gains or losses have not been included in the financial statements.

6. Ratios are not sufficient by themselves as a basis for judgment about the future.

Despite our observation that ratios are only as good as the data on which they are computed, there is a human tendency to interpret ratios as "hard" data. Such a tendency should be avoided. It is seldom desirable to carry out a ratio beyond one decimal place, as such precision encourages readers to think of ratios as accurate. One way of avoiding such precision is to interpret the soundness of a ratio within a "quality range." For example, a current ratio is satisfactory if it falls between 1.5 and 2.0.

When comparison is made with other firms or industry averages, care must be taken that all comparative data are based on a similar environment and on the same accounting principles. If not, adjustments must be made.

One could hardly expect firm A which is only five years old and has a modern new plant to have the same ratios as firm B which is 20 years old and has old plant and equipment. Firm B's long-term assets would have been purchased when prices were much lower than when firm A purchased its assets. Assume that firm B selected as short a depreciation life as possible and an accelerated method of depreciation such as double declining balance. Firm B would have a very low asset base in comparison to firm A. Other things being equal, firm B would show a much higher return on assets than firm A. Still, this knowledge does not tell the whole story for long-term decisions. Firm B may have to incur substantial expenditures in the foreseeable future to modernize its facilities. This factor alone would have tremendous influence on future cash flow, fixed assets, possibly long-term debt, retained earnings, and earnings per share.

Another accounting principle crucial to ratio analysis is inventory cost flow method (discussed in Chapter 16). Again, other things equal, a firm that uses the LIFO method instead of FIFO would have a lower inventory base and hence lower current assets, lower total assets, lower retained earnings, lower stockholders' equity, higher cost of goods sold, lower net profit, and lower earnings per share.* Any ratios computed on these data would not be comparable with the firm using FIFO.

Several other major accounting factors to look out for are methods of depreciation, deferred income taxes, recognition of prior service expenses, and obligations for pension plans. If a firm changes from one generally accepted accounting method to another, prior periods' data and ratios should be recom-

---

*LIFO stands for last in/first out; FIFO means first in/first out.

puted to reflect the new accounting principle. Recomputation is also necessary for material errors in prior periods.

Keep in mind that there is no standard series of ratios applicable to all firms. Each firm and industry must select and interpret its own ratios. Unfortunately, a few of the more common ratios such as return on investment have multiple formulas; therefore, the analyst must be aware of the formulas and the accompanying data before interpreting the results.

In our discussion of some of the more common ratios, we will discover that ratios can be classified in several ways, including the classification *liquidity ratios.*

LIQUIDITY RATIOS

Liquidity ratios measure the ability of a firm to pay its maturing obligations over the short run. There is a very close relationship between cash generated from income statement activities and the firm's ability to pay its bills. Generally, it is desirable to repeat the operating cycle as frequently as possible. Recall that the operating cycle is the period of time from cash to cash, that is, from obtaining raw materials to production, finished goods, sales, and collection of receivables.

Current Ratio

Chart 3.1

$$\text{Current ratio} = \frac{\text{Current assets}}{\text{Current liabilities}} \frac{\$97,000}{\$39,000} = 2.5 \text{ Times}$$

The current ratio measures how frequently current liabilities are covered. Will the firm have sufficient cash to pay its obligations as they come due? A ratio of 2.5 to 1 means that there is $2.50 of current assets to pay each dollar of current liabilities. Unfortunately, current liabilities tend to be more current than current assets, that is, they are due earlier than some current assets can be converted into cash. Hence, a weakness of the ratio is the liquidity of receivables and inventories.

Another way of viewing this ratio is from the perspective of working capital. Working capital is defined as current assets less current liabilities. Working capital provides the cushion of protection for short-term creditors.

Current Asset Turnover

We show here three ratios that basically measure the same thing—how much profit is generated from current assets.

Chart 3.2

(1)	Cost of goods sold and operating expenses less depreciation	$300,000
(2)	Current assets	$ 97,000
(3)	Net income	$ 12,000
(4)	Current asset turnover (Line (1) ÷ Line (2))	3.1 Times
(5)	Rate of return on current assets (Line (3) ÷ Line (2))	12%
(6)	Rate of return per turnover (Line (5) ÷ Line (4))	3.9%

A rapid turnover of current assets indicates that they are liquid; that is, inventories are not dragging the current asset ratio down. In the above illustration the current asset turnover is 3.1 times and the rate of return on current assets is 12%. A high turnover results in a higher return on current assets and total assets, if profit per turnover (3.9%) can be maintained.

Acid Test Ratio

Chart 3.3

Acid test ratio (Quick test)

$$= \frac{\text{Cash} + \text{Marketable securities} + \text{Net receivables}}{\text{Current liabilities}}$$

$$\frac{\$2000 + \$3000 + \$55,000}{\$39,000} = \underline{\underline{1.5}} \text{ Times}$$

This ratio removes inventories from current assets; hence it will be lower than the current ratio (2.5 versus 1.5). The acid test shows the availability of cash to near cash to pay current liabilities.

Defensive Interval Ratio

Chart 3.4

$$\frac{\text{Defensive}}{\text{interval ratio}} = \frac{\text{Cash} + \text{Marketable securities} + \text{Net receivable}}{\text{Projected daily operational expenditures (based on past expenditures) minus noncash charges}}$$

$$= \frac{\$2,000 + \$3,000 + \$55,000}{\$400,000} = \underline{\underline{15.\%}}$$

The defensive interval ratio of 15% measures the time a firm can operate on present liquid assets without resorting to next period's revenue.

Current and acid test ratios can be too high, thus indicating an inefficient use of current assets. Firms in high inflationary countries want low current and acid test ratios because they are losing purchasing power by holding monetary assets. We explain this concept more fully in Chapter 18.

ACTIVITY RATIOS

Activity ratios measure how quickly certain assets can be converted into cash.

Accounts Receivable Turnover

Chart 3.5

$$\text{Receivable turnover} = \frac{\text{Net sales}}{\text{Average net trade receivables}}$$

$$\frac{\$400,000}{\dfrac{\$40,000 + \$55,000}{2}} = \underline{\underline{8.4}} \text{ Times}$$

$$\text{Number of days in receivable} = \frac{365}{\text{Accounts receivable turnover}}$$

$$\frac{365}{8.4} = \underline{\underline{43.5}} \text{ Days}$$

The accounts receivable turnover ratio denotes how quickly the firm expects to convert receivables into cash and is therefore a measure of the quality of receivables. Our firm can expect its receivables to be converted into cash on an average every 43.5 days or 8.4 times a year. When evaluating this ratio, several factors must be considered.

1. Discounts offered
2. Types of customers
3. Seasonal variations
4. Credit policy of the firm
5. Credit policies of competitors
6. Relation of bad debts to profitability

Inventory Turnover

Chart 3.6

$$\text{Inventory turnover} = \frac{\text{Cost of goods sold}}{\text{Average inventory}}$$

$$\frac{\$316,000}{\dfrac{\$45,000 + \$37,000}{2}} = \underline{\underline{7.7}} \text{ Times}$$

$$\text{Number of days in inventory} = \frac{365}{\text{Inventory turnover}}$$

$$\frac{365}{7.7} = \underline{\underline{47}} \text{ Days}$$

The inventory turnover ratio of 7.7 times measures how quickly inventory is sold and provides a basis for determining if obsolete inventory or pricing problems exist. This ratio can also be converted into the average number of days of inventory on hand—in this case, 47 days. Usually, high turnover is important except when stockout costs are high. Quantity discounts must be weighed against the cost of carrying the additional inventory. High turnover is desirable only if high earnings per turnover can be sustained. The method of inventory valuation and the method of accounting for cost flow can affect turnover.

Asset Turnover

Chart 3.7

$$\text{Asset turnover} = \frac{\text{Net sales}}{\text{Average total assets}}$$

$$\frac{\$400,000}{\dfrac{\$160,000 + \$145,000}{2}} = \underline{\underline{2.6}} \text{ Times}$$

How efficiently a firm utilizes its assets is measured by asset turnover. The illustrated firm has only a 2.6 asset turnover. Generally, a high turnover is desirable. Low book values due to old assets or accelerated depreciation methods can cause the ratio to be high.

PROFITABILITY RATIOS

Profitability ratios show how well a firm has operated during the year.

Net Profit to Sales

Chart 3.8

$$\text{Net income to sales} = \frac{\text{Net income}}{\text{Net sales}}$$

$$\frac{\$12,000}{\$400,000} = 3\%$$

Net profits to sales (i.e., 3%) measures the relationship of income to sales. Other income amounts that can be related to sales include gross profit, income before taxes, income before extraordinary items, and income after extraordinary items.

Rate of Return on Assets

Chart 3.9

$$\text{Rate of return on assets} = \frac{\text{Net income}}{\text{Average total assets}}$$

$$\frac{\$12,000}{\dfrac{\$160,000 + \$145,000}{2}} = 7.9\%$$

The relationship of income to assets is measured by the rate of return on assets. Our firm experienced a 7.9% return on its average assets utilized in operations. Variations consist of removing interest and dividends after taxes from the numerator. The denominator can be revised several ways, such as net assets or plant assets plus working capital.

Rate of Return on Common Stock Equity

Chart 3.10

$$\text{Rate of return on common stock equity}$$

$$= \frac{\text{Net income minus preferred dividends}}{\text{Average common stockholders' equity}}$$

$$\frac{\$12,000 - \$1,000}{\$76,000} = 14.5\%$$

The rate of return on common stock equity relates net profit to common stock-holders' equity. The ratio of 14.5% must be evaluated against the market rate of interest. When the rate of return on total assets is lower than the rate of return on common stockholders' equity, the firm is trading on the equity. Trading on the equity consists of borrowing money at a lower interest rate than the expected return. For example:

Chart 3.11

Borrowed	$5,000,000 @ 10%	$500,000
Earned	$5,000,000 @ 14%	700,000
	Profit	$200,000

The firm pays an interest rate of 10% to obtain a return of 14%. The $200,000 profit goes to the common stockholders. Trading on the equity can be risky. Consider the situation opposite to the above—a loss. Then the $200,000 loss would be borne by the common stockholders.

Long-term debt and preferred stock are not equally efficient in generating positive leverage because interest on long-term debt is tax deductible whereas dividends paid on preferred stock is not. Consider the following situation. We have a choice of issuing 8% bonds or 8% preferred stock to obtain $500,000.

Chart 3.12

	Bonds	Preferred Stock
Earnings before interest and taxes	$ 200,000	$ 200,000
Deduct interest expense		
(8% × $500,000)	40,000	0
Net income before taxes	$ 160,000	$ 200,000
Income tax expense (40%)	64,000	80,000
Net income after tax	$ 96,000	$ 120,000
Deduct preferred dividends		
(8% × $500,000)	0	40,000
Net income for common	$ 96,000	$ 80,000
Common stockholder's equity	$1,000,000	$1,000,000
Return on common stockholders	9.6%	8.0%

You can see from the chart that issuing bonds is more efficient than preferred stock because interest expense is tax deductible. On the negative side, bonds are more risky because the interest must be paid currently, and the principal must be paid at maturity.

Earnings Per Share

Chart 3.13

$$\text{Earnings per share} = \frac{\text{Net income minus preferred dividends}}{\text{Weighted shares of common stock outstanding}}$$

$$\frac{\$12,000 - \$1,000}{25,000} = \$.44 \text{ Per Share}$$

Earnings per share tells us how much income is applicable to each share of common stock. Each share earned $.44. Its simpler formula is net income less preferred stock dividends, divided by the weighted number of shares outstanding. It is necessary to weight the denominator for the period of time the stock is outstanding to give effect to earnings generated from the funds received from the initial sale of the stock.

Earnings per share is very complicated to calculate when there are dilutive securities outstanding. A dilutive security is one which can be converted into common stock, which causes the number of shares to increase and the earnings per share to decrease. Stock options, warrants, convertible bonds, and convertible preferred stock are examples.

Stock dividends, stock splits, and reverse splits require previous periods' earnings per share to be restated. This is necessary for comparability. Earnings per share should be computed for earnings before and after extraordinary items.

Price Earnings Ratio

Chart 3.14

$$\text{Price earnings ratio} = \frac{\text{Market price of stock}}{\text{Earnings per share}}$$

$$\frac{\$10}{\$.44} = 22.7$$

The price earnings of 22.7 ratio measures how many times the market price exceeds the earnings during the period. It is used as a gauge for determining stock values.

Payout Ratio

Chart 3.15

$$\text{Payout ratio} = \frac{\text{Cash dividends}}{\text{Net income}}$$

$$\frac{\$8,000}{\$12,000} = \underline{\underline{66.7\%}}$$

The percentage of income paid to stockholders is provided by the payout ratio. The firm paid out ⅔ of its earnings as dividends. Cash dividends have the effect of liquidating a portion of the firm. Growth firms tend to have low payouts, whereas mature firms have higher payout. Obviously, the dividend policy determines the payout ratio. The desirability of payout depends in part upon the cash needs and tax bracket of the investors. Investors who depend on investment income to meet their personal bills favor a high payout. On the other hand, an individual in a high tax bracket would probably prefer that profits be retained in the firm and be reinvested by the firm in profitable activities. Other things being equal, the price of the stock would rise with such a strategy, and the investor's profit on the sale of stock would be taxed at a favorable capital gains rate.

Dividend Yield

Chart 3.16

$$\text{Dividend yield} = \frac{\text{Cash dividend per share}}{\text{Market price of stock}}$$

$$\frac{\$.32}{\$10} = \underline{\underline{3.2\%}}$$

The dividend yield measures the return on market price in cash. In the above illustration, assuming the stock was originally purchased at $10 a share, the stockholders received $.032 cash return for each dollar invested. Note that this is not the return on investment. In the short run, the return on investment is:

Chart 3.17

$$\text{ROI} = \frac{\text{Earnings per share}}{\text{Market price of stock}} = \frac{\$.44}{\$10} = \underline{\underline{4.4\%}}$$

The return on investment of 4.4% is higher than the dividend yield of 3.2% because all earnings were not distributed as dividends. Over the long run, before shareholders can determine the profitability of owning stock the potential earnings to be paid to the stockholders have to be adjusted for any capital gains or losses after disposition of the stock. The return on investment can be computed before or after income tax.

COVERAGE RATIOS

Coverage ratios tell to what extent a certain variable is covered. Coverage measures the relationship between two sets of flow. These ratios help predict long-run solvency of the firm and the amount of protection available.

Debt to Total Assets and Debt to Stockholders' Equity

Chart 3.18

$$\text{Debt to total assets} = \frac{\text{Debt}}{\text{Total assets}}$$

$$\frac{\$69,000}{\$145,000} = \underline{\underline{47.6\%}}$$

Chart 3.19

$$\text{Debt to stockholders' equity} = \frac{\text{Debt}}{\text{Stockholders' equity}}$$

$$\frac{\$69,000}{\$76,000} = \underline{\underline{90.8\%}}$$

Two ratios—debt to total assets and debt to stockholder's equity—measure the degree of leverage. These ratios can affect the company's ability to raise capital as risk increases proportionately to leverage. Stability of earning power is a major factor in determining the amount of leverage desired. The illustrated ratios of 47.6% and 90.8% show that nearly one half of the firm's assets are financed by debt and the remainder by ownership.

Times Interest Earned

Chart 3.20

$$\text{Times interest earned} = \frac{\text{Income before taxes and interest charges}}{\text{Interest}}$$

$$\frac{\$12,000 + \$3,500 + \$1,200}{\$1,200} = \underline{\underline{13.9}} \text{ Times}$$

The times interest earned ratio tells the number of times interest was earned. The firm has sufficient earnings to pay its interest 13.9 times. Keep in mind that interest must be paid each period as stated in the debt instrument. High-leverage firms will have high cash outflows from paying interest, which can cause a major cash shortage problem.

A similar ratio can be computed for preferred stock in order to determine the number of times preferred stock dividends were covered.

Number of Times Fixed Charges Were Earned

Chart 3.21

Number of times fixed charges were earned

$$= \frac{\text{Earnings before fixed charges}}{\text{Fixed charges}}$$

$$\frac{\$12,000 + \$8,000}{\$8,000} = \underline{\underline{2.5}} \text{ Times}$$

Fixed charges include all items where there is a firm commitment to pay. Examples are interest, rental payments, and preferred stock dividends. This ratio determines if a firm is able to meet its fixed-charge obligations. Generally, the higher the fixed charges, the more risky is the investment. The firm has $2.50 of earnings for each dollar of fixed charges.

Book Value Per Share

Chart 3.22

$$\text{Book value per share} = \frac{\text{Common stockholders' equity}}{\text{Outstanding shares of common stock}}$$

$$\frac{\$70,000}{25,000} = \underline{\underline{\$2.80}} \text{ Per Share}$$

Book value determines the amount each share of common stock would be worth if all balance sheet accounts were liquidated at their book value. The $2.80 per share must be interpreted with care because it is primarily based on historical cost. Book value is more meaningful when financial statements are prepared at current value. Dilutive securities (those which can be converted into common stock) when converted can substantially decrease book value.

Book value for preferred stock is the liquidation amount (which may be par or some other amount) plus dividends in arrears.

If the market value of stock materially exceeds book value, it may be an indication of overpricing. Generally, knowledge of book value is of limited value because as we discussed in the last chapter, there are many inadequacies in financial statements.

Cash Flow Per Share

Chart 3.23

$$\text{Cash flow per share} = \frac{\text{Net income} + \text{noncash adjustments}}{\text{Outstanding shares of common stock}}$$

$$\frac{\$12,000 + \$16,000}{25,000} = \underline{\underline{\$1.12}} \text{ Per Share}$$

Cash flow of $1.12 per share measures the amount of cash per share if the books were kept on a cash basis (other than depreciation expense). It does not represent the flow of cash through the enterprise for the period. Nor does it represent the amount of cash available per share if the firm liquidates. Because of misinterpretations, the American Institute of Certified Public Accountants suggests that this ratio not be included in annual reports.

HORIZONTAL ANALYSIS

Horizontal analysis means the examination of the same ratio over a period of time. It is useful in trend analysis, when the proportionate increase or decrease of an account can provide valuable information. Recall that one ratio and ratios for only one period of time are not as meaningful as a series of ratios over well-selected time periods. Most large companies include five to ten years of ratios in their annual reports so readers can observe the trend of pertinent data. Hence, the analyst can focus on the changes in the ratios in relation to modifications of products, divisions, the state of the economy, operating and marketing strategies, and a host of other factors which impact heavily on the profitability and liquidity of a firm.

It is important to relate trend ratios to the size of the firm. For example, a 1% increase in sales for a billion dollar firm results in a $10,000,000 increase, whereas it is only $10,000 for a million dollar firm. Hence for a small firm, a small change in dollars can result in significant changes in ratios. The opposite is true for large firms. An illustration of trends might look like Exhibit 3-1.

An analysis of these ratios indicates that net income and earnings per share are decreasing, even though revenue is increasing. The firm is spending more dollars to increase its revenue ($20,000,000 during the 10-year period). A con-

Exhibit 3-1
ABC COMPANY
Condensed Comparative Statements
(OOO,OOO omitted)

	1985	1984	1983	1982	1981	1975
Revenue	$80	$78	$82	$77	$75	$60
Cost of goods sold	$40	$39	$41	$35	$34	$28
Depreciation	12	12	11	11	10	8
Selling expense	5	4	4	3	3	2
G&A exp	6	7	6	5	5	4
Interest expense	7	6	7	7	5	2
Income tax	5	5	6	9	9	8
Total expenses	$75	$73	$75	$70	$66	$52
Net income	$ 5	$ 5	$ 7	$ 7	$ 9	$ 8
Earning per share	$ 5	$ 5	$ 7	$ 7	$ 9	$ 8
Cash dividend on common stock	$ 3	$ 3	$ 3	$ 3	$ 3	$ 3
Current ratio	1.7	1.6	1.9	1.7	1.6	1.9
Acid test	1.0	.9	.9	.8	1.0	.9
Debt/equity	1.9	1.7	2.6	2.3	1.3	.8
Return on total assets	25%	26%	39%	38%	64%	53%
Return on SE	71%	71%	140%	127%	150%	100%
Market price of CS	$80	$78	$94	$110	$90	$130
Price/earning	16	15	13	16	10	16

stant dividend policy is followed. The current and acid test ratios are fairly constant and indicate the firm is able to meet its obligations. The debt/equity ratio has fluctuated substantially. Although the return on total assets and return on stockholders' equity appear high, keep in mind that these ratios are computed on book value, not fair market value. One might question why the market price of the stock has not fallen lower. The price earnings tend to center around 16. There are major factors influencing stock prices, some internal and some external to the firm. Perhaps the firm has a high sales potential because of new products or was subjected to some unusual economic conditions during the early 1980s.

One sure thing is that the trend data presented do not tell the whole story. Perhaps it is more accurate to say that the data raise more questions than they answer. An analysis of the balance sheet, statement of changes in financial position, and footnotes to the financial statements should be helpful. Another technique that should be applied is vertical analysis.

Exhibit 3-2

XYZ COMPANY

Income Statements

For the Year Ended December 31, 19X1 & 19X2

(in OOO)

	19X2		19X1	
Revenue	$2,000	100%	$1,800	100%
Cost of goods sold	1,000	50	850	47
Gross profit	1,000	50	950	53
Selling expenses	300	15	290	16
General and administrative expenses	400	20	405	22
Income tax expense	200	10	122	7
Net profit after taxes	100	5%	$ 133	8%

VERTICAL ANALYSIS

Vertical analysis is expressing each item on the financial statement as a percentage of a common base. These kinds of financial statements are called common-size financial statements. Revenue is the base for most common-size income statements.

An example of a common-size income statement for the XYZ Company is Exhibit 3-2.

Of course, the data should be expanded beyond two years. The common-size income statements make it apparent that increasing revenue resulted in a higher cost of goods sold and lower profits, even though selling, and general and administrative expenses decreased in relation to revenue. The firm should investigate if its selling prices are too low or manufacturing costs too high or a combination of the two. Perhaps neither is true. Economic conditions or the company's competitive position may explain the 19X2 data. The obvious next question is whether these conditions are expected to continue into the current and future periods.

SUMMARY

We discussed interpretation of financial statements through ratio analysis. We said that ratios must be:

1. Dovetailed to the firm and industry
2. Based on comparative raw data

3. Compared with previous periods
4. Compared with industry's averages
5. Adjusted for differences in accounting principles
6. Interpreted with care

Some of the accounting principles that can distort ratios are historical cost, inventory cost flow, depreciation, deferred income taxes, and pensions. Our discussion of some common ratios was detailed by those that measure the liquidity of a firm, its ability to generate cash, its profitability, and its long-run solvency.

There are many different ratios that can be used to evaluate the soundness of a firm and the effectiveness of its managers. Which ratios are crucial depends upon the type of firm. Effective ratio analysis can go far toward uncovering a company's strengths and weaknesses, its developing problems, its profitability, and its operating efficiency.

4. Cost Concepts

Cost is one of the most nebulous words in the English language and is relatively meaningless without a modifier to indicate the type of cost. Much of the confusion and disagreement over cost is the result of an inadequate definition of terms. It is important in the discussion of the dozen or so cost concepts that follows that you understand each of them and their significance since they are very important for planning, controlling, reporting, and evaluating performance.

Basically, cost is the amount of resources given up in exchange for a good or service. The resource given up is usually measured in terms of money. Costs are either expired or unexpired. Expired costs are called expenses on the income statement. Unexpired costs are assets on the balance sheet. Sometimes, the amount of resources given up is not easy to determine. Certainly, the amount depends upon the circumstances and how cost is defined.

Suppose you read in the newspaper that the cost of sending a child to college is $15,000 a year. You may start feeling rather numb as you wonder how you will be able to finance your children's college education. How is the $15,000 sum arrived at? Published statistics tend to be silent as to the assumptions made and the factors inserted into their formulas. There are many different ways of financing higher education with substantially different costs. Let us consider three alternatives.

1. Junior could stay home, attend the local community college, and ride the bus to school. The incremental out-of-pocket cost would be for low tuition and books, maybe $500 a year.

2. Junior could stay home and go to a private university where tuition is expensive. Incremental cost could easily be $8,000.

3. Junior could attend a private university away from home. Now, $15,000 is not at all unrealistic when considering the cost of tuition, board, room, books, and transportation.

In each of the above examples, we refer to out-of-pocket cost, that is, incremental cost beyond what was expended when Junior was attending the local public high school. Incremental cost is not the same as total cash outflow, as the latter includes cash disbursements for clothing, food, entertainment, and so on. If we want total cost, we would have to add Junior's pro-rata share of common family costs such as shelter, utilities, transportation (assuming Junior resides at home). Finally, we could add opportunity cost. If Junior could earn

$12,000 a year if he were not attending college, we would add $12,000 to the cost of each alternative above.

Consider another example—a published statistic that it costs about $100,000 to raise a child in a middle-class American home. Again, how was the $100,000 computed? Is it solely incremental cost, that is, the additional cash the parents would expend over the years for items such as food and clothing for the child? Or is it total cost—meaning not only cash outlays but the child's portion of common family costs such as shelter? Surely, total cost is substantially higher than incremental cost. How do we allocate shelter cost among the individuals living in a home? Some may say in direct proportion to the number occupants. For example, if annual shelter cost is $10,000 and there are four occupants in a house, one quarter or $2,500 is assigned to each individual. What if a fifth person joins the family? Is this person's shelter cost $2,000 (⅕ of $10,000)? If so, does this mean that the shelter cost of existing occupants decreases simply because the home is shared by more individuals? Maybe the shelter cost is zero for the fifth member based on the premise that no additional shelter cost is incurred and the entire $10,000 is already allocated to the existing occupants. Is it "rational" or "equitable" to assign $2,500 to four occupants and nothing to the fifth? What if the family had to move to larger facilities in order to adequately accommodate the fifth person? Say, the new accommodations cost $12,000 a year. We could argue that the fifth person's cost should be computed:

1. One fifth of $12,000, or $2,400. This method results in each individual in the household sharing equally in the total cost.
2. $12,000 − $10,000 = $2,000. This method reflects the incremental cost assigned to the fifth occupant.
3. None. This method may be justified if the family was planning on moving anyway.

Returning to our problem of how the $100,000 cost of raising a child was computed, it is highly unlikely that it includes opportunity costs, say, the income the mother could have earned during the years she cared for the child. Assume she could have earned $15,000 a year. At the rate of $15,000 a year, the cost of raising a child to age 18 is $270,000 (unadjusted for factors such as the time value of money, employment costs, etc.). What if a woman has two children? Is the opportunity cost now $15,000 for the first child, and zero for the second child, or is it $7,500 for each, or do we ignore wages foregone completely, as society has done in general.

It is hoped that the above illustrations help you to realize that:

1. There is no one perfect way of defining cost.
2. The method of determining cost depends on the circumstances.
3. It is unlikely that all individuals will agree what costs are fair and equitable because the decision entails value judgments. Many behavioral, social, and psychological factors affect the way individuals interpret values.

To the extent practical, cost definitions should be agreed on in advance of economic events rather than afterward. If a person contracted with an automobile manufacturer to build a custom-made automobile for actual cost plus a profit, the day of delivery is hardly the time for the contracting parties to discuss the composition of actual cost. Although generally the term *actual cost* means historical cost, it is not clear what historical cost should be charged to the contract and how it should be measured. The buyer and seller would probably agree that actual direct material and direct labor are allowable, but the allocation of indirect cost (called overhead) is more troublesome. Should the buyer be expected to pay a "fair share" of the seller's independent research and development cost (R&D), especially if some of the expertise utilized in the custom-made car was the result of such R&D?

MANUFACTURING COSTS

In our consideration of various cost definitions, we start with manufacturing cost. There are three principle types of cost necessary to manufacture most products.

1. Direct material
2. Direct labor
3. Manufacturing overhead

Direct material is the cost of material that can be directly traced to the end product. If the cost of concrete, lumber, and shingles can be directly attributed to a house, these items constitute direct material. Similarly, because we can trace wheels, sheet metal, and seats directly to an automobile, these items are also direct material. For some items the cost of directly linking them to the end product is prohibitive, such as nails used in house building. For reasons of immateriality and cost–benefit, such items are classified as indirect material and become part of manufacturing overhead.

Direct labor is similar in concept to direct material. It is the amount of labor that can be directly assigned to an end product. In construction, amounts paid to the framer, electrician, and carpenter constitute direct labor cost. Some labor is more difficult to trace to a particular job. A construction foreman might be overseeing many jobs; hence his time would probably be indirect labor. Indirect labor like indirect material is part of manufacturing overhead. There are labor costs other than manufacturing, for instance, corporate salaries, compensation for individuals displaying model homes, and salesmen's commissions. How do we classify these costs? Corporate salaries are probably classified as general and administrative cost (G&A) and the other two are selling expenses.

Manufacturing overhead is all manufacturing costs that are not classified as direct material and direct labor. It consists of indirect manufacturing costs. Some of the more common manufacturing costs for a medium size company are summarized here.

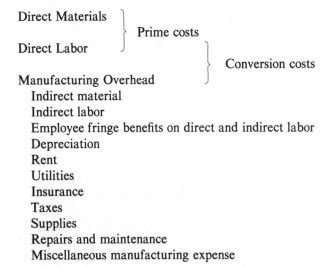

Direct Materials ⎫
                 ⎬ Prime costs
Direct Labor   ⎭
                      ⎫
                      ⎬ Conversion costs
Manufacturing Overhead ⎭
   Indirect material
   Indirect labor
   Employee fringe benefits on direct and indirect labor
   Depreciation
   Rent
   Utilities
   Insurance
   Taxes
   Supplies
   Repairs and maintenance
   Miscellaneous manufacturing expense

Direct material and direct labor are referred to as prime costs. Direct labor and manufacturing overhead make up conversion costs.

A firm cannot wait until the end of the accounting period to determine the cost of manufacturing goods. Direct material and direct labor can easily be charged to a product or job when these costs are incurred. Manufacturing overhead is more troublesome because the total actual manufacturing cost will not be known until the end of the accounting period. Hence these costs cannot be charged to products or jobs as they are incurred because there is no way of knowing which amounts are applicable to which products or jobs. This problem can be resolved by use of a predetermined manufacturing overhead rate. At the beginning of the period, we estimate expected overhead costs for the period.

Next, we select a base for spreading the expected overhead costs over units produced during the period. Direct labor hours or direct labor dollars are common overhead allocation bases. Ideally, the base selected should most equitably match the manufacturing overhead actual cost with the units produced.

The determination of an overhead base is not easy. There has probably been more disagreement over the most appropriate overhead base than any other cost-accounting concept. The base is important because the amount of indirect manufacturing cost ultimately assigned to products depends on the overhead base. Therefore, the base directly affects the amount of inventory, the cost of goods sold, and the period in which profit is recognized on the income statement.

Assume that the base is direct labor hours. The manufacturing overhead formula is:

$$\frac{\text{Estimated manufacturing overhead costs}}{\text{Estimated direct labor hours}} = \text{predetermined overhead rate}$$

Putting hypothetical numbers in the formula, the predetermined overhead rate is $2 per direct labor hour.

$$\frac{\$20,000,000}{10,000,000 \text{ hours}} = \$2$$

The firm would assign to a product or job $2 overhead for every direct labor hour incurred. The cost of manufacturing 100 widgets can be computed as follows:

Direct material	$1,300
Direct labor (100 hours at $10)	1,000
Manufacturing overhead (100 hours × $2)	200
Total manufacturing cost	$2,500
Manufacturing cost per widget $2,500/100	$25

Of course we would not offer these items for sale at $25 each. There are other costs to consider—selling expenses and general and administrative expenses. Selling expenses are marketing costs, for example, salesmen's salaries and commissions, advertising, salesmen's travel expenses, and depreciation on sales facilities and equipment. General and administrative costs include executive, organizational, and clerical costs required for the general administration of the firm. The cost of the accounting department is properly classified as G&A.

Suppose direct material dollars were selected as the overhead base in lieu of direct labor hours. Using hypothetical figures, the predetermined overhead rate is $4 per direct material dollar incurred.

$$\frac{\$20,000,000}{\$5,000,000} = \$4$$

Now the cost of manufacturing the 100 widgets is:

Direct material	$1,300
Direct labor (100 hours at $10)	1,000
Manufacturing overhead ($1,300 direct material × $4)	5,200
Total manufacturing cost	$7,500

Thus you can see in this example that the cost of the 100 widgets is $5,000 larger ($7,500 − $2,500) if direct material dollars is used as the overhead base instead of direct labor hours. No wonder selection of the base is a critical decision. Obviously, if material dollars are used as the base, products requiring a high amount of direct material dollars will carry a larger amount of overhead. Similarly, if direct labor hours is the base, highly labor-intensive products will absorb a higher amount of the overhead.

PRODUCT/PERIOD COSTS

Costs can be further defined as product or period cost. A product cost is attached to the product; that is, product cost follows the physical flow of the product. If the product is unsold, its cost is in inventory. Period cost relates to a period of time and is expensed on the income statement during the applicable period. Under generally accepted accounting principles, manufacturing costs are product costs whereas selling and G&A are period costs. Again, this differentiation is important because it tells which period of time the cost is recognized as an expense on the income statement. The following chart should help define product and period cost as they relate to financial statements.

Manufacturing Costs	*Balance Sheet*	*Income Statement*
Direct material		
Direct labor	Work-in- Finished	Cost of
	process → goods →	goods
Manufacturing overhead	inventory inventory	sold
Selling expense	→	Expense
General & administrative	→	Expense

Note that product costs are stored in inventory accounts until the product is sold. Inventory is carried on the books as an asset, that is, as an item of value. Hence, under generally accepted accounting principles it is the point of sale that measures the amount of profit and determines the period of time that it is recognized. When an inventory item is sold, its cost is transferred on the income statement from finished goods inventory to cost of goods sold.

Selling and general and administrative expenses on the other hand are immediately expensed as period cost when these costs are incurred. They are never "stored" in the inventory accounts.

We said in the introduction to this chapter that cost may be defined as expired or unexpired cost. Expired cost is an expense, that is, recognized on the income statement as a deduction from revenue. Salemen's commissions on products sold in the current period is an expense, whereas factory rent paid in advance (say for next year) is an unexpired cost. Unexpired costs are balance sheet items; expired costs are income statement accounts. Note that these concepts are similiar but not quite identical to the concept of product or period cost.

CONTROLLABLE/NONCONTROLLABLE COSTS

Costs are also classified as controllable or noncontrollable. A controllable cost can be controlled; a noncontrollable cannot be. If a cost is controllable, an individual has the power to authorize its expenditure, and therefore that individual should be held responsible for it. A person should not be held accountable for costs he or she cannot control. This principle underlies the concept of responsibility accounting. Managers should budget and control only those costs under their jurisdiction.

All costs are controllable at some level of the firm. In complex organizations classifying cost as controllable or not is extremely difficult. Many individuals, departments, and divisions may be involved in the design, production, and marketing of a product. Generally, the extent to which a cost is controllable depends upon the level of management. For example, a salesperson would not normally be responsible for advertising, the sales manager might be, and the marketing vice president is sure to be responsible. Incidently, the words *controllable* and *uncontrollable* apply to revenue too.

There are many reasons other than profit for being concerned over the controllability of cost. Under participative budgeting, managers normally budget only those items they can control. They make decisions concerning the incurring of costs, explain any differences between budgeted and actual costs, and institute whatever corrective action is required. In addition, managers may be evaluated and even compensated for their ability to control cost. Thus, "goal incongruence" is likely to develop if managers are held responsible for costs they cannot control.

ENGINEERED/DISCRETIONARY COSTS

The concept of engineered and discretionary costs is closely related to controllable and noncontrollable costs. Costs are engineered when the right or proper amount of the costs to be incurred can be estimated with a high degree of precision. Direct material and direct labor are usually considered to be engineered costs since their approximate amounts are determinable by engineering studies. Engineered costs are not to any significant degree the result of management's judgment.

Discretionary costs (also called *programmed costs* and *managed costs*) tend to be set by management; that is, they are budgeted at constant levels for particular time periods. Decisions are made annually at the beginning of the period as to how much should be expended. Examples are advertising, research, and management development programs. Obviously a firm has considerable control over advertising. If top managment commits $2 million dollars for advertising for the next period, this amount becomes fixed for all intents and purposes. Hence, discretionary costs take on the attribute of a fixed cost—they do not change with output.

Discretionary costs are more controllable in the short run than committed fixed costs, such as may arise from the construction of a new facility. The former are relatively short lived (usually one year) whereas the latter may extend over many years.

HISTORICAL/FUTURE COSTS

Historical costs are those costs that have already been incurred, whereas future costs are expected to be incurred. Recall that managerial accountants and managers are more concerned with the future than with the past because they can only change the future. Future costs are relevant to decisions; historical costs may or may not be. Here is an illustration of a situation when historical cost is irrelevant.

Suppose a firm expends $3,000 for a machine. Shortly thereafter a new model is available for $5,000, which would save $50 a widget. The old machine is worth only $100 because it is obsolete. Suppose the new machine and the old machine can both produce 200 widgets, so that the quantity of output is not the determining factor in this problem; cost is. The original cost of $3,000 is irrelevant to the decision of whether or not to trade machines. The historical cost is a sunk cost. It has no bearing on the solution to the problem, which is whether or not to trade machines. The calculations are as follows:

Savings (200 widgets × $50)	$10,000
Cost of new machine	(5,000)
Trade in value of old machine	100
Net savings	$ 5,100

Clearly it is advantageous to trade the old machine for the new machine. Note that the above illustration ignores several crucial factors: income taxes, time value of money, and opportunity cost. The effect of income tax is such a major consideration that we devote an entire chapter to taxes later in the book (Chapter 17). The time value of money is also an important consideration. A dollar earned in five years does not have the same value as a dollar earned now. We also devote an entire chapter (Chapter 14) to the time value of money and another chapter (Chapter 15) to applications. The final consideration is opportunity cost. Opportunity cost is the potential benefit that is lost when one of several alternatives is selected. Maybe the $4,900 ($5,000 cost of the new machine less $100 trade-in) cost of the new machine could be invested at 10%. The $490 potential earnings foregone is an opportunity cost. Again, opportunity cost is profit foregone because of a decision between alternatives and must be considered for each selected alternative being studied. One way of avoiding calculation of opportunity cost is to compute the total cost for all alternatives and compare the results, but this is seldom feasible in terms of effort, time, and cost.

Opportunity cost, alluded to several times already in this chapter, is a very important concept and one which is not well understood by the general public. We therefore present a couple more examples (ignoring the effects of income taxes). Suppose managers are trying to decide if they should rent a building or buy it. The down payment is $50,000. The interest income foregone on the $50,000 is an opportunity cost. If the $50,000 could have been invested at 15%, there is an opportunity cost the first year of $7,500 (15% of $50,000). The opportunity cost the second year is $8,625 (15% of $50,000 plus $7,500). Each year of the mortgage the opportunity cost increases because the original down payment, plus any interest foregone to date, is not earning a return.

Similarly, there is an opportunity cost of the down payment on homes. Interestingly, many homeowners are very concerned about the interest rates of their mortgages, but ignore or fail to realize that there is an opportunity cost of the down payment. If interest is 16% and a mortgage is $100,000 after a downpayment of $20,000, the effective interest cost for the first year (assuming annual mortgage payments) is not $16,000 but $19,200

$100,000 × 16%	$16,000
$20,000 × 16%	3,200
	$19,200

Admittedly, the cash outflow for interest is $16,000 as well as the amount deductible for income taxes, assuming the homeowner itemizes deductions.

Individuals fortunate enough to have a $120,000 home fully paid for are still suffering an annual opportunity loss of $18,000 (interest rate of 15%), plus interest foregone on opportunity cost to date. It is important that you understand that the owners have foregone the opportunity to earn $18,000 before taxes, even though their cash outflow for interest (and principle) is zero. Still, from a practical and psychological point of view, foregoing a cash inflow may be more palatable than payment of a cash outflow.

One more example: Suppose that as a university professor, I were to contemplate a trip to Europe this summer at a cost of $3,000. If I could instead teach summer school and earn $5,000, the cost of my European trip would really be $8,000 before taxes.

Opportunity costs are relevant for decisions whereas historical costs are usually irrelevant. Why then are historical costs the primary measurement base for accounting records and for published financial statements? Perhaps the major reason is that their amounts can be objectively determined. An accountant can easily determine the dollar amount of material purchased by reference to purchase orders and payment documentation. Accountants do not always know the liquidation value or replacement cost of inventory and long-term assets, and hence cannot assess opportunity costs with certainty.

Recall from Chapter 1 that managerial accountants and managers can use any measurement base for internal decision making; hence a blind adherence to historical cost is hardly managing effectively.

DIFFERENTIAL COSTS

Differential cost (also known as incremental cost) is the cost difference between two alternatives. For example, if a person receives two identical job offers except that one job requires driving an extra 20 miles a day, the cost of the additional transportation is the differential cost. To make a decision it is not necessary to compute the net revenue (salary less job related expenses) for each job because all that is required is to know the differential cost, that is, the cost of driving the extra 20 miles.

As a more sophisticated example, suppose a firm with the necessary knowhow and excess capacity receives an offer to make 100 widgets at $70. The order would require renting a special-purpose machine at $300. Assume that one half of the $16 overhead rate per direct labor hour is fixed and one half is variable. In other words overhead will increase only $8 per direct labor hour if the order is accepted. We could compute total revenue and total cost before and after the order but that is tedious and unnecessary. An easier way is to compare differential revenue with differential cost. Here are the calculations.

	UNIT COST	TOTAL COST (100 WIDGETS)
Direct material	$30	$3,000
Direct labor (2 hours at $10)	20	2,000
Manufacturing overhead (½ × $16 per direct labor hour × 2 hours)	16	1,600
	$66	$6,600
Additional rental cost		300
Differential cost		$6,900
Differential revenue (100 widgets at $70)		7,000
Differential profit		$ 100

A comparison of the additional manufacturing cost with the differential revenue shows an increase in profit of $100 if the firm accepts the order. The next step is to consider nonfinancial criteria to determine if it is preferable to accept an offer that yields a relatively low incremental profit.

Note that the differential cost listed above is not full manufacturing cost. To obtain full cost we would have to add another $1,600 (for the fixed portion of overhead) to the $6,900 to obtain a total cost of $8,500. Clearly then the order would be rejected. Many firms price their products based on full cost plus a markup, such as 15% of full cost. Full-cost pricing models are not always appropriate because in many cases profitable orders are not accepted. In the above illustration, the firm would have $100 less profit on its income statement if it rejects the order.

FIXED/VARIABLE COST

A very important breakdown of cost is fixed versus variable cost. Fixed costs do not change with output over a relevant range. It is possible for fixed costs to change with time, as happens when an increase in the real estate tax occurs during the accounting period, but fixed costs do not change with output. Variable costs change in direct proportion to output. Direct material and direct labor are examples of variable costs.

An understanding of the behavior of fixed and variable costs is critical to decision making. Assuming a variable cost of $20 a widget and a fixed cost of $100, the more widgets that are manufactured, the higher the total variable cost and the lower the average cost per unit because the fixed cost is spread over more units (see Exhibit 4-1).

Note that variable cost per unit (column 2) is constant but total variable costs (column 3) increases at the rate of $20 a unit. Total fixed cost (column 4) is constant but fixed cost per unit decreases at a diminishing rate. Total cost

Exhibit 4-1
Behavior of Fixed and Variable Costs

(1)	(2)	(3) TOTAL VARIABLE COST (COL. 1 × COL. 2)	(4)	(5) FIXED COST PER WIDGET (COL. 4/ COL. 1)	(6)	(7) AVERAGE COST PER WIDGET (COL. 6/ COL. 1)
NUMBER OF WIDGETS	VARIABLE COST PER WIDGET		TOTAL FIXED COST		TOTAL COST (COL. 3 + COL. 4)	
1	$20	$20	$100	$100	$120	$120
2	$20	$40	$100	$ 50	$140	$ 70
3	$20	$60	$100	$ 33	$160	$ 53
4	$20	$80	$100	$ 25	$180	$ 45

(column 6) increases at the rate of $20, the amount of variable cost per unit. The average cost per unit (column 7) decreases by the same amount that fixed cost per unit (column 5) decreases.

Now let us plot columns 4 and 5 from Exhibit 4-1 on a graph in Exhibit 4-2. Then the behavioral pattern of these costs becomes more evident.

Exhibit 4-2
Behavior of Total Fixed Cost and Fixed Cost per Unit of Output

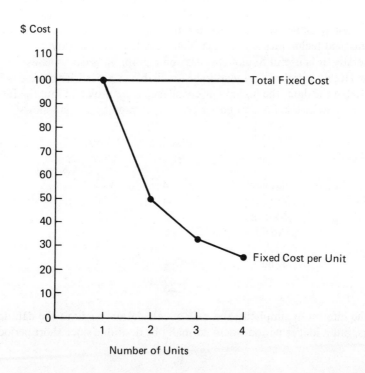

Note that the total fixed cost is a straight line because it does not vary with output, but as more units are produced, the fixed cost per unit decreases at a diminishing rate.

Variable costs behave just the opposite (see Exhibit 4-3). Now the per unit cost is a straight horizontal line whereas total variable cost increases at a constant rate of $20 per unit. Also, note that if no widgets are produced total variable cost is zero, but total fixed cost id $100 (see Exhibit 4-2).

If we superimpose the two graphs on each other and add a total cost line (Exhibit 4-4), we find that the average cost per unit behaves very much like the fixed cost per unit; that is, it decreases at a decreasing rate. The distance between average cost per unit and fixed cost per unit lines is a constant $20, the amount of the variable cost per unit. Study these graphs well because this theory forms the basis for cost-volume-profit analysis and pricing theory.

SEMIVARIABLE COSTS

Unfortunately, not all costs fall neatly into a fixed or variable category. Many are mixed (semivariable) in that they contain an element of both fixed and variable cost. For example, assume a $45 telephone bill which consists of a flat $30 per month plus charges for meter units and long-distance calls. The $30 is the fixed portion and the remaining $15 is variable. Semivariable accounts must be broken down into their fixed and variable elements. If a rational breakdown is not possible, such as with the telephone example, there are several mathematical techniques available, which we will discuss shortly.

Generally, it is useful to plot cost data on a graph in order to assess its variability. Highly variable data tend to be unreliable as a basis for decisions. The less variable the data, the higher our confidence if we project it into the future.

Assume machine hours and power cost for six months are as follows:

	Machine Hours	Power Cost
January	8	$12
February	6	10
March	5	8
April	9	12
May	10	13
June	4	7
	42	$62

In the interest of simplicity and ease of calculation, we limit the data to six months, but a longer period would normally be desirable since short periods of

Exhibit 4-3
Behavior of Total Variable Cost and Variable Cost per Unit

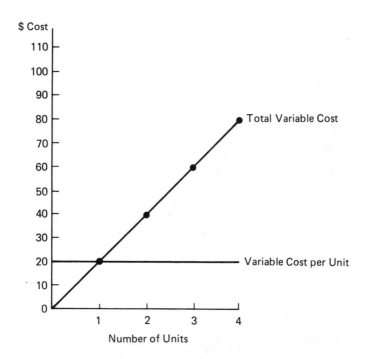

time may not be representative of the future. Here is the data plotted on a graph (Exhibit 4-5).

This type of graph is called a scattergraph. We can get a fair idea how the cost behaves by observing where the points fall on the graph. The power cost tends to increase as machine activity increases, but it is obvious that the points do not neatly fall on a straight line. If they did, we could measure the slope of the line and we could use the equation for projecting future cost. The linear equation for a straight line is of the form:

$$y = a + bx$$

where a = fixed cost and b is variable cost per machine hour. One way of arriving at a linear equation is to estimate (eyeball) the line that would best fit the data, something like Exhibit 4-6.

The fixed portion of the equation is where the line intersects the y axis and

Exhibit 4-4
Behavior of Fixed and Variable Cost

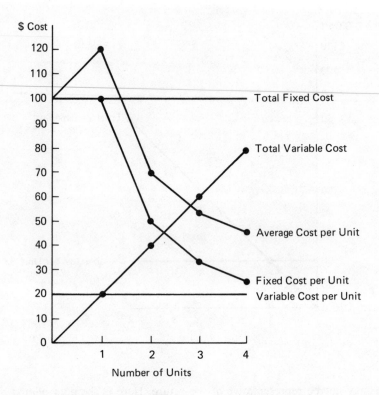

the variable portion is the slope of the line. Power cost increases approximately $1 with each machine hour. Therefore, the estimated linear equation is:

$$\text{Total power cost} = \$4 + \$1x$$

where x = number of machine hours. If more precision is desired the line can be calculated mathematically by the high-low or least squares techniques.

High-Low Method

The high-low method involves finding the highest and lowest levels of cost and changes in the activity base. Any difference in cost observed at the two

Exhibit 4-5
Scattergraph

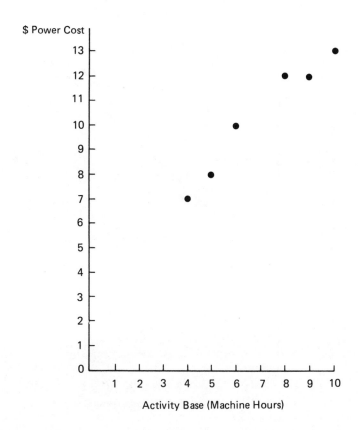

$ Power Cost

Activity Base (Machine Hours)

extremes is divided by the change in activity. The result is variable cost per unit of the activity base. We determine the fixed portion by the following steps.

1. Find the difference between the highest and lowest amounts for both cost and machine hours. The differences are six and six respectively.

	Power Cost	Machine Hours
Highest	$13	10
Lowest	7	4
Difference	$ 6	6

Exhibit 4-6
Estimated Best Fit Line

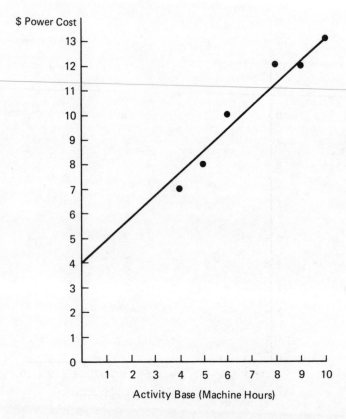

Activity Base (Machine Hours)

2. Divide the power cost difference by the change in machine hours.

$$\frac{\$6}{6} = \$1 \text{ per machine hour}$$

The variable rate is $1 per machine hours.

3. Find the fixed portion by inserting pertinent data in the familiar linear equation formula for either the highest or lowest month. Using the highest month's data the linear equation is computed:

$$\$13 = a + \$1(10)$$
$$\$13 = a + \$10$$
$$a = \$3$$

The fixed cost is $3. The formula is then:

$$\text{Total cost} = \$3 + \$1x$$

The lowest month's data will result in the same answer.

Least Squares

The least squares method is mathematically more accurate, though a bit tedious to calculate without a computer. Commercial software packages are readily available to handle the arithmetic. Least squares occurs when the sum of the squares of the deviations from the plotted points to the regression line is smaller than would be obtained from any other line fitted to the data. In other words, it is the line of best fit. Two simultaneous equations must be solved:

$$xy = a\,x + b\,x^2$$
$$y = na + b\,x$$

where

a = fixed cost
b = variable cost
n = number of observations
x = activity measure
y = total mixed cost

The calculations using the same raw data as for high-low are:

	MACHINE HOURS x	POWER COST y	xy	x^2
January	8	12	96	64
February	6	10	60	36
March	5	8	40	25
April	9	12	108	81
May	10	13	130	100
June	4	7	28	16
	42	62	462	322

Substituting numbers into the formulas:

$$462 = 42a + 322b$$
$$62 = 6a + 42b$$

The arithmetic to determine the value of b is:

$$
\begin{aligned}
2772 &= 252a + 1932b \\
\underline{2604} &= \underline{252a + 1764b} \\
168 &= 168b \\
1 &= b
\end{aligned}
$$

Substituting the value of b in one of the formulas, we can compute a:

$$
\begin{aligned}
62 &= 6a + 42(1) \\
3.33 &= a
\end{aligned}
$$

Therefore, the cost formula is:

$$\text{Cost} = \$3.33 + 1x$$

The above formula can be used to plan future expenditures. For example, if 11 machine hours are expected to be needed for production during the next month, July's power cost can be estimated at:

$$
\begin{aligned}
\text{Power cost} &= \$3.33 + \$1(11) \\
\text{Power cost} &= \$14.33
\end{aligned}
$$

UNUSUAL COST BEHAVIOR

Judgment must be exercised in each of the above ways of determining the variable portion of mixed data on the assumption that past data are indicative of the future. What do we do with a point on the graph that greatly deviates from the normal pattern, like the circled point shown in Exhibit 4-7? Do we ignore the point or include it in the raw data? First, we must determine the reason for its erratic behavior. If the cause is of a nonrecurring nature, we remove it from our model. If the reoccurrence cannot be ascertained, we must use judgment to decide if we wish to keep the deviate point in the raw data. This is important because the slope of the line is dependent upon the position of the points. We are interested in obtaining a line whereby future behavior will coincide with projected behavior.

RELEVANT RANGE

The breakdown between fixed and variable cost is only valid within a relevant range. We know from economics that over the long run all costs are variable.

Exhibit 4-7
Graph Depicting Unusual Behavior

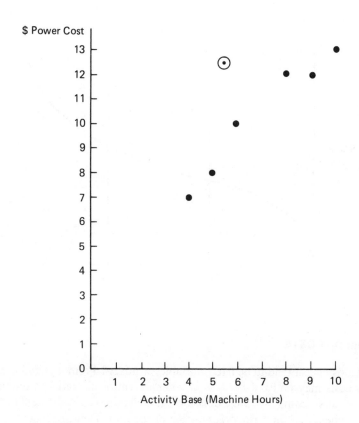

The managerial accountant is concerned with short-term as well as long-run problems. Hence, establishing the relevant range can be helpful for short-run problems. Graphically, the relevant range is indicated in Exhibit 4-8.

Note that the line is curvilinear. At very high and very low activity levels, the cost and volume do not follow a linear relationship. Although determination of the slope of a curvilinear line is possible through the use of calculus, it is tedious and unnecessary. Within the relevant range the slope is sufficiently stable that the assumption of linearity can be used without significant loss of accuracy. The graph shows that the relevant range is between 1,000 and 2,000 units. Within it, we can compute our variable and fixed cost with sufficient accuracy for decision making.

Exhibit 4-8
Illustration of Relevant Range

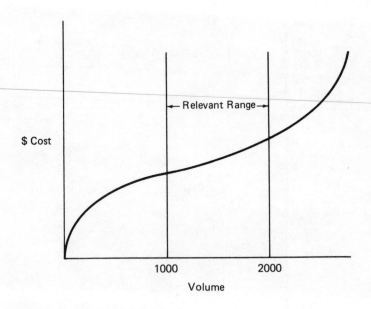

NATURE OF COSTS

What kinds of cost tend to be fixed, variable, or mixed? From a planning point of view costs may be fixed because of commitment or discretion. Committed fixed costs arise from long-range decisions on such things as investment in plant and equipment and the basic organization of the firm. Typical accounts are:

1. Depreciation of facilities and equipment
2. Real estate taxes
3. Insurance
4. Salaries of key management and operating personnel

These kinds of fixed costs generally cannot be easily reduced over the short run.

Discretionary fixed costs arise from management decisions. We talked about these earlier in this chapter. We said that they arose from annual decisions as to how much should be expended for certain programs such as advertising, research, and management development. Since discretionary costs have a fairly short-term planning horizon, they are much easier to reduce or eliminate should hard times hit the firm.

The concept of the relevant range gives fixed cost behavior something like what is shown in Exhibit 4-9. Within the relevant range fixed costs are $400, below it $300, and beyond it $500. Note that the $300 line does not reach the *y* axis because $300 is not necessarily the amount of fixed cost should the plant close down. If such an event occurred the type of fixed cost would likely change somewhat by the nature of each fixed-cost account.

Generally, prime costs of direct material and direct labor are assumed to be variable, which means that these costs are assumed to change in direct proportion to changes in activity level and that they are constant on a per unit basis. In order for a cost to be variable, it must be variable in relation to an activity base. The number of units produced is the base for direct material and direct labor. For salesmen's commissions it could be number of units sold. For

Exhibit 4-9
Behavior of Fixed Cost within Relevant Range

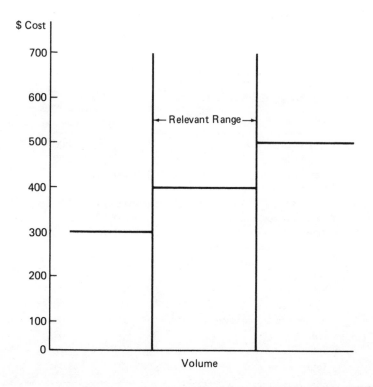

automobile expenses it could be number of miles driven. The activity base should vary in direct relationship with the variable cost.

Theoretically there are very few costs that behave 100% in accordance with an activity base, but perfect precision is not necessary for data to be useful. For example, there are many reasons why direct material does not change perfectly with changes in output, for instance:

1. Quantity discounts
2. Rush orders causing higher prices
3. Changes in suppliers
4. Abnormally high or low spoilage
5. Changes in quality of raw materials

Most manufacturing costs are semivariable or mixed and form part of manufacturing overhead. Examples include:

1. Indirect materials
2. Indirect labor
3. Factory supplies

Exhibit 4-10
Input for Linear Formula

	FIXED COST	VARIABLE COST PER UNIT
Direct material		$1.00
Direct labor		1.50
Depreciation	$20,000	
Real estate tax	2,000	
Insurance	1,000	
Salaries of key executives	8,000	
Advertising	1,000	
Research and development	2,000	
Management development	500	
Indirect material	500	.10
Indirect labor	400	.20
Factory supplies	100	.05
Repairs and maintenance	300	.08
Utilities	600	.09
Set up	100	.02
Total	$36,500	$3.04

4. Repairs and maintenance
5. Utilities
6. Set up

Once semivariable costs have been separated into fixed and variable components, a linear formula for total manufacturing cost can be computed. Exhibit 4-10 provides the input for the linear formula. The cost is $36,500 + 3.04x$ within the relevant range. Now we can project the cost of any number of units, say 10,000 units.

$$\text{Cost} = \$36,500 + \$3.04(10,000)$$
$$\text{Cost} = \$36,500 + \$30,400$$
$$\text{Cost} = \$66,900$$

This cost formula can be used for breakeven (the volume where revenue equals cost), budgeting, and pricing. Each of these applications is discussed in later chapters. Again, we would like to impress upon you that it is absolutely essential that you understand how cost behaves, both in total and on a per unit basis because knowledge of behavioral patterns is useful in solving a variety of managerial problems.

SUMMARY

In this chapter we discussed types of costs. We said that it was very important to understand their various meanings and their context. To manufacture products three types of manufacturing cost are necessary:

1. Direct material and direct labor costs can be directly traced to the end products.
2. Indirect costs cannot be identified directly with the end product. They are assigned to goods produced by means of a predetermined overhead rate.

Manufacturing costs are product costs in that they are inventoriable, meaning that they are assets while the product is unsold. After sales the inventory becomes a cost on the income statement. Costs that are expensed in the period of time they are applicable are period costs. These include selling expenses and general and administrative expenses.

If an individual authorizes expenditures the result is a controllable cost. Managers should not be held responsible for noncontrollable cost.

Historical costs are incurred actual costs, while future costs are anticipated costs. Future costs are relevant for decisions; historical costs seldom are relevant except for the income tax effect. Historical costs are frequently considered to be "sunk costs" when they have no bearing on a decision.

Opportunity costs are potential benefits foregone as a result of a particular decision. Opportunity costs are relevant to future decisions.

Engineering costs are much more determinable than discretionary costs. The former can be scientifically estimated, whereas the latter is the result of management's decisions.

Differential costs are additional costs incurred as the result of a particular decision. Usually, it is more advantageous to calculate the differential costs for alternatives instead of the total cost of each alternative.

Perhaps the most important cost distinction is between fixed and variable. Fixed costs do not change with output over a relevant range, whereas variable costs change in direct relation with output. Mixed costs must be broken down into their fixed and variable components. Now a linear formula can be developed that is immensely helpful in solving a variety of problems, including cost-volume-profit analysis.

5. Cost-Volume-Profit Relationships

Once we have separated variable and fixed costs, we can utilize the data for decision making. Let us start out by discussing *breakeven,* that is, how many units or what dollar amount of sales is necessary to have no profit or loss. Breakeven occurs when total revenue exactly equals total costs; therefore, it is the point of zero profit or loss.

Assume that we are manufacturing an item with an expected selling price of $5 per unit, variable cost of $3 per unit, and fixed costs of $10,000. The solution can be found two ways: the equation technique and the contribution margin approach.

EQUATION TECHNIQUE

The equation technique mirrors the profit and loss statement prepared under a variable-costing approach. (Chapter 6 covers variable-costing income statements.) The formula is:

$$\text{Sales} = \text{variable expenses} + \text{fixed costs} + \text{profits}$$

Let x = breakeven in units.

$$\$5x = \$3x + \$10{,}000 + 0$$
$$\$5x - \$3x = \$10{,}000$$
$$\$2x = \$10{,}000$$
$$x = \frac{\$10{,}000}{2}$$
$$x = 5{,}000 \text{ units}$$

The breakeven point is 5,000 units. Again, the equation is selling price per unit times the number of units sold is equal to the variable cost per unit times number of units sold plus total fixed cost plus zero profit.

We can easily convert the breakeven units into dollars of sales by multiplying by the expected selling price:

$$5{,}000 \times \$5 = \$25{,}000 \text{ sales to breakeven}$$

CONTRIBUTION MARGIN APPROACH

Under the contribution margin approach, the first step is to compute the contribution margin. *Contribution margin* is a very important concept, useful in many decision models. The formula for calculating the contribution margin is very simple.

Contribution margin = selling price per unit − variable cost per unit. It can also be computed on a total basis, such as:

$$\text{Contribution margin} = \text{total revenue} - \text{total variable cost}$$

We commonly say that the contribution margin is the amount that the selling price contributes to fixed cost and profit. We can easily prove this by looking at an income statement.

Sales	$10,000
Variable cost	6,400
Contribution margin	$3,600
Fixed costs	2,000
Profit	$ 1,600

Below breakeven, contribution margin is all fixed costs; above breakeven per-unit contribution margin is profit.

For breakeven calculation, we use contribution margin on a per unit basis. Substituting figures from our example into the formula we arrive at a contribution margin of $2 per unit.

$$\text{\$5 selling price} - \text{\$3 variable cost} = \text{\$2 contribution margin}$$

Now if we divide the $10,000 fixed costs by contribution margin, we have breakeven in terms of sales units.

$$\frac{\$10,000}{\$2} = 5,000 \text{ units}$$

Note that this is the same answer we arrived at earlier utilizing the equation technique.

Variable Cost/Selling Price Relationship

If the dollar amount of variable costs is unknown but the relationship of variable cost to sales is known, we can still determine breakeven, only this time in terms of sales dollars. For example, suppose we did not know that variable cost was $3 per unit or that the selling price was $5 per unit, but we knew that the relationship between the two was .60. Our calculation is:

$$\text{Revenue} = \text{fixed cost} + \text{variable cost \%} + \text{profit}$$
$$x = \$10{,}000 + .6x + 0$$
$$x - .6x = \$10{,}000$$
$$.4x = \$10{,}000$$
$$x = \$25{,}000 \text{ breakeven in sales dollars}$$

We can easily convert to units by dividing $25,000 by the selling price

$$\$25{,}000/\$5 = 5{,}000 \text{ units}$$

Cost-Volume-Profit Graph 1

We now graph this example as a breakeven chart (also called a cost-volume-profit graph). The y axis on Exhibit 5-1 represents dollars and the x axis units.

Exhibit 5-1
Breakeven Graph

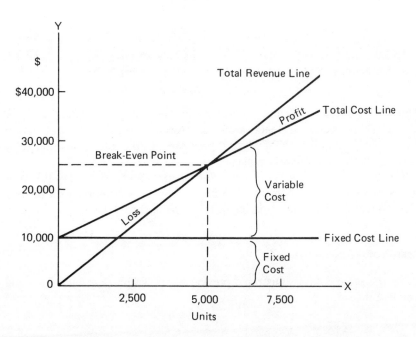

Recall that fixed cost is constant with output; therefore it will be represented by a horizontal line starting at $10,000 on the y axis. With zero sales, we would have $10,000 of cost and a $10,000 loss. Similarly, were we to have zero production, we would incur no variable cost because variable cost by definition varies with output. Therefore, the total cost line starts at $10,000 and increases by $3 for each unit sold. The distance between total cost and fixed cost is variable cost.

The revenue line commences at point zero because if there are no sales there can be no revenue. This line increases at the rate of $5 per unit, the amount of the selling price. The revenue line intersects the total cost line at breakeven (in this case, $25,000 and 5,000 units). Note that the entire area below breakeven is a loss, but that the loss decreases, the closer to breakeven. Conversely, the entire area above breakeven is profit. The distance between the total revenue and total cost lines increases as additional units beyond breakeven are sold. One way of interpreting the graph is that below breakeven the entire amount of the contribution margin consists of fixed costs, whereas after breakeven the fixed costs have been covered, so the contribution margin is profit. This explains why profit increases rapidly after breakeven. How much profit does one additional unit sold produce? The answer is $2, the amount of the contribution margin. Hence, you can readily compute the profit on any number of items sold after breakeven simply by multiplying the number of items by the contribution margain. This is powerful knowledge for decision making. Consider what would happen if the firm sold

1. 6,000 units (6,000 units — 5,000 units breakeven) × $2 $2,000
2. 8,000 units (8,000 units — 5,000 units breakeven) × $2 $6,000

The net income on the income statement would increase before taxes by $2,000 and $6,000 respectively. Hence, profit increases rapidly as additional units are sold. Keep in mind that this analysis is predicated on the assumption that 8,000 units are within the relevant range.

The two alternative ways of preparing breakeven charts display the same information we just demonstrated. Still, you should be familiar with them in order to feel comfortable preparing or using them, should you be requested to.

Cost-Profit-Volume Graph 2

Using the same data as illustrated previously, the graph (Exhibit 5-2) would look like this:

Exhibit 5-2
Breakeven Graph

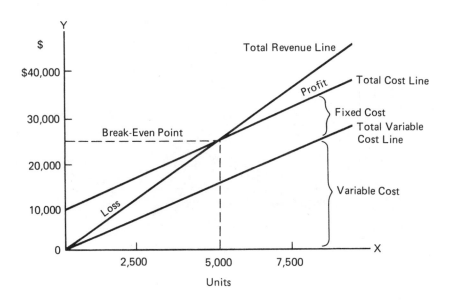

The only difference between this graph and Exhibit 5-1 is that Exhibit 5-2 shows variable cost on the bottom and fixed cost piled on top of variable cost, whereas the previous graph depicts these lines in the opposite positions. Neither graph is superior. It is simply a matter of individual preference as to which graph is easier to comprehend and utilize.

Cost–Volume–Profit Graph 3

Still, some would say that there is a simpler way of displaying breakeven; see, for instance, Exhibit 5-3. This graph shows only one line—a profit-loss line. When the firm is below breakeven, the firm is operating at a loss. Hence, the beginning point on the y axis is a negative $10,000, the amount of the fixed costs. The firm is at breakeven when the profit–loss line crosses the x axis. This is, of course, at 5,000 units. Sales above 5,000 units generate profit.

Other variations of the above models are to label the x axis as a percentage of capacity or dollars.

EXPANDING THE BREAKEVEN CONCEPT

We can expand the breakeven principle to cover a variety of situations.

Exhibit 5-3
Breakeven Graph

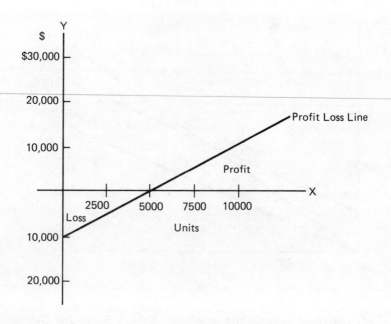

Profit

How many units must a company sell to make a profit of $8,000?

$$\text{Sales} = \text{VC} + \text{FC} + \text{profit}$$
$$\$5x = \$3x + \$10,000 + \$8,000$$
$$\$5x = \$3x + \$18,000$$
$$\$2x = \$18,000$$
$$x = 9,000 \text{ units}$$

or

$$9,000 \times \$5 = \$45,000 \text{ sales}$$

Thus, we see that the answer is 9,000 units or $45,000 sales.

Utilizing the contribution margin approach, we arrive at the same answer:

$$\frac{\text{Fixed cost} + \text{profit}}{\text{Contribution margin}}$$

$$\text{Sales} = \frac{\$10,000 + \$8,000}{\$2}$$

$$\text{Sales} = \frac{\$18,000}{\$2}$$

$$\text{Sales} = 9,000 \text{ units}$$

Percentage Increase in Sales

If we wanted to know breakeven, assuming a 20% increase in sales revenue, we would simply add 20% of sales to our formula.

$$\text{Sales} = \text{variable cost} + \text{fixed cost}$$
$$\$5x + .20\,(\$5x) = \$3x + \$10,000$$
$$\$5x + \$1x = \$3x + \$10,000$$
$$\$6x = \$3x + \$10,000$$
$$\$6x - \$3x = \$10,000$$
$$\$3x = \$10,000$$
$$x = 3.333 \text{ units}$$

Change in Fixed Cost

What would breakeven be if fixed cost changed? Recall that many fixed costs are discretionary; that is, they are set at the discretion of management. A $5,000 increase in fixed cost would cause breakeven to increase to 7,500 units.

$$\$5x = \$3x + \$15,000$$
$$x = 7,500 \text{ units}$$

Change in Variable Cost

What if variable cost increased from $3 per unit to $3.75 per unit? The new breakeven would be 8,000 units:

$$\$5x = \$10,000 + \$3.75x$$
$$x = 8,000 \text{ units}$$

Change in Selling Price

In one more simple example, we change the selling price to $4.60 per unit. Breakeven is now 6,250 units or sales of $28,750.

$$\$4.60x = \$3x + \$10,000$$
$$\$1.60x = \$10,000$$
$$x = 6,250 \text{ units}$$
$$6,250 \times \$4.60 = \$28,750 \text{ of sales}$$

Change of Several Variables

Frequently we are confronted with simultaneous changes in several variables. The breakeven formula can handle this situation too. Assume:

Fixed cost increases from $10,000 to $30,000.
Variable cost decreases from $3 to $2.60 per unit.
Target profit is $9,000.
No change in selling price.

Breakeven then equals 16,250 units.

$$\$5x = \$2.60x + \$30,000 + \$9,000$$
$$\$2.40x = \$39,000$$
$$x = 16,250 \text{ units or } \$81,250 \text{ sales}$$

Each of the above situations can readily be graphed on a breakeven chart.

MARGIN OF SAFETY

The margin of safety is the amount the firm sells in excess of breakeven. For example, if the firm sells 1,000 units and breakeven is 800 units, the margin of safety is 200 units. Margin of safety can be expressed in sales dollars or as a percentage of sales. For example, if each unit sells for $2, the margin of safety in dollars is $400 (200 units × $2), as a percentage of sales, 20%.

$$\frac{\$400}{\$2(1,000)} = 20\%$$

The margin of safety is a measure of risk. The larger the margin of safety, the lower the risk and the higher the profit. It can also be used to compare two products or two divisions. Suppose we have two divisions with income statements as shown in Exhibit 5-4. We might be tempted to conclude that the two divisions are equal because their sales and net income are equal. But Division B is operating closer to breakeven. Study Exhibit 5-5.

Division B's margin of safety is lower than Division A's. Stated another way, if volume for Division B drops more than 14%, it will be operating at a loss,

Exhibit 5-4
Divisional Income Statements

	A		B	
Sales	$5,000	100%	$5,000	100%
Variable costs	3,000	60	1,500	30
Contribution margin	2,000	40	3,500	70
Fixed costs	1,500		3,000	
Net income	$ 500		$ 500	
Breakeven in sales dollars	$3,750		$4,286	

Exhibit 5-5
Margin of Safety by Division

	DIVISION	
	A	B
Margin of safety		
($5,000 — $3,750)	$1,250	
($5,000 — $4,286)		$714
Margin of safety as % of sales		
($1,250/$5,000)	25%	
($714/$5,000)		14%

whereas Division A could tolerate a 25% decrease in sales. Thus, we conclude that Division A is less risky. This is not to say that Division A is a "better" division than Division B; sales and profits are the same. Consider what would happen if sales doubled for both divisions. Then Division B would be considerably more profitable because it has a higher contribution margin per unit.

	DIVISION	
	A	B
Sales	$10,000	$10,000
Variable costs	6,000	3,000
Contribution margin	$ 4,000	$ 7,000
Fixed cost	1,500	3,000
Net income	$ 2,500	$ 4,000

Exhibit 5-6
Operating Leverage

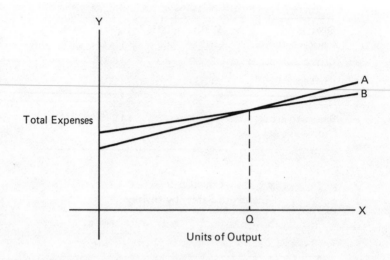

SUBSTITUTION OF TYPES OF COSTS

Sometimes it is possible to substitute fixed costs for variable costs, such as replacing labor hours by investing in a new machine. Were we to graph such a situation, we would find that the substitution would cause the total cost line to have a lower slope but a higher intercept (see Exhibit 5-6).

Note that substitution caused total fixed costs to increase but total variable cost (i.e., direct labor costs) to decrease. Firms that have high fixed costs and low variable costs have operating leverage. Although breakeven is higher, the

Exhibit 5-7
Average Contribution Margin

PRODUCT	CONTRIBUTION MARGIN	EXPECTED PERCENTAGE OF SALES	TOTAL
A	2	.20	$ .40
B	7	.50	3.50
C	5	.30	1.50
			$5.40

Average contribution margin

potential for profits are great at high levels of production. At points above Q, substitution results in lower production cost and therefore more profit.

MULIPRODUCT COMPANY BREAKEVEN

The above illustrations assumed a single product company. Multiproducts can be handled by computing an average contribution margin. To do this, we have to multiply expected percentage of sales by the unit contribution margin for each product. Then we total as illustrated in Exhibit 5-7.

The average contribution margin is $5.40. Assuming fixed cost of $42,000 breakeven is 7,778 units.

$$\frac{\$42,000}{\$5.40} = 7,778 \text{ units}$$

The 7,778 units can now be defined by product as shown in Exhibit 5-8.

Changes from Low to High Contribution Margin Products

Such an analysis can encourage managers to shift attention from low contribution margin products to high contribution margin products. For example, what would happen if the expected percentage of sales for A decreases to .10 and increases by .05 for B and C. The new average contribution margin is calculated as $5.80 in Exhibit 5-9. The new breakeven is:

$$\frac{\$42,000}{\$5.80} = 7,241 \text{ units}$$

Finally, breakeven in units and dollars of sales is shown in Exhibit 5-10. Thus, we can see that even a relatively minor shift in sales mix can decrease break-

Exhibit 5-8
Breakeven for Multiproduct Firm

PRODUCT	EXPECTED PERCENTAGE OF SALES	BREAKEVEN IN UNITS	SELLING PRICE	BREAKEVEN IN SALES $
A	.20	1,556	$10	$ 15,560
B	.50	3,889	$21	81,669
C	.30	2,333	$25	58,325
		7,778		$155,554

Exhibit 5-9

Average Contribution Margin

PRODUCT	CONTRIBUTION MARGIN	EXPECTED PERCENTAGE OF SALES	TOTAL
A	2	.10	$ .20
B	7	.55	3.85
C	5	.35	1.75
			$5.80

Average contribution margin

Exhibit 5-10

Breakeven for Multiproduct Firm

PRODUCT	EXPECTED PERCENTAGE OF SALES	BREAKEVEN IN UNITS	SELLING PRICE	BREAKEVEN IN SALES $
A	.10	724	$10	$ 7,240
B	.55	3,983	21	83,643
C	.35	2,534	25	63,350
		7,241		$154,233

even quite dramatically in terms of units and slightly more than $1,000 in sales dollars.

Changes from High to Low Contribution Margin Products

Keep in mind, however, that a shift from high contribution margin products to low contribution margin products has the opposite effect; that is, it increases breakeven in units and dollars. For example, let us assume that unforeseen environmental factors cause the sales mix shown in Exhibit 5-11. The new average contribution margin is $5.05 and breakeven is:

$$\frac{\$42,000}{\$5.05} = 8,317 \text{ units}$$

Breakeven in sales and units is according to Exhibit 5-12. Thus, you can see that it takes more dollars of sales to break even. This knowledge is important during hard times when a firm may have to push any product that it can possibly sell. So long as the product yields a positive contribution margin, additional sales of the product will generate profits.

Exhibit 5-11
Average Contribution Margin

PRODUCT	CONTRIBUTION MARGIN	EXPECTED PERCENTAGE OF SALES	TOTAL
A	2	.25	$ .50
B	7	.40	2.80
C	5	.35	1.75
			$5.05

Average contribution margin

Exhibit 5-12
Breakeven for Multiproduct Firm

PRODUCT	EXPECTED % OF SALES	BREAKEVEN IN UNITS	SELLING PRICE	BREAKEVEN IN SALES $
A	.25	2,079	$10	$ 20,790
B	.40	3,327	$21	69,867
C	.35	2,911	$25	72,775
		8,317		$163,432

OTHER FACTORS TO CONSIDER

Frequently, the simple analysis illustrated here would have to be expanded to consider factors such as:

1. Unequal effort/result ratios among products; that is, some products require more resources, risk, and effort than others.
2. No change in sales promotion.
3. No interdependency among products. For example, an increase in demand for automobiles is unlikely to cause an increase or decrease in sales of lawn mowers. Interdependency exists if camera sales correlate directly with film.

NONPROFIT ORGANIZATIONS

The contribution margin approach can be used for nonprofit organizations as well as profit enterprises. For example, assume that a city has the following annual fixed cost for a recreation park.

Administrative salaries	$4,000
Building and equipment costs	2,000
Occupancy	11,000
Total fixed cost	$17,000

Assume that variable cost per citizen visiting the park is $.80, and the entrance fee is $1.00 per visit. If 50,000 visits are made annually, the income statement prepared following a contribution margin approach is:

Revenue (50,000 × $1)	$50,000
Variable costs (50,000 × $.80)	40,000
Contribution margin	$10,000
Fixed costs	17,000
Loss	($7,000)

The park would cost the taxpayers $7,000.

What if the city wished to put the park on a nonprofit (and no loss) basis? How many visits would be required to breakeven? Utilizing the contribution margin formula, we find that 85,000 visits would be required.

$$\frac{\$17,000}{\$1.00 - \$.80} = 85,000 \text{ visits}$$

What if this number is unreasonably high? Suppose the park is not large enough to accomodate 85,000 visitors. We could consider increasing the entrance fee, say, to $1.50. Now the number of visits to breakeven is:

$$\frac{\$17,000}{\$1.50 - \$.80} = 24,286 \text{ visits}$$

This is obviously a substantial decrease from 85,000. With additional deliberations, the city officials would be able to calculate an entrance fee that would allow the park to break even or at least minimize the taxpayers' subsidy.

LIMITATIONS OF BREAKEVEN

Breakeven is not a panacea for all production and marketing problems. Rather it is a way of thinking. Knowing the cost behavior and contribution margin can be immensely helpful in solving a variety of managerial problems.

Some of the limitations of breakeven that you should be aware of are that:

1. Behavior of expenses and revenue is linear throughout the entire relevant range or at least close enough to linearity that no major distortions occur. This means that:
   a. Fixed costs will remain constant throughout the relevant range.
   b. Variable costs do not change per unit.

   c. Selling prices do not change with volume of sales; hence products have constant contribution margins.
2. Expenses can be accurately divided in fixed and variable components.
3. Cost assumptions, efficiency, and productivity do not change throughout the relevant range.
4. There is no change in sales mix.
5. Inventory levels do not change or, stated another way, production and sales volume are equal. We will explore this point more in the next chapter when we discuss direct costing income statements.

We said that one of the limitations of the breakeven model is that it assumes linear relationships. Frequently, variable cost per unit and selling price per unit are not constant in the real world. For example, many times variable cost increases at a declining rate, then, at a constant rate, and finally at an increasing rate. This is because at a certain point operating inefficiencies take place. In economics, this phenomenum is called the "law of diminishing returns." Similarly, in economic theory, the demand curve assumes that quantity demanded increases as selling price decreases. If so, the revenue line is curvilinear rather than a straight line.

A graph depicting economic theory is shown in Exhibit 5-13. Profit is max-

Exhibit 5-13
Economic Model of Breakeven

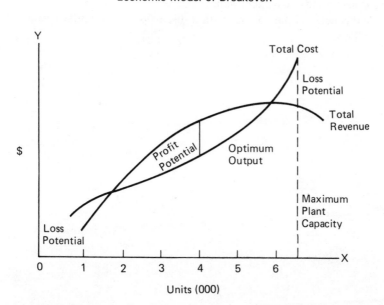

Units (000)

imized at the point of greatest distance between total revenue and total cost. Note that there are two breakevens—one at approximately 1,500 units and the other at about 6,000 units. Still, the economic model is not incompatible with the linear breakeven model when we consider the concept of relevant range. We can see visually that the total revenue and total cost lines approximate linearity at between 2,000 and 5,000 units, which is close enough to make linear models consistent with economic theory.

SUMMARY

This chapter is concerned with cost–volume–profit relationships. We computed breakeven by the equation and contribution margin methods and demonstrated breakeven by three different graphs. Then, we discussed the effects of changing factors, such as:

1. Selling price
2. Variable cost
3. Fixed cost
4. A combination of factors

Breakeven for a multiple product firm and a way for managers to maximize profits by shifting from low contribution margin products to high contribution margin products were illustrated. We assumed that because the firm's goal is to maximize profits, managers want to concentrate on the most profitable products. We concluded the chapter with a discussion of the limitations of breakeven models.

6. Contribution Margin and Direct Costing

The concept of contribution margin is one of the most important tools a manager can utilize because it forms the basis for many decision models. *Contribution margin* is defined as the difference between selling price and variable costs. This difference is the amount contributed to fixed costs; any excess is profit.

Some of the tasks the contribution margin approach can be applied to are:

1. Retention or disposition of a division or product line
2. Preparation of direct costing income statement
3. Pricing
4. Evaluation of managers
5. Budgeting
6. Cost planning and control

In this chapter we introduce you to retention/disposition decisions and explain direct-costing income statements. Other contribution margin decisions are examined in subsequent chapters, especially Chapter 12.

RETENTION/DISPOSITION OF A DIVISION

Let us start out by solving a problem as to whether a firm should retain or dispose of a division. Revenue and cost data for three divisions are provided in Exhibit 6-1.

Recall that fixed costs do not change with output over a relevant range; therefore, the $43,000 fixed cost would be incurred whether or not the division is retained. The method by which the $43,000 fixed cost was allocated to the divisions is irrelevant to the solution of the problem.

The question to be answered is which division(s) should be eliminated? Or, stated another way, which division(s) should be retained? Clearly Division C should be retained, but not because it has a $19,000 profit before taxes, but rather because it has a positive contribution margin of $35,000.

The basic rule is whenever a division has a positive contribution margin it should be retained. The dollar amount of contribution margin equals the division's effect on net income before taxes; that is, the income statement will show $35,000 more profit if Division C is retained than if it is eliminated. Applying

Exhibit 6-1
Divisional Income Statements

	A	B	C	TOTAL
		DIVISIONS		
Sales	$180,000	$160,000	$190,000	$530,000
Variable cost	170,000	165,000	155,000	490,000
Contribution margin	$10,000	$(5,000)	$35,000	$40,000
Fixed cost	15,000	12,000	16,000	43,000
Profit (loss) before taxes	$(5,000)	$(17,000)	$19,000	$ (3,000)

the rule to Division A, we conclude that Division A should also be retained since it has a $10,000 positive contribution margin. Division B should be disposed of because this division is not generating high enough revenue to cover its variable cost. Sales (quantity and/or price) are two low, variable cost is too high, or there is a combination of these two variables at work. The contribution margin is negative in the amount of $5,000.

In Exhibit 6-2 we prove our conclusion that Divisions A and C should be retained and Division B eliminated by drafting income statements under each of the seven possible alternatives.

The combined strategy of retaining only Divisions A and C actually changed a $3,000 loss into a profit of $2,000, that is, a $5,000 increase. Of course the $5,000 is in essense the amount of Division B's negative contribution margin.

Again, we repeat, a division or product should be retained if it has a positive contribution margin because the fixed cost is incurred anyhow. Do not let the loss after the allocation of fixed cost deceive you into erroneously concluding that a division should be eliminated.

The above illustration assumed that all the fixed cost would continue if a division is disposed of. This is not always the case. Fixed cost unique to the eliminated division would cease, for example, a real estate tax incurred because the division occupied a building, which would be sold if the division were eliminated. Such complexities are covered in Chapter 12.

We also assumed that there would be no changes in Division A and C's sales and variable costs if Division B were eliminated. Many times such assumptions are not valid. For example, if a grocery store eliminated its fruit and vegetable department, grocery and produce sales might drop dramatically. Sales of ladies' dresses might decline if a fashion boutique discontinued accessories.

A very important principle to remember is that a manager must be aware of the limitations and assumptions supporting a decision model. Blindly insert-

Exhibit 6-2
Income Statements Under Various Alternatives

DIVISIONS

	A, B & C	A,B	A,C	B,C	A	B	C
Sales	$530,000	$340,000	$370,000	$350,000	$180,000	$160,000	$190,000
Variable Cost	490,000	335,000	325,000	320,000	170,000	165,000	155,000
Contribution Margin	$ 40,000	$ 5,000	$ 45,000	$ 30,000	$ 10,000	$ (5,000)	$ 35,000
Fixed Cost	43,000	43,000	43,000	43,000	43,000	43,000	43,000
Profit (Loss) Before Taxes	$ (3,000)	$ (38,000)	$ 2,000	$ (13,000)	$ (33,000)	$ (48,000)	$ (8,000)

ing data into a decision model is hardly managing effectively or efficiently. The selection of the wrong decision model may result in less than optimal consequences.

DIRECT COSTING

Under a direct costing accounting system (also called *variable costing*), the accounts are classfied as variable or fixed. A direct costing accounting system can be a very important source of information because it furnishes information useful for preparing cost-volume-profit solutions, contribution margin analysis, flexible budgets, and direct costing income statements (breakeven and contribution margin have already been discussed, and we will cover flexible budgets in Chapter 10).

Many accountants and managers believe that direct costing income statements are more meaningful than full costing (absorption costing) statements. The practice of assigning all manufacturing costs (whether variable or fixed) to inventory is called absorption costing or full costing, an approach you are already familiar with. Again, under full costing, manufacturing costs that can be directly identified with the products produced are directly assigned to the inventory. All other indirect manufacturing costs are allocated by some rational base to inventory by means of a predetermined overhead rate.

Under direct costing only the variable manufacturing costs are assigned to inventory and eventually to the cost of goods sold. All fixed manufacturing costs are considered period costs and are charged off on the income statement as an expense in the period incurred. Accounting for inventory is simplified because only variable cost is inventoried; thus we are not concerned with selection of the most appropriate base to allocate fixed cost or how to handle variances.

If a standard cost system is used, inventory valuation becomes extremely easy to account for. Only standard variable costs are inventoried, and all variances (assuming the standards are properly set) are written off as an expense on the income statement. Standard cost also eliminates selection of an inventory cost flow method such as FIFO, LIFO, and so forth.

Under direct costing, inventory and retained earnings balance sheet accounts are lower than absorption costing. When sales and production are in balance during an accounting period, direct and absorption costing yield the same profit or loss. Seldom is such a desirable situation the case. We can summarize possible alternatives as follows:

1. If production exceeds sales, absorption costing shows higher profit.
2. If sales exceed production, direct costing results in higher profit.

3. Direct costing yields a constant profit figure per unit when sales volume is constant but production fluctuates because only variable costs are included in the cost of goods sold.
4. If production is constant and sales change, profits will vary under both direct and absorption costing.

Over the long run the differences mentioned above will tend to cancel out because sales cannot indefinitely exceed production or vice versa.

Product Unit Cost

Now we calculate per unit cost under both direct and absorption costing. Next we demonstrate the income statement under both approaches. Assume the following data:

Direct material per unit	$2.00
Direct labor per unit	$3.00
Variable manufacturing cost per unit	$2.50
Total fixed manufacturing cost	$20,000
Number of units produced each year	5,000

Per unit manufacturing cost under absorption and direct costing is calculated in Exhibit 6-3.

The $20,000 fixed overhead is charged off as an expense on the income statement and hence is treated as a period cost. Note the result is that the full cost per unit is $4 more than the variable cost per unit.

Exhibit 6-3

Calculation of Manufacturing Cost Per Unit Under Absorption Costing and Direct Costing

	ABSORPTION COSTING	DIRECT COSTING
Direct material	$ 2.00	$2.00
Direct labor	3.00	3.00
Variable overhead	2.50	2.50
Total variable production cost	$ 7.50	$7.50
Fixed overhead ($20,000/5,000 units)	4.00	0*
Cost per unit	$11.50	$7.50

*The $20,000 fixed overhead will be charged off the expense in total as a period cost.

Changes in Units

What if only 2,000 units are produced in lieu of 5,000? Under absorption costing the fixed overhead cost per unit is $10 ($20,000/2,000) and the total manufacturing cost is $17.50 per unit. The increase from $11.50 to $17.50 is solely the result of producing fewer units. To the extent those units are in next period's beginning inventory, profit per unit will be $6.00 less in the subsequent period (assuming FIFO inventory) because the cost of goods sold is $6.00 a unit higher. Such a situation is confusing to individuals not trained in the idiosyncrasies of financial and cost accounting. Direct costing avoids this problem as only the variable cost ($7.50) follows the inventory.

Absorption and Direct Costing Income Statements

To compile income statements under both approaches additional data are supplied. Assume:

Beginning inventory, January 1, 19X4	1,000 units
Produced in 19X4	5,000 units
Sold during 19X4	4,500 units
Selling price per unit	$20
Variable selling and administrative expense per unit	$1
Total fixed selling and administrative expense	$2,000

We know that the December 31, 19X4 ending inventory must be 1,500 units, computed as follows:

	Units
Beginning inventory	1,000
Produced	5,000
Units available for sale	6,000
Number of units sold	4,500
Ending inventory	1,500

Income statements under absorption and direct costing are presented in Exhibit 6-4. This exhibit illustrates the income statement when production units exceed sales; therefore, absorption costing will show a higher profit.

Exhibit 6-5 depicts the income statements when sales units exceed production units; then direct costing results in a higher profit.

Changes in Costs

The above illustrations assumed that in year 19X3 the cost was equal to cost incurred in year 19X4. This is seldom the case. What if fixed manufacturing cost changed from $20,000 in 19X3 to $25,000 in 19X4? Assuming sales of

Exhibit 6-4

Absorption and Direct Costing Income Statements for the Year Ended 19X4
(Production Exceeds Sales)

	INCOME STATEMENTS	
	ABSORPTION COSTING	DIRECT COSTING
Sales (4500 × $20)	$90,000	$90,000
Cost of goods sold		
Beginning inventory		
(1000 units × $11.50)	$11,500	
(1000 units × $7.50)		$ 7,500
Variable costs of production		
(5000 units × $7.50)	37,500	37,500
Fixed cost of production	20,000	0
Ending inventory		
(1500 units × $11.50)	(17,250)	
(1500 units × $7.50)		(11,250)
Cost of goods sold	$51,750	$33,750
Gross margin	$38,250	$56,250
Variable selling and administrative		
expense per unit (4500 × $1)	4,500	4,500
Contribution margin		$51,750
Fixed manufacturing cost	0	20,000
Fixed selling and administrative expense	2,000	2,000
Net income before taxes	$31,750	$29,750
Difference		$2,000
Consists of the difference between beginning and ending inventory times fixed manufacturing cost per unit		
(1000 − 1500) × $4		$2,000

5,500 units in 19X4, production of 4,500 in both years, final profit under direct
costing is $36,250, whereas under absorption costing the profit is $34,750 or a
difference of $1,500. Therefore, profit under direct costing will exceed absorp-
tion costing by $1,500. A short cut calculation is:

	UNITS	FIXED COST
Beginning inventory (1,000 × $4)	1,000	$4,000
Ending inventory $\left(500 \text{ units} \times \dfrac{\$25,000}{5,000}\right)$	500	2,500
Net change	500	$1,500

Exhibit 6-5

Absorption and Direct Costing Income Statements for the Year Ended 19X4
(Sales Exceed Production)

	INCOME STATEMENTS	
	ABSORPTION COSTING	DIRECT COSTING
Sales (5500 × $20)	$110,000	$110,000
Cost of goods sold		
Beginning inventory		
(1000 units × $11.50)	$ 11,500	
(1000 units × $7.50)		$ 7,500
Variable cost of production		
(5000 units × $7.50)	37,500	37,500
Fixed cost of production	20,000	0
Ending inventory		
(500 units × $11.50)	(5,750)	
(500 units × $7.50)		(3,750)
Cost of goods sold	$ 63,250	$ 41,250
Gross margin	$ 46,750	$ 68,750
Variable selling and administrative expense per unit (5500 × $1)	5,500	5,500
Contribution margin		$ 63,250
Fixed manufacturing costs	0	20,000
Fixed selling and administrative expense	2,000	2,000
Net income before taxes	$ 39,250	$ 41,250
Difference	$2,000	
Consists of the difference between beginning and ending inventory times fixed manufacturing cost per unit (1000 − 500) × $4	$2,000	

Disadvantages of Direct Costing

Direct costing has been an extremely controversial concept among practitioners, theorists, and academicians. Those who oppose it maintain that:

1. Direct costing is not permitted for published financial statements under generally accepted accounting theory.
2. It is not acceptable by the Internal Revenue Service or the Securities and Exchange Commission.
3. Costs are not properly matched against revenue on the income statement.
4. Many costs cannot be accurately separated into fixed and variable components.

5. Direct costing income statements confuse readers trained to work with absorption costing statements.
6. Such statements may disclose confidential information to competitors.
7. Total costs may be overlooked when making decisions. It is absolutely essential that over the long run, all fixed costs must be covered if a firm is to survive. Direct costing puts too much emphasis on short-run decisions. There may be a tendency to assume that variable costs must be recovered first and that fixed costs are relatively unimportant.
8. The balance sheet inventory and retained earning accounts are understated by the amount of fixed costs that should have been allocated to inventory. All ratios where inventory, profit, or retained earnings are part of the formulas are also distorted.

Advantages of Direct Costing

On the other hand, advocates of direct costing say:

1. Managers currently have to work with two sets of data, which is confusing.
2. Direct costing income statements more closely parallel data used for profit planning and decision making, and with flexible budgeting.
3. Emphasis is placed on the impact of fixed cost on profit since all fixed cost is immediately expensed.
4. Under direct costing only the variable cost of manufacturing an item is included in inventory. Variable cost is the "real" inventory cost; fixed cost should be treated as a period cost since it is primarily a function of time.
5. Allocation of fixed cost to inventory can distort data used for decisions such as appraising products or divisions.
6. Profits are directly influenced by changes in sales volume under direct costing instead of being effected by changes in inventory levels, as is the case under absorption costing.

SUMMARY

Contribution margin is the difference between selling price and variable cost. Retaining divisions or products with positive contribution margin increases a firm's overall profits to the extent of the positive contribution margin. The practice of assigning only variable manufacturing cost to inventory and expensing all fixed manufacturing cost is called variable (direct) costing, a concept that can be immensely helpful in solving cost–volume–profit problems and understanding the profit relationship between sales volume and production volume.

7. Cost-Accounting Systems

Now we turn our attention to how costs are accumulated in accounting records. Our purpose is not to teach you to be a cost accountant. Rather is it to make you sufficiently familiar with cost accounting that you understand (1) how costs are entered into accounting records, (2) how costs are accumulated, and (3) how they are transferred from one account to another. You need to understand how to convert raw data into relevant information and know what additional data are or could be available upon request.

There are two basic kinds of cost systems: job order costing and process costing. Job order costing is used when each job or product is unique and easily identifiable, for examples, aircraft, furniture, and buildings. When a contract requires that actual costs be identified, as is frequently the case with government contracts, a job order is set up to accumulate costs as they are incurred.

Process costing is used when there is mass production of identical units. Usually there is a continuous flow of material through a production line. Examples include processing of food, refining of petroleum, and manufacturing of chemicals and paint.

It is important to understand that job order and process costing are not two mutually exclusive and distinct systems. There are many variations of the two systems. Still, if you acquire a basic understanding of these two general systems, it is relatively easy to adapt your thinking to a modified system.

MANUFACTURING COST FLOW

To the greatest extent possible, the flow of costs through the accounting records (T accounts) should match the physical flow of a product through manufacturing. Before we demonstrate job order and processing costing, let us start out by tracing cost flow through the T accounts. Exhibit 7-1 shows that there are three inventory accounts: *raw material, work-in-process* and *finished goods*. When items are sold, their costs are transferred from finished goods inventory to *cost of goods sold*.

When raw materials are physically received, they are stored in a warehouse and their costs recorded on the left-hand side of the raw material inventory account. As the items are physically moved to production, their costs are removed from the raw material inventory account by putting the costs on the right-hand side of the account. If the material is directly identifiable with an item manufactured, its cost is entered as direct material to the work-in-process inventory. The cost of indirect material used goes to *manufacturing overhead*. The *labor distribution* account shows the gross wages earned (before deductions and withholdings) during the period. Gross wages are then distributed to the appropriate accounts. The cost of labor that can be directly identified with a product is assigned as direct labor to work-in-process and indirect labor increases manufacturing overhead. All other indirect manufacturing costs incurred (i.e., utilities, rent, insurance, etc.) are put initially in manufacturing overhead. By use of a predetermined overhead rate (which we explained previously), manufacturing overhead is transferred to work-in-process inventory. The balance at the end of the accounting period in the manufacturing overhead is the under- or overabsorbed overhead.

Returning to the work-in-process inventory, you can see that the costs of manufacturing an item consist of direct material, direct labor, and manufacturing overhead. When an item is physically complete, it is physically transferred from the factory to a finished goods warehouse. The cost is removed from the work-in-process inventory to the finished goods inventory. Similarly, when an item is sold it is physically transferred to the buyer. Its cost is transferred from finished goods inventory (an asset) to cost of goods sold (an expense).

You might be wondering what this description has to do with job order and process costing. The problem is how to measure the amount of cost to relieve

Exhibit 7-1
Manufacturing Cost Flow

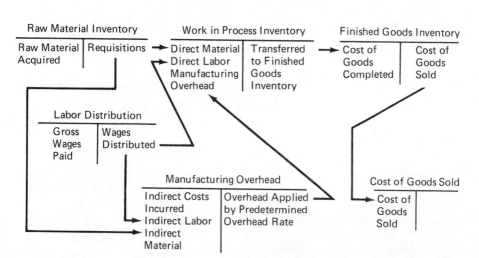

one account and increase another account, especially the work-in-process inventory account. Job order and process costing are cost measurement systems.

JOB ORDER COSTING

In job order costing, for each job there is job cost sheet that is used to accumulate cost by element, that is, direct material, direct labor, and manufacturing overhead. These job cost sheets form a subsidiary (supporting) ledger to the work-in-process inventory general ledger T account. In other words, when the accumulated costs to date from all the individual job cost sheets are totaled, the sum must agree with the balance in the work-in-process inventory.

There is no one standardized format for a job cost sheet. It can be simple or complex. A typical format is shown as Exhibit 7-2.

Note the amount of detail on the job card. The item manufactured is a 12-inch blade. The stock number, number of items made, and the date started and

Exhibit 7-2
ABC COMPANY
Job Cost Sheet

Job Number 846

Stock No. 9B

Item 12-inch blade

Date Started. 8/1/X4

Date Completed. 8/15/X4

Units Completed. 400

| DEPARTMENT | DIRECT MATERIAL | | | DIRECT LABOR | | | OVERHEAD 150% DL$ |
	DATE	REF	AMOUNT	DATE	REF	AMOUNT	
	19X4			19X4			
Grinding	8/1	66	$4,000	8/2	B1	$2,700	$4050
	8/3	92	600	8/5	B18	300	450
			$4,600			$3,000	$4500
Polishing			0	8/9	B81	$ 400	$ 600
				8/10	B90	800	1200
				8/14	B99	1,200	1800
			0			$2,400	$3600
Total			$4,600			$5,400	$8100

Summary: Direct material	$4600
Direct labor	5400
Manufacturing overhead	8100
Total manufacturing costs	$18,100
Average cost per unit ($18,100/400)	$45.25

completed are provided. In the material columns there are the date, requisition number of the document requesting raw material from the warehouse, and the amount of each requisition. The total of $4,600 is the cost of the raw material used to produce the blades.

Labor costs are accumulated in a similar fashion. The *reference* column refers to a weekly labor distribution report. The dollar amount consists of the number of hours times the employees' wage rates.

Recall earlier our mentioning that manufacturing overhead is applied according to a predetermined overhead rate because it consists of indirect costs that cannot be identified with a particular job. The overhead rate used in this illustration is 150% of direct labor cost. One hundred and fifty percent is the predetermined overhead rate, and direct labor dollars is the base. The manufacturing overhead of August 2 of $4,050 is arrived at by multiplying the direct labor cost of $2,700 by 150%. Other overhead figures are computed similarly. The bottom of the job cost sheet summarizes costs and shows a per unit cost. The $18,100 is the total cost of manufacturing 400 12-inch blades and the average per unit cost is $45.25.

The means of transferring cost in accounting records is by journal entry. Hence, the $18,100 is recorded:

Finished goods inventory	$18,100	
Work-in-process inventory		$18,100
To transfer cost of job number 846		
completed on 8/15/X4 to finished goods		
inventory		

Obviously, when the products are sold, the cost of each item sold is transferred out of finished goods inventory to cost of goods sold at $45.25 per unit.

PROCESS COSTING

Process costing is quite a bit more complicated than job order costing. This cost system is based on the *equivalent unit* concept. It is absolutely essential that you understand what equivalent units are and how to compute them.

Equivalent Unit Example 1

We introduce this theory with an elementary example, first, then progressing to more complicated examples. Assume that we operate a pastry counter and sell cake by the piece or whole cake. We have on hand:

8 cakes	60% sold
50 cakes	not sold

How many equivalent cakes do we have?

8 × 40% (not sold)*	3.2
50 × 100% (not sold)	50.0
Number of equivalent cakes	53.2

Suppose we then bake 30 more cakes and at the end of the second day have only 10 left, ⅔ sold. How many equivalent cakes do we have on hand?

$$10 \times \frac{1}{3} = 3\frac{1}{3} \text{ equivalent cakes on hand}$$

How many equivalent cakes were sold?

8 × 40%	3.2
50 × 100%	50.0
(30 − 10) × 100%	20.0
10 × ⅔	6.7
Number of equivalent cakes sold	79.9

Equivalent Unit Example 2

Let us try a harder example. Product A goes through two processes: mixing and molding. Mixing must be done before molding. Pertinent data are:

	MIXING		MODLING	
	NO. OF UNITS	PERCENTAGE COMPLETED	NO. OF UNITS	PERCENTAGE COMPLETED
Beginning inventory	100	60%	200	70%
Started	1000			
Ending inventory	200	10%	150	20%

We calculate the equivalent units produced this period as follows:

Mixing
Beginning inventory (100 × 40%)[a]	40
Started and completed (1000 − 200) × 100%	800
Ending inventory (200 × 10%)	20
Number of equivalent units	860

---

*Note that if 60% is sold, 40% (100 − 60%) must be on hand.
[a]Amount finished this period

Molding

Beginning inventory (200 × 30%)[a]	60
Transferred in from Mixing (900[c] − 150[b]) × 100%	750
Ending inventory (150 × 20%)	30
Number of equivalent units	840

Note that equivalent units must be computed separately by departments. They must also be computed separately by material, labor, and overhead. The reporting document tends to take the form of a cost of production report.

COST OF PRODUCTION REPORT

The *cost of production report* summarizes production costs for a particular time interval at a specific process center; therefore, there is a separate production report for each department. Assume that we are manufacturing candy which goes through three processes:

In January 19X4 we started 100,000 units in the mixing department; 90,000 units were completed and transferred to cooking. The 10,000 units still in process were 50% complete as to material and 25% as to labor and manufacturing overhead. Exhibit 7-3 is the cost of production report for mixing for the month of January.

First, we must account for all units started in production. We know that the 100,000 units started, 90,000 units were finished insofar as the Mixing Department is concerned, and the remaining 10,000 units are still in process. The accounting records show that $233,750 of costs were incurred this period and charged to the Mixing Department. In order to compute the unit cost it is necessary to know the number of equivalent units by cost element (see the bottom of Exhibit 7-3). For material the 90,000 units are 100% complete and the 10,000 units are 50% complete; therefore, the number of equivalent units is 95,000 for material. Now we compute a per unit cost for material by dividing material cost incurred, $95,000, by the number of equivalent units. The answer is $1.00.

---

[b]In ending inventory
[c]Consists of 800 units started and completed in the mixing process plus 100 units of beginning inventory in the same process.

Exhibit 7-3

Mixing Department Cost of Production Report for the Month of January 19X4

Quantity schedule

Units started in production	100,000
Units transferred to the Cooking Department	90,000
Units still in process in Mixing Department	10,000
Total units to account for	100,000

COSTS CHARGED TO THE DEPARTMENT	TOTAL COSTS	UNIT COST
Cost added by department		
Material	$95,000(a)	$1.00(a)
Labor	64,750(b)	.70(b)
Manufacturing overhead	74,000(b)	.80(c)
Total costs to account for	$233,750	$2.50

Cost accounted for

Transferred to Cooking Department (90,000 units × $2.50)	$225,000
Work-in-process ending inventory	
Material [.50(10,000 units) × $1.00]	5,000
Labor [.25(10,000 units) × $.70]	1,750
Manufacturing overhead [.25(10,000 units) × $.80]	2,000
Total costs accounted for	$233,750

Work-in-process inventory	
Material ($5,000) + labor ($1,750) + overhead ($2,000)	$8,750

Equivalent units

Material = 90,000 + .50(10,000) = 95,000
Labor and manufacturing overhead = 90,000 + .25(10,000) = 92,500

Unit Costs

(a) Material $\dfrac{\$95,000}{95,000\ (1)} = \$1.00$

(b) Labor $\dfrac{\$64,750}{92,500\ (2)} = \$.70$

(c) Overhead $\dfrac{\$74,000}{92,500\ (2)} = \$.80$

Labor and manufacturing overhead per unit are calculated in a similar fashion. Remember that it is absolutely essential that the number of equivalent units be computed separately for each cost element when costs are incurred at different stages of production. If direct material, direct labor, and manufacturing overhead were entered at the same rate (which is seldon the case), we would use the same equivalent units for all three cost elements.

When the three per unit figures (direct material, direct labor, and manufacturing overhead) are added, the total cost is $2.50 for each unit in the Mixing Department. Now we can easily compute the cost of units transferred from mixing to cooking: 90,000 units at $2.50 each or $225,000. The journal entry is:

Work-in-process inventory—Cooking
Department $225,000
Work-in-process inventory—Mixing
Department $225,000

The cost of uncompleted items as of the end of January is $8,750. Note that the cost of production report details this amount by material, labor, and overhead.

COOKING DEPARTMENT COST OF PRODUCTION REPORT

The Cooking and Cooling Departments have cost of production reports too. One important addition is that the costs charged to these departments include costs incurred for the preceding department(s). For example, the Cooking Department's costs for January include the $225,000 transferred-in cost from the Mixing Department. To the $225,000 is added the cost incurred by the Cooking Department for material, labor, and overhead. The Cooking Department cost of production report for the month of January is shown in Exhibit 7-4.

The journal entry to transfer the cost from Cooking to Cooling is:

Work-in-process inventory—Cooling
Department $283,500
Work-in-process inventory—Cooling
Department $283,500

The cost of production report for the Cooling Department is similar to that of the Cooking Department. Keep in mind that *total* transfer of costs from preceding departments must be considered.

Cost transferred out from the last department in the manufacturing process goes to finished goods inventory. Accurate computation is essential because errors made in determining per unit cost early in a multidepartment chain carry through all departments and can be very complicated to correct.

If its departments have a beginning inventory (which would normally be the case), a firm has to select an inventory cost flow method, such as first-in/first-

Exhibit 7-4

Cooking Department Cost of Production Report for the Month of January 19X4

Quantity schedule

Units started in production (transferred in from mixing department)	90,000
Units transferred to cooling department	70,000
Units still in process	20,000
Total units to account for	90,000

Costs Charged to Department	Total Costs	Unit Costs
Costs transferred in from mixing department (90,000 units)	$225,000	$2.50
Costs added by cooking department		
Material	45,000	.50(a)
Labor	54,000	.75(b)
Manufacturing overhead	21,600	.30(c)
Total costs to account for	$345,600	$4.05

Costs Accounted For

Transferred to cooling department (70,000 units × $4.05)	$283,500
Work-in-process ending inventory	
Transferred-in cost (20,000 units × $2.50)	50,000
Material (20,000 × $.50)	10,000
Labor [.10(20,000) × $.75]	1,500
Manufacturing overhead [.10(20,000) × $.30)]	600
Total costs accounted for	$345,600

Work-in-Process Inventory

Transferred-in costs ($50,000) + material ($10,000) + labor ($1,500) + overhead ($600)	$62,100

Equivalent units

(1) Material (90,000)100% = 90,000

(2) Labor and manufacturing overhead = 70,000 + .10(20,000) = 72,000

(a) Material $\dfrac{\$45,000}{90,000 \ (1)} = \$.50$

(b) Labor $\dfrac{\$54,000}{72,000 \ (2)} = \$.75$

(c) Overhead $\dfrac{\$21,600}{72,000 \ (2)} = \$.30$

out or weighted average to determine the cost of items transferred to another department (and ending inventory) or to finished goods inventory. Inventory cost flow methods are discussed in Chapter 16.

DIFFICULTIES WITH PROCESS COSTING

Process costing can sometimes be troublesome, and unless adequate care is taken, gross distortions can occur. Accuracy depends upon the proper determination of production quantities and their stages of completion. The way shrinkage, spoilage, defective items, and evaporation are handled can affect the costs of goods transferred to finished goods inventory as well as charges to the current period's income statement. Direct and indirect material costs transferred from raw material inventory to work-in-process inventory are dependent on the inventory cost flow method (this is also true for job order costing). Finally, many products accounted for under process costing are joint products and the complexities of allocating common costs can be overwhelming.

SPOILAGE AND DEFECTIVE ITEMS

Normal spoilage (results of an efficient production process) is frequently treated as part of overhead. Assuming the amount of normal spoilage is immaterial, an easy way of handling revenue from the sale of normal scrap is to reduce the overhead account accordingly. Abnormal spoilage (any excess over what is usual for a particular production process) is controllable by line personnel, and they should be held responsible for it. Hence, abnormal spoilage costs are listed as a separate inventory item on the cost of production report. Full cost to the point of spoilage is removed from the work-in-process inventory account, and its residual value is classified as spoiled goods inventory, with the difference between cost and residual value recognized as an immediate loss. When the spoiled goods are sold, the difference between revenue and residual value is reported as a gain (loss) on the income statement.

Defective items are reworked to put them into a salable condition. The cost to rework a "normal" amount of defective items is appropriately charged to work-in-process inventory. The cost of reworking "abnormal" defective goods should be shown on the income statement as a loss. What is normal or abnormal depends on past experience adjusted for future expectations.

BY-PRODUCTS AND JOINT PRODUCTS

Two problems frequently encountered in accounting for manufacturing costs are how to handle by-products or joint products. A by-product is one of relatively small total value produced simultaneously with higher-value products, for example, saw dust in a lumber mill. Common ways of handling by-products include:

1. Income from sales of by-product is shown on the income statement as:
   a. Other income
   b. Included in sales revenue
   c. A deduction from cost of goods sold or manufacturing costs
2. Allocating a portion of the manufacturing costs to the by-product and treating it as a main product.
3. Only charging additional processing costs, if any, to the by-product.

By definition, the by-product revenue will be small. Based on the generally accepted accounting principle of immateriality, it does not matter which method is used because the impact on net profit in any accounting period is too insignificant to affect decisions.

Sometimes because of technological changes, a by-product becomes a joint product or maybe the nature of the products results in joint products, such as in meat packing. Joint products are produced simultaneously as common cost to a point of physical separation. The problem is then how to allocate the common cost to each product at the point of separation. Perhaps the most well-known method is the relative sales value method.

Assume A, B, and C are joint products, and common costs incurred to the split-off point are $250,000. The allocation of the $250,000 common costs to the three joint products is demonstrated in Exhibit 7-5.

The last column of Exhibit 7-5 shows the amount allocated to each of the three products. Other methods that may prove satisfactory include:

Exhibit 7-5
Allocation of Joint Costs Using Relative Sales Value Method

JOINT PRODUCTS	NUMBER OF UNITS PRODUCED	MARKET VALUE PER UNIT	TOTAL MARKET VALUE (a)	COST TO COMPLETE	RELATIVE SALES VALUE (b)	RATIO OF PRODUCT TO RELATIVE SALES VALUE (c)	ALLOCATION OF JOINT COSTS (d)
(1)	(2)	(3)	(4)	(5)	(6)	(7)	(8)
A	10,000	$20	$200,000	$50,000	$150,000	41.43%	$103,575
B	15,000	8	$120,000	$10,000	110,000	30.39	75,975
C	12,000	11	132,000	30,000	102,000	28.18	70,450
	37,000		$452,000	$90,000	$362,000	100.00%	$250,000

(a) Col. (2) $\times$ Col. (3)
(b) Col. (4) $-$ Col. (5)
(c) Ratio for A $150,000/$362,000 = 41.43%
(d) For A, $250,000 $\times$ 41.43%

1. Sales value method—same as above exclusive of cost to complete
2. A physical measurement such as weight, volume, and so forth.
3. Average unit cost
4. Use of a predetermined standard or index

SUMMARY

This chapter explains the physical flow and cost flow of a product through manufacturing. We explained and illustrated job order and process cost accounting systems, including calculation of equivalent units, and we concluded with an explanation of the appropriate treatments of by-products and joint products.

8. Budgeting

Budgeting is one of the most important planning and control tools used by managers. This chapter is devoted to the planning aspects of budgeting, and in subsequent chapters we will explore the control ramifications. Budgeting is essential because without some form of formal planning, managers spend too much of their time solving daily problems instead of controlling the future.

Nearly all firms budget, however informally. Ideally, budgets should be in writing, disseminated to managers affected by the budget, and comprehensive in scope. Long-term budgets up to five or ten years (sometimes called long-term planning) are usually desirable. The most current year of the long-term budget should be the current period's operating budget. In other words, long-term and short-term budgets should not be independent of each other.

What is a budget? Basically, it is a plan of action stated in monetary terms and usually for a period of a year. Yearly budgets are often detailed by month or quarter. Budgets are based on agreed-upon objectives that have the commitment and approval of managers and higher authority. A primary feature of budgets is that actual performance is compared with the budget, and differences are analyzed as to cause. If warranted, corrective action should be immediately undertaken.

DIFFERENCES BETWEEN FORECASTS AND BUDGETS

Forecasts are frequently confused with budgeting. Forecasts play an important role in the budgeting process, especially in projecting sales, but they are not the same as budgets. For example:

1. Budgets are usually stated in monetary terms, but forecasts may or may not be.

2. A forecast can be for any period of time, whereas a budget is usually for one year. As mentioned previously, if a long-range plan in prepared, the most current part should be this period's budget.

3. Managers are committed to meeting budgets since they are a control tool. Managers may be evaluated on their ability to meet budgets. Forecasters do not accept responsibility for meeting projections.

4. Since managers are committed to budgets, variances are analyzed and reasons for deviations determined and possibly corrected. No variance analysis is done with forecasts.

5. As soon as conditions of change are known, forecasts are immediately updated. Budgets may or may not be revised. Too frequent updating of budgets is costly and results in confusion. It creates a tendency to revise budgets to avoid accounting for and explaining unfavorable variances. Often it is more effective to let deviations resulting from environmental changes appear in the variance rather than update the budget.

6. Budgets are usually approved by higher management, but at a minimum by the next lower level of supervision. Often approval comes from a high-level budget committee and/or top management. A budget is the company's plan of operation. Forecasts are seldom approved by higher authority.

BUDGET COMMITTEES

Large firms frequently establish budget committees to oversee budget preparation and coordination. The committee reviews the budget for reasonableness and makes recommendations designed to improve efficiency. Other duties include (1) dissemination of information concerning corporate goals and objectives, (2) establishment of budget procedures, (3) preparation of a budget manual, and (4) settlement of budget conflicts among managers. Its membership consists of heads of various departments and other high-level executives.

TYPES OF RESPONSIBILITY CENTERS

Before demonstrating budgets let us briefly review responsibility centers. Since one of the purposes of budgets is to hold managers responsible for variances, budgets need to be detailed by responsibility center. There are four general kinds of responsibility centers.

1. *Revenue*. Here managers are responsible for revenue only. A sales division is an example.

2. *Expense*. Managers are responsible for expenses only, for example, the accounting department is an expense center.

3. *Profit*. Since profit (loss) by definition is the difference between revenue and expenses, managers are responsible for both elements. If a sales division purchases merchandise and incurs operating expenses, it is a profit center.

4. *Investment*. The managers control both profit and investment. Frequently, a return on investment percentage is calculated to determine if the investment is yielding a satisfactory return. The formula is

$$\frac{\text{Profit}}{\text{Investment}} = \text{return on investment}$$

There are many ways of defining investment. Some common ways are: total assets, net assets, and long-term assets (before and after accumulated depreciation). When comparing the return on investment among companies, divisions, and so on, it is essential that the same definition of investment be utilized; otherwise the comparison is invalid. Also, be aware that all historically based models suffer from the inadequacies of generally accepted accounting principles.

MASTER BUDGET

The larger the firm, the more essential is the soundness of the budgeting process. A firm does not have one budget, rather it has a series or package of budgets which are coordinated. This package is called a master budget. The master budget for a hypothetical firm, Sun Toys, is presented in Exhibit 8-1.

This schematic demonstrates how the budgeting process begins with sales and terminates with budgeted financial statements. The sales budget shows the number of units to be sold. Then the firm calculates the numbers of units on hand and the desired ending inventory level. There are separate budgets for the three factors of production: direct labor, direct material, and manufacturing overhead. Now, budgeted cost of goods sold can be computed. Adding marketing and administrative expense budgets, we can project the three basic financial statements. A capital expenditure budget is based on the long-range goals of the firm. To control cash flow, a cash budget is prepared. We demonstrate each of these individual budgets, and, for simplicity, assume that Sun Toys makes two products: dolls and teddy bears. It operates on a calendar year and budgets quarterly. Prior to budgeting the company must have established its goals and objectives. Preferably these should be stated in writing and in a measurable form. For example, a vague goal such as to supply customers with high-quality merchandise is difficult to evaluate and control. Examples of measureable objectives are:

1. To achieve a net income after taxes of 15% of the common stockholders' equity as reported on the balance sheet at the end of the year.
2. To increase sales dollars for product X by 5%.

It may be necessary to set priorities among multiple or conflicting goals. After-the-fact actual performance should be compared with stated objectives.

To the greatest extent feasible, it is usually preferable to have lower-level employees or managers participate in budgeting. This philosophy is called *participative budgeting*. Studies tend to show that motivation and acceptance of budgets are higher when such individuals participate in the budgeting process.

SALES BUDGET

The sales forecast is by far the most important part of the sales budget as it ultimately determines not only the number of units to be sold but also how

Exhibit 8-1
Sun Toys
Master Budget

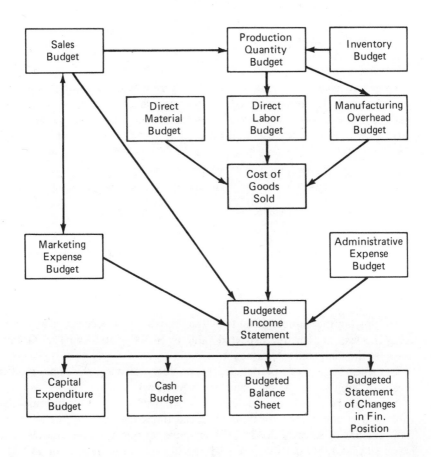

many units to produce, and the amount of raw material, labor, and overhead. There are many ways sales can be forecasted and many factors to consider, some of which are:

Macro-level
1. Demand for industry
2. Demand for firm
3. Mathematical models
4. Probability models
5. General economy
6. Competitive position

Micro-level
1. Projection of past sales
2. Sales force input
3. Market research studies
4. Advertising
5. Sales promotion
6. Price changes

To reduce uncertainty some firms have experimented with probablistic budgets, especially for projecting sales and approach that relies on probability analysis. For example, assume that the sales force estimates the probability of various levels of sales to be as follows:

NUMBER OF UNITS	PROBABILITY	EXPECTED VALUE
10,000	.15	1,500
12,000	.25	3,000
14,000	.50	7,000
18,000	.10	1,800
		13,300

Multiplying the number of units by the probability of occurrence and summing the last column, the expected value is 13,300 units. The 13,300 units becomes the budgeted sales amount.

The sales budget can be detailed by product, territory, division, or other means. Exhibit 8-2 is the sales budget for Sun Toys.

Note that the sales budget is detailed by product: dolls and teddy bears. For each quarter the number of units produced times the selling price gives the total amount of sales in dollars. For example, during the first quarter, it is expected that 1,000 dolls will be sold at $10 each for total sales of $10,000. Total sales in dollars for both products for the first quarter is expected to be $42,000.

PRODUCTION BUDGET

As mentioned previously the sales budget provides data as to the number of units to be sold. The production budget determines the number of units to be produced in order to meet expected sales demand as well as provide a reasonable level of ending inventory; therefore, the firm must first estimate ending inventory requirements. In Chapter 16, we will discuss some of the models and

Exhibit 8-2
SUN TOYS
Sales Budget
for the Year Ended December 31, 19X5

| | QUARTER | | | | |
	1	2	3	4	TOTAL
Dolls					
Number of units	1,000	800	1,200	2,000	5,000
Sales @ $10	$10,000	$ 8,000	$12,000	$20,000	$ 50,000
Teddy bears					
Number of units	4,000	3,000	1,800	5,000	13,8000
Sales @ $8	$32,000	$24,000	$14,400	$40,000	$110,400
Total sales	$42,000	$32,000	$26,400	$60,000	$160,400

analytical tools helpful in establishing the optimal amount of production lots and ending inventory. Ending inventories for finished goods and raw material for Sun Toys are given in Exhibit 8-3.

The production budget is also by product. See Exhibit 8-4.

For each quarter we have determined the number of units to be produced. For the first quarter, Sun Toys' production division must supply 1,000 dolls to be sold, and a desired ending inventory, 200, for a total of 1,200 dolls. Since it has 250 dolls on hand at the beginning of the period, it does not have to make

Exhibit 8-3
SUN TOYS
Ending Inventory Budget
for the Year Ended December 31, 19X5

| | QUARTER | | | | |
	1	2	3	4	
Finished goods (in units)					
Dolls	200	100	300	250	
Teddy bears	400	300	180	500	
					Price per lb
Raw material (in lb)					
1	100	50	60	100	$1
2	40	10	20	20	$2
3	80	90	70	60	$. 60
4	110	115	125	120	$1.20

Exhibit 8-4
SUN TOYS
Production Budget
for the Year Ended December 31, 19X5

| | QUARTER | | | | |
	1	2	3	4	TOTAL
Dolls					
Budgeted sales in units (Exhibit 8-2)	1,000	800	1,200	2,000	5,000
Desired ending inventory (Exhibit 8-3)	200	100	300	250	250
Total requirements	1,200	900	1,500	2,250	5,250
Beginning inventory	250*	200	100	300	250
Budgeted production	950	700	1,400	1,950	5,000
Teddy Bears					
Budgeted sales in units (Exhibit 8-2)	4,000	3,000	1,800	5,000	13,800
Desired ending inventory (Exhibit 8-3)	400	300	180	500	500
Total requirements	4,400	3,300	1,980	5,500	14,300
Beginning inventory	350[a]	400	300	180	350
Budgeted production	4,050	2,900	1,680	5,320	13,950

[a]Assumed.

the entire 1,200. The 250 units in beginning inventory is subtracted from 1,200 to arrive at the number of dolls to be manufactured in the first quarter, 950 dolls.

Note that the desired ending inventory becomes the expected beginning inventory for the next quarter. The 200 units at the end of the quarter 1 is the beginning inventory for quarter 2. Production requirements for the remaining three quarters are computed the same way as for the first quarter.

RAW MATERIAL BUDGET

Recall that products are composed of direct material, direct labor, and manufacturing overhead. For each of these cost elements, a budget is needed.

The raw material budget provides information on the units and cost of raw materials. This budget is not by product produced, but by types of raw material because it is the raw material that is purchased to make a product. In our illustration, raw material requirements are:

Dolls
Material 1   ½ lb
Material 2   ½ lb
Material 3   1½ lb
Teddy bears
Material 3   1 lb
Material 4   ½ lb

As with the production budget, the company must establish a desired amount of ending inventory for each kind of raw material. This information is supplied in Exhibit 8-3. The raw material budget is presented in Exhibit 8-5.

To determine the number of units (pounds) to be purchased, we first find the quantity needed for production. Then we add the desired ending inventory to the production requirement and subtract the beginning inventory. You will

Exhibit 8-5
SUN TOYS
Raw Material Budget
for the Year Ended December 31, 19X5

| | QUARTER | | | | |
	1	2	3	4	TOTAL
Material 1					
Material required for current production					
Number of units to be produced (Exhibit 8-4)	950	700	1,400	1,950	5,000
Pounds per doll	½	½	½	½	½
Pounds needed for production	475	350	700	975	2,500
Ending inv. (Exhibit 8-3)	100	50	60	100	100
Total pounds required	575	400	760	1,075	2,600
Beginning inventory	50[a]	100	50	60	50
Current quarter purchases	525	300	710	1,015	2,550
Unit purchase price	$1	$1	$1	$1	$1
Cost of purchased material 1	$525	$300	$710	$1,015	$2,550
Cost of purchases[b]					
material 2	990	640	1,420	1,950	5,000
material 3	3,303	2,376	2,256	4,941	12,876
material 4	2,466	1,746	1,020	3,186	8,418
Total cost	$7,284	$5,062	$5,406	$11,092	$28,844

[a]Assumed
[b]Details are computed the same as for material 1.

recognize that this is the same formula as for the production budget. For the first quarter, 475 pounds of material 1 (950 units to be produced multiplied by ½ pound per doll) are required for production. Desired ending inventory is 100 pounds. Subtracting the beginning inventory of 50 pounds, we find that the firm needs to purchase 525 pounds during the first quarter. We can easily convert this figure into dollars by multiplying by the unit purchase price of $1 a pound. The result, $525, is useful in preparing the cash budget. Material cost for materials 2, 3, and 4 are computed similarly; hence the detail is not shown here. Obviously for material 3, we must compute the amount of material required for both the dolls and teddy bears because material 3 goes into both products. Please be sure you trace through the calculations in order that you understand the derivation of each number.

LABOR BUDGET

Preparation of the labor budget is similar to the raw material budget. Requirements are:

Dolls—½ hour
Teddy bears—¼ hour

The direct labor budget is Exhibit 8-6.

The first step in preparing the labor budget is to determine the number of direct hours needed. This is done by multiplying the number of units budgeted by the estimated direct hours per unit. For example, in quarter 1, Sun Toys expects to produce 950 dolls. This number times ½ hour per doll gives the direct labor hours for dolls, 475. Again, this figure can easily be converted into a dollar amount by multiplying it by the expected labor rate of $9 an hour.

MANUFACTURING OVERHEAD

Ideally, the manufacturing overhead budget is organized by variable and fixed costs, as illustrated in Exhibit 8-7.

Variable cost can be calculated on a base, or it can be projected as the number of units to be manufactured times an estimated variable overhead cost per unit. In our illustration direct labor hours serve as the base for variable and fixed manufacturing overhead. To obtain the dollar amount of variable cost per account in Exhibit 8-7, we simply multiply the estimated number of labor hours by the variable rate per hour. For example, we assume that indirect material increases at the rate of five cents per direct labor hour; hence budgeted indirect material for quarter 1 is five cents multiplied by the expected direct labor hours in Exhibit 8-6.

Exhibit 8-6
SUN TOYS
Direct Labor Budget
for the Year Ended December 31,19X5

| | QUARTER | | | | |
	1	2	3	4	TOTAL
Dolls					
Budgeted production (Exhibit 8-4)	950	700	1,400	1,950	5,000
Direct labor hours per unit	½	½	½	½	½
	475	350	700	975	2,500
Hourly rate	$9	$9	$9	$9	$9
Direct labor costs	$4,275	$3,150	$6,300	$8,775	$22,500
Teddy bears					
Budgeted production (Exhibit 8-4)	4,050	2,900	1,680	5,320	13,950
Direct labor hours per unit	¼	¼	¼	¼	¼
	1,013*	725	420	1,330	3,488*
Hourly rate	$9	$9	$9	$9	$9
Direct labor costs	$9,117	$6,525	$3,780	$11,970	$31,392
Total direct labor hours	1,488	1,075	1,120	2,305	5,988
Total direct labor costs	$13,392	$9,675	$10,080	$20,745	$53,892

*Rounded

Fixed costs do not change with output. These costs are assumed to be a constant amount for each quarter. Now a predetermined overhead rate for the year can be calculated. We expect manufacturing overhead to be $24,998 and direct labor hours to be 5,988. Dividing the $24,998 by 5,988, we arrive at a manufacturing overhead rate of $4.175 (rounded) per direct labor hour.

COST OF GOODS SOLD BUDGET

The cost of goods sold budget (Exhibit 8-8) summarizes the data needed for the cost of goods sold section of the income statement. Beginning inventory plus 19X5 production costs gives the total dollar amount of inventory that can be sold during the year. Items unsold at the end of the year (ending inventory) are deducted from this amount, leaving the difference as the cost of inventory

Exhibit 8-7

SUN TOYS

Manufacturing Overhead Budget

for the Year Ended December 31, 19X5

	PER HOUR	QUARTER 1	2	3	4	TOTAL
Direct labor hours (Exhibit 8-6)		1,488	1,075	1,120	2,305	5,988
Variable costs:						
Indirect material	.05	$ 75	$54	$56	$115	$300
Indirect labor	.10	149	108	112	231	600
Fringe benefits	.80	1,190	860	896	1,844	4,790
Payroll taxes	.65	967	699	728	1,498	3,892
Utilities	.15	223	161	168	346	898
Repairs	.07	104	75	78	161	418
Total variable cost	$1.82	$2,708	$1,957	$2,038	$4,195	$10,898
Fixed Costs:						
Insurance		$150	$150	$150	$150	$600
Maintenance		125	125	125	125	500
Real estate taxes		750	750	750	750	3,000
Supervision		500	500	500	500	2,000
Depreciation		2,000	2,000	2,000	2,000	8,000
Total fixed cost		$3,525	$3,525	$3,525	$3,525	$14,100
Total manufacturing overhead		$6,233	$5,482	$5,563	7,720	$24,998

Manufacturing overhead rate $\dfrac{\$24,998}{5,988 \text{ direct labor hours}}$ = $4.175 per direct labor hour (rounded)

sold in 19X5. For simplicity we assume that the unit cost of beginning inventory is the same as the current period's production cost. This is rarely the case. In Chapter 16, we will explain various inventory cost flow methods should inventory cost change.

ADMINISTRATIVE EXPENSE BUDGET AND MARKETING EXPENSE BUDGET

The administrative expense budget (Exhibit 8-9) and the marketing expense budget (Exhibit 8-10) are easy to prepare. They simply consist of a listing of the expected cost by account.

Exhibit 8-8
SUN TOYS
Cost of Goods Sold Budget
for the Year Ended December 31, 19X5

	DOLLS		BEARS		TOTAL
Beginning inventory in units (Exhibit 8-4)	250		350		
Unit cost	$8.99ᵃ	$ 2,248	$4.49ᵃ	$1,572	$3,820
19X5 production (Exhibit 8-4)	5,000		13,950		
Unit cost	$8.99ᵇ	44,950	$4.49ᵃ	62,636	107,586
Total available		$47,198		$64,208	$111,406
Less ending inventory in units (Exhibit 8-3)	250		500		
Unit cost	$8.99ᵇ	2,248	$4.49ᵇ	2,245	4,493
Cost of goods sold		$44,950		$61,963	$106,913

ᵃAssumed the same as current period.
ᵇComputed as follows:

Material 1	(½ lb @ $1)	$ .50		
Material 2	(½ lb @ $2)	1.00		
Material 3	(1½ lb @ $.60)	.90	(1 lb @ $.60	$ .60
Material 4			(½ @ $1.20)	.60
Direct material		$2.40		$1.20
Direct labor	(½ hr @ $9)	4.50	(¼ hour @ $9)	2.25
Manufacturing overhead	(½ hour @ $4.175)	2.09	(¼ hour @ $4.175)	1.04
Manufacturing costs		$8.99		$4.49

Exhibit 8-9
SUN TOYS
Administrative Expense Budget
for the Year Ended December 31, 19X5

Administrative salaries	$ 9,000
Clerical salaries	2,000
Employee fringe benefits and payroll taxes	2,150
Repairs and maintenance	200
Insurance	400
Property taxes	600
Office supplies	250
Depreciation	400
Total administrative expense	$15,000

Exhibit 8-10

SUN TOYS

Marketing Expense Budget

for the Year Ended December 31, 19X5

Salaries and commissions	$13,550
Clerical salaries	2,000
Employee fringe benefits and payroll taxes	3,500
Advertising	1,900
Entertainment	2,000
Insurance	500
Repairs and maintenance	200
Office supplies	350
Travel	1,000
Rent	400
Depreciation	600
Total marketing expense budget	$26,000

BUDGETED INCOME STATEMENT

Now we are ready to project net income by means of a budgeted income statement, Exhibit 8-11.

All figures except for income tax are transferred from one of the budgets we described:

1. Sales from the sales budget (Exhibit 8-2)
2. Cost of goods sold from the cost of goods sold budget (Exhibit 8-8)
3. Administrative expenses from administrative expense budget (Exhibit 8-9)
4. Marketing expenses from the marketing expense budget (Exhibit 8-10)

The sales less estimated uncollectible accounts and cost of goods sold result in a gross profit of $50,273. After deducting administrative and marketing expenses, income before taxes is $9,273. The income tax expense is estimated at 25% of $9,273. Hence, Sun Toys expects its profit after tax for 19X5 to be $6,953.

CAPITAL EXPENDITURE BUDGET

The firm must project its capital acquisitions and payment schedule for the year. Sun Toys has a very simple capital budget—only a listing of expected capital expenditures by quarter, Exhibit 8-12.

In Chapter 15 we will discuss methods of evaluating capital proposals.

Exhibit 8-11
SUN TOYS
Budgeted Income Statement
for the Year Ended December 31, 19X5

Sales (Exhibit 8-2)	$160,400
Uncollectible accounts	3,214
Cost of goods sold (Exhibit 8-8)	106,913
Gross profit	$ 50,273
Administrative expense (Exhibit 8-9)	15,000
Marketing expense (Exhibit 8-10)	26,000
Net income before taxes	$ 9,273
Income tax expense (25% average rate assumed)	2,320
Net income after taxes	$ 6,953

CASH BUDGET

We are now in a position to prepare a cash budget. Cash budgeting is critically important because it helps management utilize the scarce resource of cash to optimal advantage. Cash shortages are to be avoided. A high cash surplus should be invested in high-yield securities. Sun Toys' cash budget is shown as Exhibit 8-13.

Exhibit 8-12
SUN TOYS
Capital Expenditure Budget
for the Year Ended December 31, 19X5

	QUARTER				
PROJECT	1	2	3	4	TOTAL
Office equipment	$1,000	$5,000			$ 6,000
Delivery equipment			$10,000[a]		10,000
Manufacturing equipment	2,000	12,000[a]	1,000	$2,000	17,000
	$3,000	$17,000	$11,000	$2,000	$33,000

[a]These items are payable equally over four quarters. All other aquisitions are paid in the same quarter purchased.

Exhibit 8-13
SUN TOYS
Cash Budget
for the Year Ended December 31, 19X5

| | QUARTER | | | | |
	1	2	3	4	TOTAL
Beginning balance	$3,000[a]	$16,311	$14,672	$6,543	$ 3,000
Collection from sales[b]					
Prior period .38	26,600[c]	15,960	12,160	10,032	64,752
Current quarter .60	25,200	19,200	15,840	36,000	96,240
Total cash available without financing	$54,800	$51,471	$42,672	$52,575	$163,992
Cash disbursements:					
Direct material (Exhibit 8-5)[d]	$7,284	$5,062	$5,406	$11,092	$28,844
Direct labor (Exhibit 8-6)[d]	13,392	9,675	10,080	20,745	53,892
Manufacturing overhead (Exhibit 8-7)[d]	4,233	3,482	3,563	5,720	16,998[f]
Administrative expense (Exhibit 8-9)[e]	3,650	3,650	3,650	3,650	14,600[f]
Marketing expense (Exhibit 8-10)	6,350	6,350	6,350	6,350	25,400[f]
Income tax expense (Exhibit 8-11)	580	580	580	580	2,320
Total disbursements	$35,489	$28,799	$29,629	$48,137	$142,054
Next cash available	$19,311	$22,672	$13,043	$4,438	$21,938
Capital expenditures[g]	3,000	8,000	6,500	7,500	$25,000
Note payable				(4,000)	(4,000)
Ending cash balance	$16,311	$14,672	$6,543	$938	$938

[a]Assumed.

[b]Assumed .60 in month of sales, .38 the following month and .02 uncollectible.

[c]Prior quarter's sales assumed to be $70,000.

[d]Assumed paid in period incurred.

[e]Assumed incurred evenly.

[f]Depreciation has been removed since it is not paid in cash.

| | QUARTER | | | |
	1	2	3	4
[g]Office	$1,000	$5,000		
Manufacturing (installments)		3,000	$3,000	$3,000
Delivery (installments)			2,500	2,500
Manufacturing	2,000		1,000	2,000
	$3,000	$8,000	$6,500	$7,500

Note that the first quarter of the cash budget begins with the cash on hand. To this we add all cash receipts. The amount received depends upon the collection policy and experience of the firm. For this firm 60% of sales are assumed to be collected in the quarter of sales, 2% are deemed to be uncollectible, and the remaining 38% is collectible in the next quarter.

All cash disbursements are taken from the respective expense budget and capital expenditure budget. At the end of the first quarter the ending cash balance is expected to be $16,311, which becomes the beginning cash balance for the second quarter. At the end of 19X5 Sun Toys should have cash on hand (and consequently listed as such on the balance sheet) of $938.

One of the main purposes of the cash budget is that it shows cash available at the end of each quarter. If more detail is required, this budget could be computed by month or even by day. The treasurer should judge whether or not $16,311 is too much cash to hold at the end of quarter 1. If so, it should be invested in short-term securities (since much of it will be needed in the third quarter and the fourth quarter). It appears that the firm will be forced to borrow $4,000 in quarter 4. An analysis should be performed whether $938 at the end of the fourth quarter is sufficient to meet unexpected expenditures and emergencies.

A word of caution concerning depreciation. Depreciation is an allocation of the cost of a long-term asset over its expected life. Depreciation does not result in cash outflow (nor does it result in cash inflow). Cash outflow takes place when capital items are paid for and not when they are depreciated. Therefore, the manufacturing overhead budget, administrative expense budget, and marketing expense budget are decreased by their respective amounts of depreciation to arrive at the cash disbursement.

BUDGETED BALANCE SHEET

The balance sheet as of December 31, 19X4 can be updated by incorporating data from the budgets to arrive at a December 31, 19X5 balance sheet, (Exhibit 8-14).

Many of the figures can be traced to previous budgets. For example, cash can be traced to the cash budget. Accounts receivable is 38% of the last quarter's sales. The inventory figures are based on the inventory budgets. Fixed assets have been increased by the amount of the capital expenditure budget and accumulated depreciation was increased by the amount of depreciation expense for the year. We netted the plant assets with accumulated depreciation. Common stock is the same as last year. Finally, retained earnings are increased by the amount of profit on the income statement.

Exhibit 8-14

SUN TOYS

Budgeted Balance Sheet

as of December 31, 19X5

ASSETS

Current assets	
Cash (Exhibit 8-13)	$938
Accounts receivable (net) (38% × $60,000)	22,800
Inventories, raw material [a]	320
finished goods (Exhibit 8-8)	4,493
Total current assets	$28,551
Plant, property and equipment	
Land	10,000
Plant assets (net of accumulated depreciation)	100,000
Total assets	$138,551

LIBABILITIES AND CAPITAL

Payable on capital acquisitions	$8,000
Short-term note payable (Exhibit 8-13)	4,000
Total liabilities	$12,000
Capital stock	50,000
Retained earnings	76,551
Total liabilities and capital	$138,551

[a]Raw material inventory is computed as follows:

Material	Quantity (Ex. 8-3)	Cost per unit (Ex. 8-3)	Total
1	100	$1	$100
2	20	$2	40
3	60	$.60	36
4	120	$1.20	144
			$320

BUDGETED STATEMENT OF CHANGES IN FINANCIAL POSITION

The statement of changes in financial position measures and explains the change in funds from one accounting period to the next. Funds can be defined as the change in cash or working capital (current assets less current liabilities). Sun Toys chooses the working capital method, Exhibit 8-15.

Note that the net decrease in working capital during the year is $17,047. A decrease is possible even though the firm expects to generate a profit. Resources provided (increase in working capital) include net income adjusted for depreciation. Recall that depreciation does not result in a cash outflow.

Exhibit 8-15

SUN TOYS

Budgeted Statement of Changes in Financial
Position (working capital concept)
for the Year Ended December 31, 19X5

Resources provided			
Net income (Exhibit 8-11)			$ 6,953
Add: depreciation[a]			9,000
Working capital from operations and total resources provided			$15,953
Resources expended			
Purchase of capital assets (Exhibit 8-12)			$33,000
Decrease in working capital			($17,047)

	DEC. 31, 19X4	DEC. 31, 19X5	WORKING CAPITAL
Cash (Exhibit 8-13)	$ 3,000	$ 938	($2,062)
Accounts receivable (Exhibit 8-13)	26,600	22,800	(3,800)
Raw material inventory	178	320	142
Finished goods inventory (Exhibit 8-8)	3,820	4,493	673
Payables for aquisitions	0	(8,000)	(8,000)
Note payable	0	(4,000)	(4,000)
	$33,598	$16,551	($17,047)
[a]Manufacturing depreciation (Exhibit 8-7)			$ 8,000
Administrative (Exhibit 8-9)			400
Marketing (Exhibit 8-10)			600
			$9,000

Working capital decreases because the firm elects to purchase $33,000 of new capital assets, which will be financed by cash and short-term debt. For a more sophisticated organization, this financial statement would be considerably more complex.

This completes our comprehensive example of the budgeting process. Keep in mind that budgeting is not the clean neat process we demonstrate here. It requries, much time, paperwork, communication, and negotiation. A great deal of judgment and cooperation is needed. Obviously, budgeting does not eliminate the administrative role of managers since budgets are not meant to be a rigid dictator of behavior, but a plan to achieve corporate goals. Budgets may travel the chain of command several times before agreement is reached as to contents and amounts. Some of the behavioral aspects of budgeting are examined in Chapter 19.

ADVANTAGES OF BUDGETING

We close this chapter by listing some of the advantages of budgeting. Budgeting:

1. Provides a disciplined approach to managing in that it forces managers to plan ahead.
2. Requires the establishment of definitive goals and objectives which managers can work toward.
3. Aids in coordinating and correlating the activities of the firm.
4. Pinpoints potential weaknesses and bottlenecks before they occur.
5. Provides a yardstick for measuring actual performance.
6. Develops an atmosphere of profit-mindedness and cost control.
7. Motivates managers and employees.
8. Aids in directing capital and effort into the most profitable areas.
9. Affords a means of appraising all facets of the organization and managers.
10. May serve as a basis for distributing rewards.
11. Satisfies legal and contractual requirements.

SUMMARY

We discussed budgets and their usefulness, as well as the differences between forecasting and budgeting. Most of the chapter was devoted to demonstrating a comprehensive budgeting system for a small toy manufacturer. The principles illustrated are equally applicable to large firms. The volume of data required for a sophisticated budgeting system would require computer capability.

9. Standard Costs and Material and Labor Variance Analysis

Many manufacturing firms utilize a standard cost system. A standard is a pre-determined amount, the cost expected to be incurred for producing a particular product under normal conditions. Obviously, standards must be set separately for the three cost elements: direct material, direct labor, and manufacturing overhead. Assume that the composition of cost to make one widget is as follows:

1. Direct material (standard material quantity × standard material price) (3 pounds × $8 per pound) $24.00
2. Direct labor (standard labor hours × standard labor rate) (4 hours × $9 per hour) 36.00
3. Manufacturing overhead (projected cost divided by a standard base × standard base per unit)

$$\frac{\$500,000 \text{ projected costs}}{100,000 \text{ standard labor hours}} = \$5$$

(4 hours × $5 overhead rate) 20.00

Total standard manufacturing cost $80.00

Note the composition of the total standard cost of $80.00. Standard material consists of a standard quantity times a standard price per unit. Similarly, standard direct labor consists of standard hours times a standard labor rate. The overhead is calculated by applying the predetermined overhead rate to the standard base per unit.

When a firm has a complete standard cost system, costs are recorded in the accounting records at both standard and actual. The difference between the two amounts is put in a variance account. For example, if raw material with a standard of $10 is purchased for $11, the journal entry is:

Raw material inventory $10
Material price variance $ 1
    Cash (or Accounts payable) $11

The standard is recorded in the raw material inventory account, and of course cash or accounts payable must reflect the actual purchase price. The $1 difference is an unfavorable price variance because the firm paid more for the order than it expected. If the opposite situation occurs, the results would be a favorable price variance. The total of the charges to the inventory account plus the price variance represents actual cost. Actual cost, not standard cost, is usually shown on published financial statements.

Some firms do not have complete cost systems. For example, they may keep their books at actual cost supplemented by memo books for standard. Such practices usually lose much of the value of a standard system because variances may be difficult to compute or cannot be calculated at all. Another undesirable practice is to compute variances at the end of the accounting period after their significance is too late for decision making. Old data seldom contain much usable information.

PURPOSES OF STANDARD COSTS

Why do firms have standard cost systems? Isn't it just a lot of extra work and expense? We probably have to say "yes" on both counts. Still, if the benefits exceed the costs, a standard system should be used. Let us now examine some of these benefits. The first one, record keeping, has already been mentioned.

Cost Control

A standard cost system constitutes a powerful cost control system. To a large extent the control is only as valid as the accuracy of the standards supporting it. A good standard system should recognize a variance as soon as it is incurred and pinpoint the person(s) responsible for it. Standard cost systems utilize the principle of "management by exception", that is, material deviations from what is normal are investigated while less attention is given when actual costs closely parallel standard costs. The sooner a purchasing manager is aware that a major price variance has occurred, the sooner he or she can investigate the cause and take corrective action if warranted. Not all variances call for corrective action since there can be valid explanations for their occurrence.

A comment or two about the phrases *favorable* and *unfavorable* variances. It is easy to fall into the trap of thinking about them as "good" or "bad," on the assumption that favorable variances deserve praise and unfavorable variances deserve censure. Such reasoning should be avoided. The purpose of standards and budgets is not to dole out praise or blame (although many times they are used that way), but to help managers control more efficiently and effectively. A manager can be incompetent in spite of a favorable variance. For example, if a purchasing manager could have purchased an item for $8 (which was purchased for $9 and has a standard cost of $10), the purchasing manager failed to act prudently. The accounting records will show a favorable price variance of $1 ($10 − $9) when it should have been $2 ($10 − $8).

Favorable variances should be investigated as well as unfavorable because if a practice is found that reduces cost, it may be desirable to continue such practice in the future. For example, if a new supplier sells raw material below standard cost or if price breaks are allowed when a buyer meets certain criteria, a firm would want to take advantage of such opportunities to minimize the costs of raw material.

Valuing Inventory

Standards provide a means for valuing inventory. Some theorists argue that variances should be recognized as such and not as part of inventory costs; hence, variances should be written off on the income statements. They say that if standards are properly set, deviations are the result of inefficiencies (if unfavorable) or superior performance (if favorable). Remember, however, actual costs (standard plus variances) are required for published financial statements.

Budgeting

Standards can be very useful in the budgeting process. For example, if standards exist they can be used to budget material and labor quantity, rates and overhead. In addition, when actual costs are known deviation from budgeted cost can be easily calculated. Such a budgeting system is much superior to a budget based on estimated expected cost because if the composition of the budgeted amount is not known, there is no way of effectively evaluating variances.

Pricing

Although there are many good pricing models other than full cost (discussed in Chapter 13), still, knowledge of full cost is essential for pricing. If a firm is to be profitable over the long run, it must recover full cost, as well as make a profit. A standard system makes a price proposal very easy to prepare with a minimum of effort. Many sales are lost because firms do not get their price proposals prepared in time. Some price proposals, such as those submitted by defense contractors to government agencies, require an audit by government auditors. Standard-cost-based proposals are usually easier to justify than most other pricing models.

An elementary example of a price quotation based on standard cost for a potential order of 100 widgets is given below.

Direct material (100 units × 2 pounds × $8)	$1,600
Direct labor (100 units × 4 hours × $6)	2,400
Variable manufacturing overhead (100% of standard direct labor cost)	2,400
Total variable cost	$6,400

Fixed manufacturing overhead (25% of total variable cost)	1,600
Fixed selling, general and administrative overhead (20% of total variable cost)	1,280
Total full cost	$9,280

Note that the price proposal, because it is prepared in a variable-cost format, aids pricing decisions. Any amount negotiated in excess of $6,400 would increase the firm's overall profit as reported on the income statement. This theory is called variable costing. If a full-cost model is used, the desired profit (based on such elements as risk, fixed assets requirement, opportunity loss from facilities' not being available for other products, etc.) is added to the total full cost of $9,280. For example, if a profit of 20% of full cost is desired, $1,856 (20% × $9,280) is added, resulting in a final price quotation of $11,136.

Evaluation and Compensation of Managers

Finally, standards are frequently used to evaluate and compensate managers, perhaps the most controversial purpose of standards. To the extent that managers disagree with tight standards, we can expect morale to decrease. Therefore, standard setting is like budgeting—the participation of the employees affected is usually a desirable management practice.

SETTING STANDARDS

There are many points of view regarding how tight standards should be set. Some of the more common are:

1. *Ideal standards*—demand maximum efficiency with no allowance for errors, such as delays, decrease in worker efficiency, or breakdown of equipment. Unfavorable variances are expected most of the time.
2. *Attainable standards*—set at practical or realistic level of performance. These standards are high but attainable.
3. *Expected standards*—are based on the mean or average level of performance. Variances should be small.
4. *Historical standards*—are based on the past regardless of inefficiencies, workers, changes in methods, and so forth.
5. *Loose standards*—require a minimum level of efficiency. Because employees should be able to meet the standards, variances should be favorable.

Research tends to show that standards should be set slightly above the mean (average) to motivate employees to meet them. Standards set too tight discourage employees and result in unfavorable variances. Loose standards are not challenging enough and result in favorable variances.

Some of the methods used for setting standards include:

1. Past experience (historical data). The major weakness is that all inefficiencies of the past are incorporated into the standard.
2. Price quotations, catalog prices, and so on. Used primarily for material.
3. Time and motion studies for labor hour standard. Employees may attempt to distort the standard by working slower than normal during observation period.
4. Published industry standards. Used mostly for standardized products or operations.
5. Union contracts. Used primarily for labor rates but can be used for labor hours.
6. Standards committee. Members should include management, accountant, and a representative from the area affected by the standard.
7. Best educated guess. The guesses should be updated when more reliable information is available.
8. Engineering blueprints. Most often used for new products.
9. Simulation studies. Requires a computer and a substantial data base.
10. Pilot product projects. These standards tend to be high because of a lack of learning.
11. Learning curves. Here the firm applies a learning curve to the historical time for making initial units.

The rework time for unavoidable spoilage should be incorporated in the standard. The cost of avoidable spoilage should be treated as a period loss.

UPDATING STANDARDS

Some firms constantly update standards, whereas other firms seldom do. Obviously, the size of variances depends upon the firm's philosophy. For static products, there should be little need to change material and labor quantity standards. However, in an inflationary economy, the material price standard and labor rate standard should be updated to include the effect of price increases; otherwise increasingly unfavorable variances would largely be caused by inflation.

Keep in mind that an obsolete standard may be more dangerous than no standard because it leads to erroneous decisions and possibly deteriorating morale. A frequent problem to be on the lookout for is "creeping change," which consists of a series of small changes over a relatively long period of time whose cumulative effect becomes significant.

Exhibit 9-1
Learning Curve

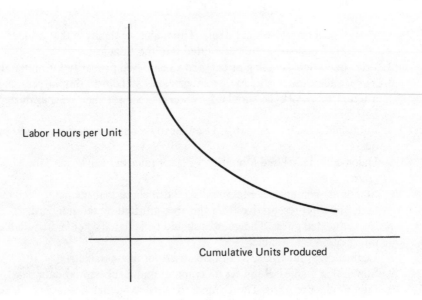

Labor Hours per Unit

Cumulative Units Produced

   Standards should be set after employee learning has taken place. A new labor standard will soon become obsolete if it does not provide for the learning curve effect. Most people perform more efficiently the second time they perform a task than the first time and better the third time than the second and so on. This phenomenon is called a learning curve, which graphically looks something like Exhibit 9-1. The idea behind the curve is that the first unit takes a relatively long period of time to make, but as a worker makes more and more units, he or she becomes more and more efficient until little or no additional learning takes place. Note that the curve tends to flatten out as a higher number of units are produced. This rate of learning can be measured mathematically. It is not our purpose here to teach you how to compute the slope of the line (this can be studied in many mathematics textbooks) but rather to warn you that learning curves are important for labor standards. If set high on the curve, the standard will be loose. Conversely, if set low, it may be too tight for new and inexperienced employees.

TYPES OF VARIANCES

A variance is the difference between standard cost and actual cost and can be divided into two kinds for both material and labor: quantity and price. Usually, we give different titles to material and labor variances, although in substance they are the same. The material price variance is like the labor rate variance, and the material quantity variance is like the labor efficiency variance. The formulas (with assumed data) are:

Material

Price variance = (standard material price − actual material price) × actual material quantity	$ 20 U
Quantity variance = (standard material quantity − actual material quantity) × standard material price	156 F
Total material variance = (total standard cost − total actual cost)	$136 F

Labor

Rate variance = (standard labor rate − actual labor rate) × actual hours	$ 16 F
Efficiency variance = (standard labor hours − actual labor hours) × standard labor rate	30 U
Total labor variance = (total standard cost − total actual cost)	$ 14 U

Material Variances

Exhibit 9-2 illustrates a material variance. Graphically, the material variance looks like Exhibit 9-3. Note that there is a joint variance of $4. Generally, the

Exhibit 9-2
Material Variance Breakdown

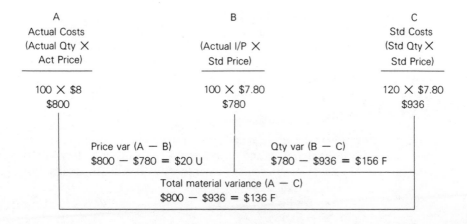

Exhibit 9-3

Graph of Material Variances

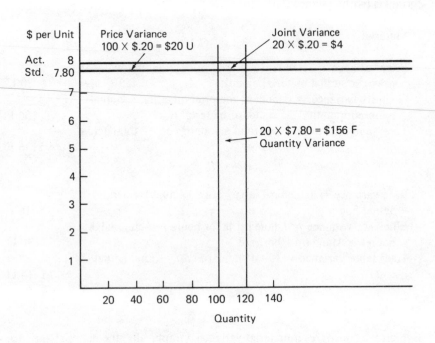

joint variance is too small to be relevant to decision making and is thus usually included as part of the overall price variance.

The journal entries to record material transactions are:

Raw material inventory	$780	
Material price variance	$ 20	
Cash or accounts payable		$800
Work-in-process inventory	$936	
Material quantity variance		$156
Raw material inventory		$780

We now look at how the material cost flows through the accounts. Note that the charges to raw material inventory and work-in-process inventory are at standard. You need not concern yourself extensively with debits or credits. Just follow the flow of cost in Exhibit 9-4.

Exhibit 9-4
Material Cost Flow

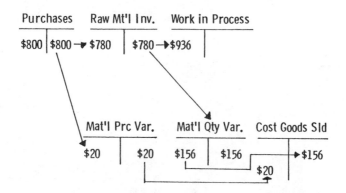

Labor Variances

The analyses of labor and material are similar. Consider the situation in Exhibit 9-5.

The journal entry to record the transaction is:

Work-in-process inventory	$450	
Labor efficiency variance	$ 30 U	
Labor rate variance		$ 16 F
Payroll		$464

If you are uncertain how a graph for labor looks or how the labor cost flows through the accounts, try working this out for yourself using material as a pattern.

MIX AND YIELD VARIANCES

Material quantity variance and labor efficiency variance can be further broken down into mix and yield variances. For some products the material input can be varied without changing the nature of the product, and different combinations of labor than those budgeted can be used. Such situations result in a mix and/or yield variance. The formulas to compute these variances are:

Mix variance = (standard quantity − actual quantity) × (standard cost of the individual input − standard average cost of all inputs)
Yield variance = (actual quantity of inputs during the period × standard

Exhibit 9-5
Labor Variance Breakdown

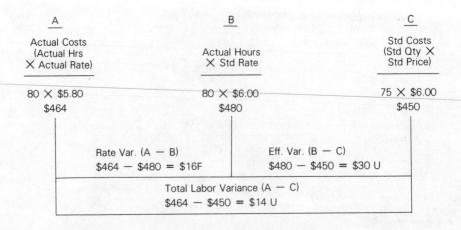

average cost of inputs) — (actual quantity of outputs for the period ×
standard cost of outputs)

The material mix variance indicates whether changing from a standard mix to
an alternate mix will affect the material cost. The material yield variance is
the difference between actual yield and expected yield from some actual
amount of input. Hence, yield is the relationship between inputs and outputs.
The labor yield variance is similar to the material yield variance in that it measures the amount that actual yield deviates from expected yield. The labor mix
variance tells if changing the composition of workers has any impact on
efficiency.

If the products produced have a high level of interchangeability of material
and labor and the effect is likely to be of measureable consequence, calculation
of yield and mix variances is probably worthwhile. If the opposite is true, it is
highly unlikely that the benefits of such information would exceed the cost.

CAUSES OF VARIANCES

What do we do with these variances once they are computed? Recall that the
total favorable material variance of $136 is separated into a small unfavorable
price variance of $20 and a relatively large favorable quantity variance of $156.
Apparently, the actual quantity needed was considerably less than expected.

The next step in the variance analysis is to obtain an explanation from the person responsible for the cost. Should corrective action be needed, it should be done at this time. Although we demonstrate standards and variances with very simple examples, keep in mind that many times firms establish standards and record actual costs by department, which enables them to pinpoint the individual(s) responsible for the variance. Similarly, with a computer we can easily compute material variances by product or operation, and labor variances by employee, types of labor, supervisor, and so forth. Care must be exercised that the benefits of such refinements exceed the cost.

The material price variance should be recognized when purchases are made instead of when raw materials are transferred to work in process. We repeat an important principle: Variances should be recognized as early as possible.

Material price variances are usually the responsibility of the purchasing department whereas material quantity and labor efficiency variances are normally the responsibility of production. The labor rate variance is the responsibility of whoever establishes labor rates, be it top management, line management, or personnel.

Sometimes the person responsible for a variance may not be the usual person. For example, when shoddy purchasing practices cause high spoilage and increased production time, the purchasing department should be held responsible for both the material quantity and labor efficiency variance. Similarly, a rush order demanded by the sales force may result in higher costs incurred because of shorter lead time, scheduling conflicts, overtime, and so forth; hence the marketing department should be held responsible for any material price variance and both labor variances.

We now list some of the causes for material and labor variances other than the erroneous setting of standards. These lists are not intended to be all-inclusive.

Material Price Variance

1. Inflation
2. New vendors
3. Vendor strikes
4. Poor purchasing practices
5. Rush orders
6. Change in order size, cash discounts, delivery dates or other terms

Material Quantity Variance

1. Change in quality of raw material
2. Worn machinery

3. Defalcations
4. Untrained workers
5. Poor supervision

Labor Rate Variance

1. Inflation
2. New employees
3. Change in mix of employees
4. Overtime at premium rates

Labor Efficiency Variance

1. Machine breakdowns
2. Less-efficient workers being assigned to job
3. Poor supervision
4. Strikes or other work interruptions
5. Abnormal environment affecting employees, for instance, a very hot day
6. Inferior raw material
7. Changes in production methods
8. Poor blueprints
9. Poorly trained workers

NONMANUFACTURING STANDARDS

Standard cost systems are not limited to manufacturing installations. They are applicable to many organizations, including nonprofit organizations, retail stores, and service companies. For example, assume we operate a service business in which 15 minutes is required to service one customer. The standard variable cost per hour is $8, and our budgeted fixed cost is $15,000. The number of customers expected during the year is 10,000. A standard cost per customer is computed at $3.50.

Variable cost (¼ hour × $8 per hour)	$2.00
Fixed cost ($15,000/10,000 customers)	1.50
Standard cost per customer	$3.50

Assume that 9,000 customers actually visit the shop during the year, and direct time charged to customers is 2,600 hours. Actual variable cost is $17,900 and actual fixed cost is as budgeted. We analyze the total unfavorable variance of $1,400 (actual $32,900 — standard for 9,000 customers $31,500) as follows :

Actual variable costs	$17,900	
Budgeted variable cost for 2,600 actual hours		
× $8	20,800	
Favorable spending variance		$2,900 F
Budgeted variable cost	$20,800	
Budgeted variable cost for 9,000 customers ×		
$2	18,000	
Unfavorable efficiency variance		2,800 U
Actual fixed overhead	$15,000	
Fixed overhead absorbed (9,000 × $1.50)	13,500	
Unfavorable capacity variance		1,500 U
Unfavorable total variance		$1,400 U

SUMMARY

We defined standards, examined their purposes, and explained the philosophies and methods of setting them. We took note of the issues involved in updating standards. Formulas for material and labor variances were provided and illustrated. Variances must be identifiable by responsibility centers in order that the causes of variances can be determined and corrective action instituted if needed. The latter portion of the chapter covered the common causes of material and labor variances.

10. Flexible Budgeting and Overhead Variance Analysis

In the last two chapters we discussed budgeting, standards, and the variance analysis of material and labor. Now, we turn our attention to flexible budgeting, overhead variances, and zero base budgeting, beginning with a review of some of the characteristics of a good planning and control reporting system. Our first question is, What do we expect from reports?

REPORTING SYSTEM

A good reporting system:

1. *Identifies variances by types and causes.* To determine cause it is usually desirable to describe variances as finely as possible. For example, total material variance is divided into a price and quantity variance. The individual(s) responsible for them and the factor(s) causing them can then be identified. Once the causes are known, corrective action can be taken if necessary. In this chapter we analyze the total overhead variance by subdividing it into four separate components. For each, the cause and correction of variances can be quite different.

2. *Includes an annual forecast.* The differences between budgeting and forecasting were explained in Chapter 8.

3. *Pinpoints the person(s) responsible for variances.* All variances should be explained by the individual(s) responsible for their occurrences and not by the controller, cost accountant, or preparer of reports.

4. *Identifies the corrective action to be taken for unfavorable variances.* A nonrecurring variance would not require correction, but unless something is done to improve recurring unfavorable variances, reporting them is wasted effort.

5. *Specifies the time frame for corrective action.* Many inefficiencies cannot be corrected overnight. Some corrections take a relatively short period of time, such as revising material price standards, whereas others may require a longer period of time, such as training personnel to prevent labor inefficiencies.

WEAKNESS OF STATIC BUDGETS

We said previously that one of the purposes of budgeting is control through variance analysis. So far we discussed the static budget, but now we turn our attention to flexible budgeting. Suppose comparison of actual with budgeted manufacturing variable overhead resulted in the variances shown in Exhibit 10-1.

The firm budgeted 20,000 hours to produce 5,000 units but expended only 18,000 hours to make 4,500 units. Yet if we look at the variance column we find that most of the variances are favorable. Our first impression might be that the company has performed well during the month. Recall in the last chapter we mentioned that favorable variances do not necessarily mean superior performance. In Exhibit 10-1 most of the variances are caused by the firm's operating below budgeted production. This becomes clear from an analysis of one of the variable overhead accounts, say, indirect materials. A similar analysis could be made of any of the variable overhead accounts. Now look at Exhibit 10-2. Of the $1,100 total favorable variance, $1,000 is because the firm operated at less than budgeted direct labor hours, or put another way, it only manufactured 4,500 units when it budgeted 5,000. The remaining $100 is the true spending variance.

The above situation depicts the major weakness of a static budget—the static budget does not consider the volume variance. Although it is possible to break the total variance of each overhead account into its components, this is a very time-consuming task and results in a great deal of paperwork. A better way to resolve the volume problem is to remove the volume variance from the budget with a technique called flexible budgeting.

Exhibit 10-1
ABC COMPANY
Performance Report
Month of April 19X8

	VARIABLE COST LABOR HOUR	BUDGET	ACTUAL	VARIANCE
Units manufactured		5,000	4,500	500
Labor hours		20,000	18,000	2,000 F
Variable overhead costs				
Indirect materials	$ .50	$10,000	$8,900	$1,100 F
Indirect labor	.40	8,000	7,300	700 F
Employees fringe benefits	.20	4,000	3,550	450 F
Payroll taxes	.10	2,000	1,800	200 F
Utilities	.15	3,000	2,680	320 F
Maintenance	.13	2,600	2,710	110 U
	$1.48	$29,600	$26,940	$2,660 F

Exhibit 10-2
Analysis of Indirect Material Variance

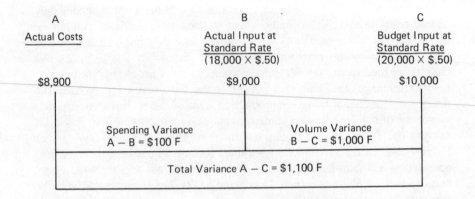

A	B	C
Actual Costs	Actual Input at Standard Rate (18,000 X $.50)	Budget Input at Standard Rate (20,000 X $.50)
$8,900	$9,000	$10,000

Spending Variance
A − B = $100 F

Volume Variance
B − C = $1,000 F

Total Variance A − C = $1,100 F

CAPACITY CONCEPTS

Before we illustrate flexible budgeting, let us spend a few minutes on capacity concepts. Recall that a predetermined overhead rate really consists of two elements: variable and fixed. For example, assume a different set of data than used for Exhibit 10-1, such as the following:

	Per Unit
Variable manufacturing overhead	$10
Fixed manufacturing overhead ($100,000/25,000 direct labor hours)	4
Total manufacturing overhead rate	$14

How do we select the 25,000 direct labor hours? One way is to calculate the number of standard direct labor hours required to produce the units budgeted. Recall from Chapter 8 how to budget units to be produced and how to prepare a direct labor budget. The direct labor budget consists of the direct labor hours required to manufacture the budgeted units.

What if in year 1 we expect to incur 40,000 direct labor hours and in year 2, only 25,000 direct labor hours? This will cause the fixed portion of the overhead to vary substantially from year 1 to year 2. For example, assuming no change in fixed manufacturing dollars, the projected fixed overhead rates are:

Year	
1 $100,000/40,000	$2.50
2 $100,000/25,000	$4.00

The consequence is that the year 2 widget will "cost" $1.50 more to produce than the year 1 widget. Unless the selling price is raised accordingly, year 2 widgets will result in $1.50 less profit per unit than year 1. Does such a situation makes sense? Of course, you know the reason why from Chapter 4. As more units are produced, the fixed cost per unit decreases because it is spread over more units.

Carrying the example a bit further, what if in year 3, 45,000 hours are incurred? Now, assuming we keep the manufacturing cost constant at $100,000, the fixed overhead rate is $2.22 per direct labor hour ($100,000/ 45,000). Could a customer demand a year-3 widget because it is $1.78 cheaper ($4 − $2.22) than the year-2 widget? If so, the customer is arguing in essence that the cost differential should be passed on to him or her.

This problem of fixed cost per unit leads to the issue of capacity. Put another way, how do we determine the amount of the base? Theoretically, fixed cost measures the capacity to make and sell within the relevant range. It is the selection of one of the several concepts of capacity that determines the amount of the overhead base, the dollar amount of overhead charged to jobs (products), and the volume variance. Capacity can be defined in the following terms:

1. Normal activity is the level at which the firm expects to operate over a relatively long period of time, say, five years. It makes allowances for factors such as seasonal or cyclical changes in consumer demand.

2. Expected annual activity for the year, a method discussed earlier, is based on the amount budgeted solely for the year. As we demonstrated, its main weakness is that the overhead rates tend to fluctuate from one period to the next. If volume does not change greatly from year to year, this is a rational base because it tends to coincide with normal activity.

3. Practical capacity is the maximum level at which the plant can operate efficiently. Keep in mind that this can seldom be defined precisely. Factors such as overtime and subcontracting can expand production capacity. Many times, practical capacity is defined by management for planning and control purposes rather than by a particular set of criteria.

Capacity can be defined by number of items that can be produced or in terms of resources, such as direct labor hours. The capacity definition selected will affect the amount of fixed overhead charged to individual products and variances. For example, if capacity is defined as 25,000 direct labor hours, the fixed overhead rate is $4, assuming $100,000 of indirect cost.

$$\frac{\$100,000}{25,000} = \$4$$

Assume actual production is 20,000 direct labor hours. The actual overhead rate for the fixed cost is $5.

$$\frac{\$100,000}{20,000} = \$5$$

When we use the predetermined rate of $4 to charge manufacturing overhead to work-in-process inventory (20,000 × $4), the result is an unfavorable volume variance of $20,000.

Actual overhead incurred	$100,000
Amount charged to work in process (20,000 × $4)	80,000
Unfavorable volume variance	$ 20,000

Treatment of the $20,000 on financial statements and disposition on the books are discussed later in the chapter.

FLEXIBLE BUDGETING

Now we return to the concept of flexible budgeting. Under flexible budgeting we prepare separate budgets at various levels of operation within the relevant range, that is, the range of production in which the firm expects to operate during the forthcoming period. Consider Exhibit 10-3.

The flexible budget assumes that the relevant range is between 4,500 and 5,250 units and that 4 direct labor hours are needed to produce each widget. Therefore, the relevant range in labor hours is between 18,000 and 21,000 direct labor hours. It is usually preferable to prepare a flexible budget in terms of direct labor hours than units manufactured because in a multiproduct company, it is difficult to work with number of units. Note that the flexible budget is broken down by variable and fixed overhead. If actual labor incurred should be 19,500 in lieu of any level on the flexible budget, we could simply redraft the budget after the fact by utilizing the cost formula provided in the flexible budget. The total budgeted cost for 19,500 units is $1.48(19,500) + $22,400 or $51,260.

PERFORMANCE REPORT

Now we are in a better position to redraft the performance report (Exhibit 10-1) for April. See Exhibit 10-4. In essence we have removed the effect of the volume variance from each overhead account. Thus the entire variance column is the variable overhead spending variance. The next step is to investigate reasons for the variances. Usually, we focus attention on large variances and ignore small amounts in accordance with the principle of management by exception. Certainly, we would want to take a look at what caused the overrun

Exhibit 10-3
ABC COMPANY
Flexible Budget
Month of April 19X8

		RANGE OF PRODUCTION (IN UNITS)			
	COST PER DLH	4500	4750	5000	5250
Direct labor hours (4 per unit)		18,000	19,000	20,000	21,000
Variable costs					
Indirect material	$ .50	$9,000	$9,500	$10,000	$10,500
Indirect labor	.40	7,200	7,600	8,000	8,400
Fringe benefits	.20	3,600	3,800	4,000	4,200
Payroll taxes	.10	1,800	1,900	2,000	2,100
Utilities	.15	2,700	2,850	3,000	3,150
Maintenance	.13	2,340	2,470	2,600	2,730
Total variable costs	$1.48	$26,640	$28,120	$29,600	$31,080
Fixed costs					
Supervision		$ 9,400	$ 9,400	$ 9,400	$ 9,400
Depreciation		7,000	7,000	7,000	7,000
Maintenance		3,000	3,000	3,000	3,000
Property tax		2,000	2,000	2,000	2,000
Insurance		1,000	1,000	1,000	1,000
Total fixed costs		$22,400	$22,400	$22,400	$22,400
Total manufacturing overhead		$49,040	$50,520	$52,000	$53,480

Predetermined overhead rate with direct labor hours as the base, assuming operation level to be 20,000 direct labor hours.

Variable element	$29,600	$1.48
	20,000	
Fixed element	$22,400	$1.12
	20,000	
Total mfg overhead		$2.60

Exhibit 10-4
ABC COMPANY
Performance Report
Month of April 19X8

	BUDGET	ACTUAL	VARIANCE
Direct labor hrs	18,000	18,000	0
Variable overhead costs			
Indirect materials	$ 9,000	$ 8,900	$100 F
Indirect labor	7,200	7,300	100 U
Benefits	3,600	3,550	50 F
Payroll taxes	1,800	1,800	0
Utilities	2,700	2,680	20 F
Maintenance	2,340	2,710	370 U
	$26,640	$26,940	$300 U

of $370 for maintenance. The performance report can easily be expanded to include a "cause" or "comment" column.

OVERHEAD VARIANCE ANALYSIS

Variances can be caused by deviations from actual costs of either the numerator or the denominator portion of the predetermined rate. For example,

$$\frac{\$52,000 \text{ estimated costs}}{20,000 \text{ direct labor hours}}$$

$$= \$2.60 \text{ predetermined manufacturing overhead rate}$$

If actual costs deviate from $52,000 we have a numerator variance. This variance can be divided into a fixed portion and a variable portion. Similarly, the denominator may not reflect actual labor hours. The denominator variance can be separated into the volume variance and an efficiency variance.

Standard Cost

Now return your attention to standard costs, discussed in Chapter 9. Recall that under a standard cost system we record cost in the inventory accounts at standard instead of actual costs; therefore, the work-in-process inventory is charged for overhead at standard direct labor hours times the predetermined overhead rate (assuming direct labor hours is the base). What happens when standard direct labor hours are not the same as actual direct labor hours? Such a situation causes overhead to be either over- or underabsorbed, depending on the direction of the direct labor hours variance. Here is an example. Assume that a firm manufactures 5,000 widgets. Other pertinent data are:

Budgeted standard direct labor hours	20,000	
Actual direct labor hours incurred	20,300	
Actual manufacturing overhead incurred		
Variable	$29,820	
Fixed	$23,000	
Predetermined manufacturing overhead		
Variable portion	$1.48	
Fixed portion	1.12	$2.60

The manufacturing overhead account would consist of:

Manufacturing Overhead

Actual overhead cost incurred	Applied overhead cost —
Variable $29,820 Fixed $23,000	Standard direct labor hours allowed for output × predetermined overhead rate 20,000 × $1.48 = $29,600 20,000 × $1.12 = $22,400
Balance — underapplied overhead $820	

The manufacturing overhead account is charged (debited) with actual cost incurred. We deliberately differentiated the data by variable and fixed cost to enable readers to trace these figures through the variance calculations, although such detail would probably not be shown in practice. The account is relieved by crediting it for standard labor hours times the predetermined overhead rate. The journal entry to record charging manufacturing overhead to work-in-process inventory is:

Work-in-process inventory (20,000 × $2.60)	$52,000	
Manufacturing overhead		$52,000

Disposition of Under- and Overapplied Overhead

You are probably wondering what we do with the $820 underapplied overhead. During the interim period, that is, for monthly financial statements, it is appropriate to adjust the under- and overapplied amount to work-in-process inventory. Underapplied overhead is added and overapplied overhead is subtracted from work-in-process inventory. In this case, since there is a debit figure in the account we add it to the work-in-process inventory on the balance sheet. At the end of the accounting period the under- or overapplied overhead can be either written off entirely to cost of goods sold on the income statement or allocated among work-in-process inventory, finished goods inventory, and cost of goods sold, according to the balances in these accounts. Conceptually, the latter method is preferable, but difficulties can be encountered in allocating the correct amount to jobs currently in production. If a good job was done of estimating the predetermined overhead rate, the over- or underapplied balance should be sufficiently small that it does not matter how it is disposed of. If predetermined overhead rates are updated during the year whenever new information indicates they are no longer accurate, the amount of variance at year end should be immaterial.

Exhibit 10-5 shows a breakdown of variances for variable and fixed overhead. The variable overhead variance is divided into spending and volume variances, whereas the fixed overhead variance is divided into price and denominator variances. Please be sure you understand the formulas on the top of each column and the calculations illustrated. Note that the total underapplied overhead agrees with the manufacturing overhead account.

Variable underapplied overhead	$220 U
Fixed underapplied overhead	600 U
Total underapplied overhead	$820 U

The variable overhead spending variance is caused when actual prices are different than expected and by the efficiency (or inefficiency) of management. For example, in this case the favorable variance of $224 may indicate that management was able to acquire the resources for less than expected and that management was more efficient in cutting waste or excessive use of overhead items than anticipated.

The $444 unfavorable volume variance is strictly the result of the base, direct labor hours being more than what they should have been; that is, 20,300 hours were incurred instead of the 20,000 budgeted. From the viewpoint of control, emphasis should be placed on the direct labor hours rather than the variable overhead volume variance since the latter follows the former.

The $264 unfavorable fixed overhead price variance is caused by the expen-

Exhibit 1O-5

Analysis of Overhead Variance

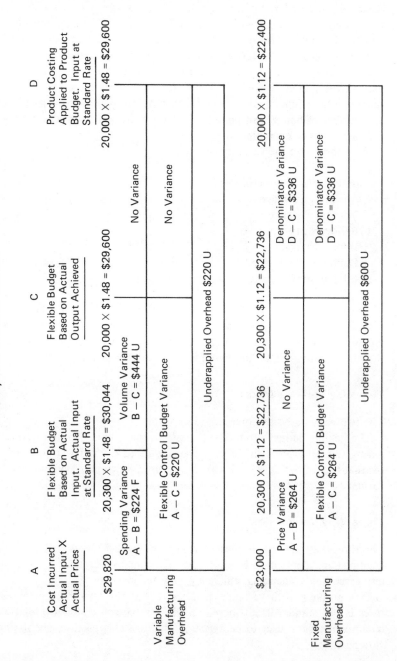

diture of more dollars for fixed overhead than expected. Recall that fixed overhead does not change with output over a relevant range, but the dollars expended can differ from the amount budgeted because of changes in costs.

The reason for the $336 unfavorable fixed overhead denominator variance is that actual direct labor hours are larger than estimated direct labor hours used in the predetermined overhead rate. Whenever these two figures differ, there will be a denominator variance because fixed cost is spread over a different number of hours than planned. The term *denominator variance* is used to indicate that the denominator is in error.

We summarize the variances as follows:

Variable overhead variances	
Spending variance	$224 F
Volume variance	444 U
Fixed overhead variances	
Price variance	264 U
Denominator variance	336 U
Total overhead variance—underapplied	$820 U

There are two other popular methods of breaking down overhead variances than the four-way method just illustrated: the two-way and three-way variance models. The following illustrations of a two-way and three-way analysis utilizes the same assumed data illustrated in the four-way analysis.

Two-Way Variance Model

The two-way analysis is presented in Exhibit 10-6.

The flexible budget variance is sometimes called controllable variance. Comparing the two-way with the four-way model (Exhibit 10-5) you can readily see that the former does not break the variance down into spending and volume variances.

Three-Way Variance Model

The three-way analysis is presented in Exhibit 10-7. Note that the columnar headings are identical to Exhibit 10-5. This analysis breaks the total variance into three kinds: spending, efficiency, and denominator.

One problem with variance analysis is that the terminology for variance titles is not standardized; therefore, for comparison and interpretation, it is incumbent on the user to be aware of the formulas used in calculating each variance.

Exhibit 10-6
Two-way Analysis of Overhead Variance

A

Cost Incurred
Actual Input
X Actual Prices

V $29,820
F 23,000
  $52,820

C

Flexible Budget
Based on Actual
Output Achieved

V 20,000 × $1.48 = $29,600
F 20,300 × $1.12 = 22,736
                   $52,336

D

Product Costing
Applied to Product
Budget Input at
Standard Rate

V 20,000 × $1.48 = $29,600
F 20,000 × $1.12 = 22,400
                   $52,000

Flexible Budget Variance
A − C

V $29,820 − $29,600 = $220 U
F $23,000 − $22,736 = 264 U
                      $484 U

Denominator Variance
C − D

V $29,600 − $29,600 = $ 0
F $22,736 − $22,400 = 336 U
                      $336 U

Underapplied Overhead
A − D

V $29,820 − $29,600 = $220 U
F $23,000 − $22,400 = 600 U
                      $820 U

Exhibit 1O-7
Three-Way Analysis of Overhead Variance

A	B	C	D
Cost Incurred Actual Input X Actual Prices	Flexible Budget Based on Actual Input. Actual Input at Standard Rate	Flexible Budget Based on Actual Output Achieved	Product Costing Applied to Product Budget Input at Standard Rate
V $29,820 F 23,000 $52,820	V 20,300 × $1.48 = $30,044 F 20,300 × $1.12 = 22,736 $52,780	V 20,000 × $1.48 = $29,600 F 20,300 × $1.12 = 22,736 $52,336	V 20,000 × $1.48 = $29,600 F 20,000 × $1.12 = 22,400 $52,000

Spending Variance
A – B
V $29,820 – $30,044 = $224 F
F $23,000 – $22,736 = 264 U
$ 40 U

Efficiency Variance
B – C
V $30,044 – $29,600 = $444 U
F $22,736 – $22,736 = 0
$444 U

Denominator Variance
C – D
V $29,600 – $29,600 = $ 0
F $22,736 – $22,400 = 336 U
$336 U

Underapplied Overhead
A – D
V $29,820 – $29,600 = $220 U
F $23,000 – $22,400 = 600 U
$820 U

SELLING AND GENERAL AND ADMINISTRATIVE CONTROL

Selling and general and administrative expense can be controlled by a comparison of actual costs with budgeted costs. Usually, this review is sufficient to control these accounts, but if more detail is needed, the variance can be divided in a way similar to that illustrated for indirect material.

INCOME STATEMENT CONTROL

Variances for the entire income statement can be analyzed. For example, assume that actual performance, flexible budget, and static budget are as shown in Exhibit 10-8.

This exhibit demonstrates the effect of removing the sales volume variance from the budgeted income statement. Column 5 is the static budgeted income statement at 6,000 units. However, sales of only 5,000 units were made (column 1). The flexible budget based on 5,000 units is restated in column 3; hence column 4 is totally the result of the 1,000 units (6,000 − 5,000) decrease in sales volume.

Now comparing column 3 with actual performance (column 1) we note:

1. An unfavorable sales variance of $5,000 is the result of the selling price being $1 less than budgeted; hence, the $5,000 is a selling price variance.
2. The unfavorable variable cost of $1,000 is the result of spending more dollars for variable cost than estimated.
3. A $6,000 unfavorable contribution margin is the result of the selling price variance and variable cost variance.
4. The $500 favorable fixed cost variance is the result of spending less for fixed cost than projected.
5. $5,500 unfavorable operating income is the difference between the flexible budget income and actual income. It is also the arithmetic residual of the variances discussed above and therefore it can be explained by them.

All of the above variances can be further defined. For example, the sale price variance can be subdivided by division, product, customer, salespersons, and so on. The total sales variance of $16,000 ($66,000 − $50,000, Exhibit 10-8) can be further differentiated into sales mix, sales price, and sales volume. The extent to which such refinements are desired is dependent upon their usefulness for planning and control.

RESPONSIBILITIES FOR VARIANCES

Perhaps throughout our rather lengthy discussion of budgets and variance analysis, we led you to believe that these activities are the simple, rational pro-

Exhibit 1O-8

Income Statement Variance Analysis

	(1) Actual	(2) Flexible Budget Variance	(3) Flexible Budget	(4) Sales Volumes Variance	(5) Static Budget
Number of Units	5,000		5,000	1,000 U	6,000
Sales	(5,000 × $10) $50,000	$5,000 U	(5,000 × $11) $55,000	$11,000 U	(6,000 × $11) $66,000
Variable Cost	(5,000 × $6) 30,000	1,000 U	(5,000 × $5,80) 29,000	5,800 F	(6,000 × $5,80) 34,800
Contribution Margin	$20,000	$6,000 U	$26,000	$ 5,200 U	$31,200
Fixed Cost	12,000	500 F	12,500	—	12,500
Operating Income	$ 8,000	$5,500 U	$13,500	$ 5,200 U	$18.700

Flexible Budget Variance $5,500 U   Sales Volume Variance $5,200 U

Operating Income Variance $10,700 U

Sales Volume Variance $10,700 U

cess we demonstrated. Seldom is the real world so simple. Many behavioral and practical problems exist. To hold an individual manager responsible for total actual cost is not always wise. The following factors are crucial in determining the extent to which a manager should be held responsible.

1. *The degree of discretion that can be exercised by a manager.* To say that a production foreman is totally responsible for material quantity does not make sense. Obviously, some material is needed to make the product. Perhaps for an engineered standard of two pounds of material per item produced, the range of actual requisitioning of raw material could only vary from 1.6 to 2.2 pounds; therefore the favorable variance could be a maximum of .4 and the unfavorable variance a maximum of .2. These boundaries form the limit of management's responsibility.
2. *The extent to which a manager can control critical performance variables.* For example, a sales manager cannot control the general level of the country's economy or most activities of competitors.
3. *The risk or uncertainty that surround a critical variable.* The research and development manager of a medical center can hardly be held responsible for determining public reaction to an issue as controversial as gene control.
4. *The time span of decisions.* Obviously, the risk of purchasing a new division is quite different from the risk of selecting a new vendor for material. The former decision may encompass 20 years, whereas the latter may concern a very short period of time. Generally, the longer the time span, the higher the risk.
5. *The extent of early warning.* If a decision has an immediate feedback, corrective action can be taken more quickly. Certainly, a manufacturer of glass beer bottles would receive a faster feedback on inferior quality than would an automobile manufacturer.

ZERO BASE BUDGETING

Before we leave budgeting and overhead control, we introduce zero base budgeting. This relatively new technique was hailed during the 1970s as the answer to budgeting woes. Zero base budgeting assumes that operations can be broken down into decision packages. Starting with point zero, a budget is prepared for each decision package. Then they are ranked according to their order of importance. If cutbacks are needed the low-ranking decision packages would be eliminated first.

Unfortunately zero base budgeting has not proved successful for many firms. Operations do not neatly fall into decision packages, nor do costs. There is lack of agreement on priority. The technique is costly, time consuming and laden with many behavioral problems. Still, for some companies it has proved to be an effective control technique.

SUMMARY

One weakness of static budgets is that the volume effect appears in the variance. To overcome this weakness a flexible budget is prepared at various levels of output, which simplifies variance analysis. Understanding capacity concepts is critical to flexible budgeting.

In this chapter we illustrated a flexible budget. Then we calculated a four-way, three-way, and two-way manufacturing overhead variance analysis for a standard cost system and explained the causes of variances. Managers can be held responsible for variances to a limited extent. We discussed these limitations and closed the chapter with a short summary of zero base budgeting.

11. Control of Decentralized Operations

In this chapter on the control of responsibility centers, special attention is given to service departments and divisions. Divisions may be centralized or decentralized. Centralization and decentralization are authority/responsibility concepts that reflect opposing ends of a continuum.

←——→

Centralization   Decentralization

The higher on the organizational chart decision making occurs, the higher the degree of centralization. In extremely decentralized operations, decision making is distributed as far as possible throughout the organization. There are many variations of these extremes. For example, top management might maintain tight control over capital acquisitions and research and development expenditures, but delegate almost complete authority for operations (sales and production) to divisional managers. How the costs of service departments are allocated is one aspect of control and is the issue to which we now turn.

SERVICE DEPARTMENTS

Service departments provide assistance to producing departments. Examples are cafeterias, personnel, medical facilities, and maintenance. Although these departments do not work directly to produce goods, if their existence is essential to production, then their cost must be included in the cost of goods manufactured. Service departments have several unique characteristics that make cost control difficult. They tend to be labor intensive and have little or no inventory; therefore, quantity and quality of output are difficult to measure.

Usually service department costs are allocated to the user departments because the exact amount utilized by each individual is unknown. For example, the personnel department might serve manufacturing, selling, administration, or some other service departments. Its cost should be allocated among the various departments served. If personnel cost is $50,000, the allocation based on number of employees might be as follows:

Manufacturing	$35,000
Selling	5,000
Administrative	10,000
	$50,000

The $35,000 allocated to manufacturing is included in manufacturing overhead just as any other indirect manufacturing cost.

ALLOCATION BASES

Service department costs are also allocated to departments or divisions for accounting and for performance-reporting purposes; hence managers are very concerned with the allocation base. There is of course no perfect allocation base. The basic guideline for selection of a base is that it should reflect as accurately as possible the benefits received by recipients from the services rendered. Meter usage may be an effective method of allocating power plant costs, whereas direct labor hours might be more appropriate for engineering costs. Usually, sales dollars constitute a poor allocation base because they are likely to vary substantially from one period to the other, whereas the costs being allocated are often largely fixed and therefore constant in amount. Still, sales dollars may be an appropriate base if there is a direct causal relationship between sales dollars and the service department costs.

To the extent possible the allocated amounts should be separated into their variable and fixed components because such a separation may reveal a causal relationship with a potential base. Correlation analysis can be very effective in measuring the strength of the relationship between variable accounts and a particular base.

An erroneous base can result in serious inequities and severe problems with employee behavior; therefore the selection of a base is a long-term decision and should not be made lightly. Whenever possible, reciprocal services among departments should be recognized. Sometimes a series of allocations are required to effect the most equitable allocation.

We now present several examples. Assume two departments, A and B, with selected data as follows:

| | DEPARTMENTS | | |
	A	B	TOTAL
Inventory	$10,000	$15,000	$25,000
Equipment	$40,000	$20,000	$60,000
Payroll	$ 8,000	$ 8,000	$16,000
Square feet of floor space	20,000	15,000	35,000

In the first example, assume $10,000 of equipment depreciation is to be allocated, for which the best base is probably cost of equipment. To determine the amount to allocate to Department A, the numerator is the cost of Department A's equipment, $40,000, and the denominator is the total equipment cost, $60,000. This ratio times $10,000 is allocated to Department A. For Department B, the numerator is Department B's equipment cost; the denominator is the total equipment cost. Again, we multiply this ratio times $10,000. Obviously, the total of the amounts allocated to Departments A and B must equal the total depreciation, $10,000.

A $\quad \dfrac{\$40,000}{\$60,000} \times \$10,000$ $\qquad$ $ 6,667

B $\quad \dfrac{\$20,000}{\$60,000} \times \$10,000$ $\qquad$ $\dfrac{\quad 3,333}{\$10,000}$

Depreciation expense can often be directly charged to departments by identifying the equipment with the user departments.

Here is another example. Suppose real estate taxes are $5,000. Now we select square footage as the best base. (A strong case could be made for using property valuation of Departments A and B as the base if these figures were known.)

A $\quad \dfrac{20,000}{35,000} \times \$5,000$ $\qquad$ $2,857

B $\quad \dfrac{15,000}{35,000} \times \$5,000$ $\qquad$ $\dfrac{\quad 2,143}{\$5,000}$

In our third example, personal property taxes are allocated over inventory and equipment cost.

A $\quad \dfrac{\$50,000}{\$85,000} \times \$2,000$ $\qquad$ $1,176

B $\quad \dfrac{\$35,000}{\$85,000} \times \$2,000$ $\qquad$ $\dfrac{\quad 824}{\$2,000}$

In our last example we select payroll as the most appropriate base to allocate personnel costs.

A $\quad \dfrac{\$8,000}{\$16,000} \times \$4,000$ $\qquad$ $2,000

B $\quad \dfrac{\$8,000}{\$16,000} \times \$4,000$ $\qquad$ $\dfrac{\quad 2,000}{\$4,000}$

Exhibit 11-1
Common Costs Allocation by Direct Method

	TOTAL COSTS	SERVICE		PRODUCTION	
		NO. 1	NO. 2	A	B
Common overhead ($\frac{4}{10}$, $\frac{1}{10}$, $\frac{3}{10}$, $\frac{2}{10}$)	$10,000	$4,000	$1,000	$3,000	$2,000
Allocation of service department No. 1 ($\frac{1}{2}$, $\frac{1}{2}$)		(4,000)		2,000	2,000
Allocation of service department No. 2 ($\frac{1}{4}$, $\frac{3}{4}$)			(1,000)	250	750
Total allocated costs				$5,250	$4,750

Cost allocation becomes considerably more complex when mutual services are rendered among service departments as well as production departments. For example, if a power plant furnishes power to other service departments and some of these service departments (e.g., personnel) provide services to the power plant, how should these kinds of reciprocal services be handled? There are three common methods of cost allocation: the direct method, the step method, and the reciprocal method.

Direct Method

Under the direct method costs are directly allocated to departments, and no consideration is given to reciprocal services rendered by one service department to another. Assume we have four departments: service departments 1 and 2, and production departments A and B. The common overhead would first be allocated among the four departments. Then the service departments' portions would be reallocated solely to the two production departments. Exhibit 11-1 shows allocation of total common overhead of $10,000.

Step Method

The step method recognizes services rendered by one department to another. Note in Exhibit 11-2 that the $10,000 is first allocated to the four departments. Then Service Department 1's cost is spread to the three remaining departments. Finally Service Department 2's cost is reallocated to the two production divisions. See Exhibit 11-2.

Exhibit 11-2
Common Costs Allocation by Step Method

	TOTAL COSTS	SERVICE		PRODUCTION	
		NO. 1	NO. 2	A	B
Common overhead (4/10, 1/10, 3/10, 2/10)	$10,000	$4,000	$1,000	$3,000	$2,000
Allocation of service department No. 1 (1/3, 1/3, 1/3)		(4,000)	1,333	1,333	1,333
			$2,333	$4,333	$3,333
Allocation of service department No. 2 (1/4, 3/4)			(2,333)	583	1,750
Total allocated costs				$4,916	$5,083

Reciprocal Method

This method (also called algebraic method) is theoretically more sound than the direct and step methods as it recognizes mutual services rendered by the departments. It requires the use of simultaneous equations (matrix algebra for multiple reciprocal departments). A very simple example will illustrate the technique. We assume the cost of operating Service Department 1 is $30,000 and Service Department 2 is $10,000. Each of these departments provides service to each other and to Production Departments A and B. The allocation of costs to the production departments is shown in Exhibit 11-3. A comparison of the reciprocal method with the step and direct methods is provided in Exhibit 11-4.

If the use of linear algebra results in a material difference from the direct or step-down methods, there is strong justification for its use. The arithmetic can easily be handled with commercial computer software packages.

RESPONSIBILITY CENTERS

Control over service departments and divisions depends on whether they are considered to be a cost center, profit center, or investment center. Each is also a responsibility center. The general guideline for responsibility accounting is that a responsibility center manager should only be held responsible for items which he or she can directly control. There are various degrees of control, however. It would be exceedingly rare in today's complex organizations to find one individual with *absolute* control over any major activity.

Exhibit 11-3
Common Costs Allocation by Reciprocal Method

	SERVICE		PRODUCTION	
	NO. 1	NO. 2	A	B
Percentage of service		1/6	3/6	2/6
Units of service department No. 2 consumed	1/4		1/2	1/4
Assumed costs of operations	$30,000	$10,000		
Service department No. 1	(31,146) P	5,191	$15,573	$10,382
Service department No. 2	1,146	(15,191)T	9,363	4,682
Total allocated costs	0	0	$24,936	$15,064

P = total cost of department No. 1
T = total cost of department No. 2
$P = \$30{,}000 + \frac{1}{4}T$
$T = \$10{,}000 + \frac{1}{6}P$
$P = \$30{,}000 + \frac{1}{4}(\$10{,}000 + \frac{1}{6}P)$
$P = \$31{,}146$
$T = \$10{,}000 + \frac{1}{6}(\$31{,}146)$
$T = \$15{,}191$

Exhibit 11-4
Comparison of Step, Direct and Reciprocal Methods

	SERVICE		PRODUCTION	
	NO. 1	NO. 2	A	B
Step Method				
Common overhead	$30,000	$10,000		
Allocation of service No. 1	(30,000)	5,000	$15,000	$10,000
Allocation of service No. 2		(15,000)	9,000	6,000
Total allocated cost—step method			$24,000	$16,000
Direct method				
Common overhead	$30,000	$10,000		
Allocation of service No. 1	(30,000)		$18,000	$12,000
Allocation of service No. 2		(10,000)	6,667	3,333
Total allocated costs—direct method			$24,667	$15,333
Total allocated costs—reciprocal method (Exhibit 11-3)			$24,936	$15,064

Noncontrollable costs should not be shown on responsibility center performance reports, or if shown, they should be listed at the bottom and clearly identified as noncontrollable. One of the arguments for listing them is to make managers aware that there are many common costs that reduce the firm's overall profitability.

A firm's objectives partially determine the input, contents, and format of divisional reports. Objectives must be clearly defined and communicated. These objectives would probably include the basis for evaluation of the quality of managers' performance (including the reward structure) and the extent to which divisions contribute to the goals of the total organization.

Behavioral theorists further advocate that

1. Managers should participate in setting the objectives.
2. Objectives should be reasonably attainable.
3. Managers should receive timely feedback.

A good responsibility accounting system is based on a sound organizational structure. There are many ways in which an organization can be structured, for instance, by function, geographic location, product line, and customer. The lines of authority and the degree of responsibility must be clearly established. Firms also need a means of tracing costs and revenue to individual managers as well as products, departments, and so on. A multiple digit chart of accounts can be devised such that digits represent specific codes. For example, a five-digit account number might be analyzed thus:

Digit
1 Major financial statement classification (asset, liability, etc.)
2 Account classification (type of expense)
3 Division
4 Department
5 Product

Account 69017 might be interpreted as

6 Income statement expense
9 Repairs and maintenance
0 Division D
1 Department 1
7 Product B

Exhibit 11-5
Painting Department
Performance Report for the Month of April 19X5

	STANDARD COSTS	ACTUAL COSTS	VARIANCE
Direct material	$ 500,000	$ 510,000	($10,000) U
Direct labor	600,000	570,000	30,000 F
Manufacturing overhead	300,000	285,000	15,000 F
	$1,400,000	$1,365,000	$35,000 F

Cost Center

A cost center is an organizational unit in which the manager is held responsible only for costs incurred. Usually, there is little or no revenue (e.g., personnel). Most service departments are cost centers, although some can be converted to profit centers through sale of their products or services. For example, data processing can sell its service to users. A cafeteria is almost certain to sell part or all of its products; hence, it can be a profit center even though it may not be a profit maximization center.

Control of a cost center tends to take the form of comparisons of budgeted costs with actual costs. Variances are analyzed as to cause. Budgeting is especially difficult for a cost center when most of the costs are discretionary, that is, when there is no scientific way of deciding what the "right" amount of costs should be. Engineered costs are much easier to budget because we can determine the right or proper amount. A performance report for a cost center might look like Exhibit 11-5.

This report in turn would be absorbed into the next level of reporting, Exhibit 11-6.

Exhibit 11-6
Products Productions Division

DEPARTMENT	STANDARD COSTS	ACTUAL COSTS	VARIANCE
Machining	$1,000,000	$1,050,000	($50,000) U
Welding	2,200,000	2,210,000	(10,000) U
Assembly	3,000,000	2,930,000	70,000 F
Finishing	1,800,000	1,800,000	—
Painting	1,400,000	1,365,000	35,000 F
	$9,400,000	$9,355,000	$45,000 F

Control over administrative staffs is especially difficult because:

1. The value of the output cannot be measured accurately. The salary paid to a professional does not necessarily measure the person's worth.
2. Lack of goal congruence. The goals of the department manager and staff may not agree with those of the firm. For example, a frequent complaint is that managers cannot get timely reports from the information department.

Control over research and development expenses are also troublesome because:

1. Results are difficult to measure quantitatively.
2. Time element. Most research and development expenditures are of a long term nature; hence they cannot be controlled effectively on an annual basis. It can take many years to know if dollars expended resulted in profitable products.
3. Lack of goal congruence. Many researchers do not identify as strongly with sound business practices as with solving their own research interests.

Profit Center

In a profit center, because managers are responsible for both revenue and costs, they must have control over both of these elements. In reality a profit center is a miniature business. Managers are evaluated on their ability to make a profit. The performance report would take the appearance of an income statement.

Investment Center

An organizational unit in which managers are responsible for a return on resources is an investment center. The investment center includes an additional element of responsibility beyond a profit center—capital investment. A common return on investment (ROI) formula is:

$$ROI = \frac{\text{Investment center profit}}{\text{Investment center assets}}$$

The numerator is computed in the same way as a profit center's income. For the denominator there are many different investment bases, some of which are:

1. Total divisional assets, either with or without accumulated depreciation deducted

2. Total net assets, exclusive of investments and nonoperating assets
3. Stockholders' equity
4. Working capital
5. Long-term assets

All of these bases except working capital suffer from twin weaknesses: The age of the assets and the method of depreciation can greatly affect the size of the base and therefore the return on investment. Assets are usually recorded on the books at historical cost. In an inflationary economy, the older the asset the lower is the cost and higher the accumulated depreciation. Other things being equal, older assets will result in a much higher return on investments than recently acquired assets.

Another weakness of return on investment is that some managers may be reluctant to undertake a new product with a lower return on investment than the division's return on investment even though the new product would be beneficial to the firm as a whole. For example, if Division A's normal return on investment is 20%, its manager might be reluctant to invest in a 15% return project, because his or her return would decrease below 20%.

Residual Income

When profitability is assessed according to residual income, divisional managers are levied a capital charge on investment which reduces net profit. As with return on investment the firm must define its investment base. Managers are assumed to be efficient if they have a positive residual income. This approach has a tendency to highlight the divisions that generate the largest profits. Study Exhibit 11-7. Since all divisions have a positive residual income all divisions have met the firm's minimum requirement of a 20% return on net

Exhibit 11-7
Residual Income

	DIVISIONS		
	A	B	C
Total net assets	$200,000	$500,000	$1,000,000
Net income	$ 50,000	$110,000	$ 280,000
Target net income at 20% return on investment	40,000	100,000	200,000
Residual income	$ 10,000	$ 10,000	$ 80,000
Return on investment	25%	22%	28%

assets. Managers will undertake new projects yielding more than a 20% return on investment.

Sometimes managers are evaluated on the amount of the residual income, and they may receive a portion of it as a bonus. Such a practice may create goal incongruence by giving managers an incentive to maximize their residual income.

The residual-income approach makes it difficult to determine which division utilizes its assets most efficiently. One solution is to add return-on-investment calculations to residual-income reports.

The amount of return on investment and residual income can be improved by one or a combination of the following:

1. An increase in revenue
2. A decrease in expenses
3. A decrease in assets used in the investment base

CRITERIA FOR REPORTING PERFORMANCE

Frequently managers must rely heavily on reports to measure how well a divisional or departmental manager is performing. These reports are subsets of the company's overall performance report which is the income statement.

Contribution Margin

A frequently used reporting method is the contribution margin approach. Recall that contribution margin is the difference between revenue and variable cost. The advantages of this method are that it stresses cost behavior patterns and presents information so as to facilitate decisions and performance evaluation.

Managers must spend their limited resources in areas that promise the largest increase in income per dollar expended. Contribution margin provides information as to which decisions contribute the most dollars to fixed cost and profit. When multiple segments are competing for limited common resources, such as advertising or employee development dollars, top management can calculate the optimal allocation by inserting contribution margin data into a linear programming model.

Exhibit 11-8 presents a typical performance report.

The revenue and variable cost allocations present no problem as they are directly identifiable with activities of a particular division. The average contribution margin is 45% ($900/$2,000) for the company as a whole, which means that on average every additional dollar of sales increases profit by 45 cents before taxes. This is powerful information for decision making.

Exhibit 11-8
Divisional Performance Report
Contribution Margin Approach

	COMPANY TOTAL	DIVISIONS A	DIVISIONS B
Net sales	$2,000	$700	$1,300
Variable manufacturing cost of sales	800	300	500
Manufacturing contribution margin	$1,200	$400	$ 800
Variable selling and administrative costs	300	100	200
Contribution margin	$ 900	$300	$ 600
Fixed costs controllable by divisional manager	200	50	150
Contribution controllable by divisional manager	$ 700	$250	$ 450
Fixed costs controllable by other individuals than divisional manager	100	30	70
Contribution by division	$ 600	$220	$ 380
Unallocated costs	180		
Income before taxes	$ 420		

The fixed cost is described in terms of the amount controllable by the divisional manager or others. Expenses controllable by the divisional manager include such items as sales promotion, salesmen's salaries and commissions, research, and supervisory cost. Costs controllable by others are insurance, taxes, depreciation on facilities, and interest expense. Divisional manager A should be evaluated on the contribution of $250 because that is the part controllable by him or her.

The unallocated costs such as president's salary and head-office expenses are not applicable to any division. There may not be a meaningful basis to assign these common costs. Listing the $180 on the bottom of the report reminds the divisional manager that there are additional corporate costs incurred by the firm beyond those generated by the division.

Reporting Standards

Departmental or divisional reports should be sufficiently detailed to answer questions such as:

1. What portion of the firm's profit is contributed by the segment?
2. Are pricing and sales policies sound?

3. Are expenses reasonable?
4. Do sales and expenses agree with the budget?
5. Are variances explained satisfactorily?
6. Who is responsible for variances?
7. What corrective actions or controls are needed?
8. Should a segment be expanded or discontinued?
9. What additional effort or resources, if any, should be expended to make a segment more profitable?

PUBLIC SEGMENT REPORTING

In 1976 the Financial Accounting Standards Board Statement no. 14 was issued, which requires certain large companies to publish segment data in their annual reports. FASB no. 14 allows firms substantial room as to how to define their segments, such as product, division, geographic area, or customer. Generally, a segment is considered significant for reporting purposes if it constitutes 10% or more of any one of:

1. Combined revenue of all segments
2. Operating profit or loss of all segments
3. Identifiable assets of all segments

The information required for each segment consists only of revenue, profit, and identifiable assets; still, the reporting requirements can be difficult when there is a large amount of common costs and extensive transfer pricing among divisions. Critics contend that additional records must be maintained and the furnishing of too much data results in information overload. They further contend that managers should be evaluated by financial statement users on the firm's overall profitability rather than portions of it and that segment reporting might disclose confidential information to competitors.

Advocates of segment reporting argue that segment information:

1. Allows a better evaluation of the past and can aid in forecasting the future.
2. Enables readers to better assess each division/product since a total net income figure combines profitable and nonprofitable divisions or products.
3. Enables a better evaluation of corporate management on performance of its stewardship function.
4. Will entail minimum additional cost because a well-managed company should have most if not all of the information required by FASB no. 14 in its internal reports or accounting records.

TRANSFER PRICING

When a division supplies goods or services to another division, the question arises as to what transfer price to charge for the goods or services. Just as with bases for cost allocation, there is no perfect answer. Some common methods are:

1. *Market price.* If there are competitive market prices available market price is probably the best transfer price. Its advantage is that the selling division receives its fair share of profit and the buying division does not overpay. It is easy to administer and low cost, and disputes are unlikely. Unfortunately, competitive market prices do not exist for many products.

2. *Full cost.* The two primary weaknesses with this method are that the selling division receives zero profits, while the buying division that ultimately markets the products receives all the profit. Disputes are likely to arise over definition of cost, especially allocated cost, and cost control becomes extremely difficult.

3. *Variable costs.* This method reduces disagreements over cost definition, but it still has the weakness that only the division that makes the final sale receives the profit. While variable costing tends to ensure good utilization of facilities in the short run, there is a danger that the division will become unprofitable over the longer term when full costs are considered.

4. *Negotiated market price.* Highly decentralized divisions often negotiate because they tend to behave as autonomous divisions. Negotiating can be highly effective if the buyer and seller can agree on the transfer price. If either manager is difficult to deal with, this method can be very costly and can cause considerable hard feelings.

5. *Opportunity cost.* Consideration must be given to the selling division's opportunity cost. If the selling division has excess capacity, its opportunity cost is zero. If the selling division is operating at full capacity, its opportunity cost is the amount it can sell its product for to outside customers. Therefore, the transfer price should never be less than the selling price to outside customers less costs avoided as a result of inside sales.

The question often arises as to how much autonomy divisions should have in setting transfer prices. For highly centralized firms transfer prices can be established by top management. But as divisions move toward decentralization, should divisions be allowed to maximize their own profit even if it results in suboptimization to the firm? Generally, the answer is "yes" because suboptimization is one of the penalties paid for decentralization. If carried to extremes, however, the firm should take a serious look at whether its method of organization is compatible with its goals.

A related question is whether divisions should be forced to deal with each other. One philosophy often advanced is that the buying division is free to purchase outside unless the selling division wants the order and is willing to meet all bona fide outside suppliers' prices and terms. The selling division can elect to sell inside or out because the firm's profit is maximized when the selling division obtains the highest price possible. Transfer pricing disputes are settled by an impartial arbitration board.

Transfer Prices for Foreign Divisions

Additional factors beyond goal congruence must be considered when establishing transfer pricing policies for foreign divisions. Some of these are:

1. *Income tax implications.* Income should be minimized in countries with high tax rates.
2. *Tariffs.* The lower the price, the lower the tariff.
3. *Government regulations.* These must be complied with by both the buying and selling divisions.
4. *Funds.* Transfer prices can be a way of shifting funds into or out of countries with stringent stipulations on fund flow. Royalties, service charges, and funds loaned are other possible ways of shifting profits and funds from one country to the next.

CONTROL OF FOREIGN DIVISIONS

Problems with control of foreign divisions extend well beyond transfer pricing. Prominent problem areas are:

1. Foreign currency
2. Inflation
3. Taxes and tariffs
4. Cultural differences and language barriers
5. Legal and government regulations

We now discuss each of these in more detail.

Foreign Currency

Control over foreign currency takes three forms:

1. Foreign currency financial statements
2. Foreign currency transactions
3. Exchange gains or losses

The Financial Accounting Standards Board has intensively studied the problem of how best to translate foreign currency into American dollars for financial statement presentation. Most of the Fortune 500 companies are multinational in scope; they have foreign divisions or at least rely on foreign markets for sales or resources. Hence, consolidating foreign currency accounts with dollars can be troublesome. FASB no. 52 is the latest attempt to resolve financial statement translation problems.

This FASB publication states that accounting for translation depends on the definition of the foreign division's functional currency. "An entity's functional currency is the currency of the primary economic environment in which the entity operates."[1] If the functional currency is not the U.S. dollar, the accounts are remeasured by the temporal method (described below) into the functional currency with the exchange gain or loss reported on the income statement. Then the financial statements are translated using *current* rates into U.S. dollars. The translation gain or loss resulting from this second process is shown in the stockholders' equity section of the balance sheet.

If the U.S. dollar is defined as the functional currency of the foreign division, the temporal method is used for translating foreign financial statements. Basically, the temporal method requires that accounts in foreign statements be translated in a manner that retains their measurement base. For example:

1. Accounts recorded on the books at historical cost (that is, past exchange or past prices) shall be translated at historical rates. Examples include plant, property, and equipment, and related depreciation accounts.
2. Accounts carried at prices in current purchases or sale exchange or future exchange shall be translated at the current rate, for example, cash, accounts receivable, and accounts payable.
3. Revenue and expense accounts shall be translated at rates that approximate the dollars which would have resulted if translated on transaction dates. For many profit and loss statement accounts, such as sales and most expenses, an average rate is appropriate. For other expenses (e.g., depreciation) the rate used is the historical rate in effect at the time of the acquisition of the asset being depreciated.

We now illustrate a balance sheet translated by the temporal method (Exhibit 11-9).

---

[1]FASB Statement no. 52, *Foreign Currency Translation,* Financial Accounting Standards Board, 1981.

Exhibit 11-9
ABC COMPANY
Balance Sheet
as of December 31, 19X9

	HISTORICAL (IN FRANCS)	CONVERSION RATE	HISTORICAL (IN DOLLARS)
Assets			
Cash	F 2,000	1.4[a]	$ 2,800
Receivables	8,000	1.4[a]	11,200
Inventory, at cost	10,000	1.3[b]	13,000
Building (net)	60,000	.8[c]	48,000
Land	20,000	.7[d]	14,000
Total assets	F 100,000		$89,000
Liabilities and Capital			
Accounts payable	F 5,000	1.4[a]	$ 7,000
Mortgage payable	30,000	1.4[a]	42,000
Common stock	50,000	.7[d]	35,000
Retained earnings	15,000		5,000
Total liabilities and capital	F 100,000		$89,000

[a]Current rate, December 31, 19X9
[b]Historical rate when item was acquired in 19X6
[c]Historical rate when item was acquired in 19X4
[d]Historical rate when item was acquired in 19X1

The temporal method requires exchange gains and losses to be reported on the current period's income statement.

In Exhibit 11-9 we assumed that the U.S. dollar was the functional currency. If the franc was the functional currency the financial statements would be translated by the current method, that basically means that all non capital (stockholders equity) accounts are translated at the rate in effect as of the balance sheet date. This method of translating the balance sheet is illustrated in Exhibit 11-10.

Exchange gains and losses can also result from economic transactions with foreign companies. These kinds of currency gains or losses are always shown on the income statement in the appropriate period. To illustrate this, assume the exchange rates for conversion of a British pound to a U.S. dollar is:

January 2, 19X9	$2.00
January 30, 19X9	$1.90
February 18, 19X9	$1.92

Exhibit 11-10
ABC COMPANY
Balance Sheet
as of December 31, 19X9

	HISTORICAL (IN FRANCS)	CONVERSION RATE	HISTORICAL (IN DOLLARS)
Assets			
Cash	F 2,000	1.4[a]	$ 2,800
Receivables	8,000	1.4[a]	11,200
Inventory, at cost	10,000	1.4[a]	14,000
Building (net)	60,000	1.4[a]	84,000
Land	20,000	1.4[a]	28,000
Total assets	100,000		$140,000
Liabilities and Capital			
Accounts payable	F 5,000	1.4[a]	7,000
Mortgage payable	30,000	1.4[a]	42,000
Common stock	50,000	.7[b]	35,000
Retained earnings	15,000	[c]	30,000
Equity adjustment translation of financial statements		[d]	26,000
Total liabilities and capital	F 100,000		$140,000

[a]Current rate, December 31, 19X9
[b]Historical rate when stock was issued
[c]From Retained Earnings Statement (not provided)
[d]Forced amount

On January 2, 19X9, we buy foreign goods for 2,000 British pounds. We record the transaction as follows:

Purchases	$4,000	
Accounts payable		$4,000
(2,000 × $2.00)		

On January 30, 19X9, we adjust the accounts for preparation of monthly financial statements.

Accounts payable	$200	
Exchange gain		$200
(2,000 × [$2.00 − $1.90])		

On February 15, 19X9, we pay the account

Accounts payable	$3,800	
Exchange loss	40	
Cash (2,000 × $1.92)		$3,840

The January 31, 19X9 income statement should report an exchange gain of $200. For the two months ended February 28, the amount of the net exchange gain is $160 ($200 − $40).

One way of avoiding transaction gains or losses is through foreign exchange contracts. If the purpose of the forward contract is to hedge an identifiable foreign currency commitment, then temporary currency gains or losses are deferred on the balance sheet until settlement of the contract. Hedges for speculation purposes require current recognition of currency gains or losses on the income statement.

Inflation

Chapter 18 is entirely devoted to inflation. At this time you should be aware that countries do not experience the same rate of inflation, nor are the exchange rates fully adjusted for differences among countries for inflation. Therefore, managers must consider both the exchange rate and inflation in their decisions.

Taxes

Taxes are of several types. The most well known is the income tax for which rates vary substantially from one country to another. Surcharges on income exceeding a specified base is common in many countries. A purchase tax is levied in some countries at different stages of the production–consumption cycle. Obviously, knowledge of the point of levy is important for decisions about where and when to produce or sell. Turnover or value-added taxes are similar in that a tax is levied at the point that value is added to an item. The taxable base and timing are crucial variables since they determine the amount of tax. Taxation is such a major problem that use of highly trained specialists are needed to advise on operating and investment decisions, including the use of tax havens.

Cultural Differences and Language Barriers

Cultural differences and language barriers include understanding the political environment. Each country has its own national interests. Ours may be profits, a high standard of living, speed, efficiency, and mass production. Not all countries agree with these values, however. Attitudes toward right and wrong, personal duties and responsibilities, questions about the future and predestination can cause people to behave quite differently. Each of these can cause conflicts and varying government regulations.

Legal and Government Regulations

Legal and government regulations must be complied with. In some countries their complexities discourage foreign sources of capital. Thus, multinational organizations operate and are subjected to many different legal environments. Different accounting methods, forms, documents, and accounts may be required. Hence, the information system and the control system may have to be designed to accommodate several sets of criteria.

Generally, profit centers are not suitable for performance evaluation of foreign divisions. The divisional manager usually has limited authority over sales and resources as major profitability policies are set by top management. Transfer prices may be established for many different reasons than to measure profitability. Division managers are encouraged to maximize company objectives rather than their own.

Any evaluation system must include consideration of local conditions. Control systems must rely heavily on budgets and frequent reporting, as opportunities for site inspection are much more limited than for domestic divisions. It is also essential that the basic information system for all divisions be global in scope and supplemented by local requirements.

SUMMARY

In this chapter we discussed cost control systems for service departments and decentralized divisions. Attention was given to methods of allocating common costs. The advantages and disadvantages of expense centers, profit centers and investment centers were investigated. Residual income is one method of overcoming the return-on-investment controversy. We discussed transfer pricing in detail. Finally, considerable discussion was devoted to problems unique to foreign divisions.

12. Decision Making

Decision making is the process of choosing among two or more alternatives. We continue to assume that the criterion for selection is profit maximization. Of course, many other factors can affect a decision other than those measurable in dollars and other than those with a direct impact on profits. Although these factors should also be considered in the decision-making process, they are beyond the scope of this book.

COST IDENTIFICATION

The first step in cost analysis problems is to identify all costs associated with each alternative being considered. Costs that are sunk should be eliminated. Recall that previously we defined sunk costs as those that have already been incurred and are unavoidable regardless what action is taken.

Costs that are identical for all alternatives can also be eliminated. Their inclusion would not result in the wrong decision, but does complicate the data. We are interested in differential costs and differential revenue, that is, those items that help us to differentiate among the alternatives being considered. Then we are in a position to make a decision. We now consider several types of problems (income taxes are ignored because taxes is the subject of Chapter 17).

PURCHASE OF A LABOR-SAVING MACHINE

The first problem is determining whether a firm should buy a new labor-saving machine. Assume the following facts for one year:

	PRESENT COST	COST WITH NEW MACHINE
Units produced	2,000	2,000
Sales price per unit	$20	$20
Direct material per unit	$5	$5
Direct labor per unit	$4	$2.50
Variable overhead per unit	$1	$1
Fixed cost exclusive of new machine	$5,000	$5,000
Fixed cost applicable solely to new machine	0	$2,000

The only two relevant items are the direct labor per unit and the fixed cost applicable to the new machine. All other data are identical for both alternatives and can be ignored. The solution is:

Direct labor saving, 2000 units at $1.50 ($4 − $2.50)	$3,000
Fixed cost applicable to new machine	2,000
Annual savings from new machine	$1,000

The conclusion is that the firm should buy the new machine because it increases net income by $1,000 a year. The total savings is $1,000 times the number of years the new machine will be in operation.

EQUIPMENT REPLACEMENT

To make the example more complicated, in lieu of buying a labor-saving machine, what if the firm traded the old machine for a new one? The pertinent data are:

	OLD MACHINE
Original cost	$50,000
Remaining book value (original cost $50,000 − accumulated depreciation $20,000)	$30,000
Remaining life	5 years
Salvage value now	$ 8,000
Salvage value in 5 years	$ 1,000
Annual variable expenses to operate	$ 35,000
Annual revenue from sales	$100,000

	NEW MACHINE
List price	$ 76,000
Expected life	5 years
Salvage value in 5 years	$ 1,000
Annual variable expenses to operate	$ 51,000
Annual revenue from sales	$120,000

If the old machine were sold now, the company would suffer an accounting loss of $22,000.

Remaining book value	$30,000
Salvage value now	8,000
Accounting loss	$22,000

Exhibit 12-1
Analysis of equipment Replacement

	KEEP OLD MACHINE	DIFFERENTIAL REVENUE/COSTS	PURCHASE NEW MACHINE
Sales	$500,000	$100,000	$600,000
Variable expenses	(175,000)	(80,000)	(255,000)
Depreciation on new machine $76,000 − $1000	0	(75,000)	(75,000)
Depreciation on old machine $30,000 − $1000	($29,000)	0	(29,000)
Disposal value of old machine	0	8,000	8,000
Total net income over next 5 years	$296,000	($47,000)	$249,000

Still, the undepreciated book value of $30,000 is a sunk cost and should not be considered as a differential item. Note that the current salvage of $8,000 is relevant because it is a future cash inflow if the new machine is purchased. An analysis of the problem is shown in Exhibit 12-1.

The firm is $47,000 worse off by selling the old machine and purchasing a new one. Actually, we only need the data in the second column of Exhibit 12-1 to solve the problem. Columns 1 and 3 are provided to help you see how column 2's figures are arrived at and why the answer is the correct solution. The $47,000 does not include the time value of money. We discuss present-value concepts and capital budgeting decisions in Chapters 14 and 15, respectively.

MAKE VERSUS BUY

Here, the problem is whether the company should make a product in house or buy it from an outside supplier. We illustrate with several examples.

Make Versus Buy Example 1

Let us assume that the firm has the necessary capacity and know-how and that all fixed cost will remain unchanged. The relevant calculations are presented in Exhibit 12-2. Analysis of the data shows that the firm would save $40,000 by making the item in house.

Make Versus Buy Example 2

We now expand the data by assuming that the company's fixed cost would decrease by $5 a unit if the product is sourced outside. Now the differential

Exhibit 12-2

Analysis of Make Versus Buy Example No. 1

| | PER UNIT DIFFERENTIAL COSTS | | 10,000 UNITS | |
COST OF PURCHASING	MAKE	BUY	MAKE	BUY
Cost of purchasing		$50		$500,000
Direct material	$16		$160,000	
Direct labor	10		100,000	
Variable overhead	20		200,000	
Fixed overhead (all $8/unit will be incurred if make or buy)	0			
	$46	$50	$460,000	$500,000
Difference in favor of making	$4		$40,000	

cost to make is $51. A cost savings of $1 a unit favors buying, and would total $10,000, as shown in Exhibit 12-3.

Make Versus Buy Example 3

What if the firm could use the space to make another product that would yield a contribution margin of $70,000? The $70,000 is an opportunity cost because the firm would forego profit of $70,000 if it continues to make the original product instead of buying it. Going back to the original data, according to Exhibit 12-4 the conclusion is that it is more advantageous to purchase from an outside vendor.

Exhibit 12-3

Analysis of Make Versus Buy Example No. 2

Variable costs	$	46
Fixed cost		5
Differential cost to make	$	51
Differential cost to buy		50
Difference in favor of buying—per unit	$	1
Number of units		10,000
Total cost savings from buying		$10,000

Exhibit 12-4

Analysis of Make Versus Buy Example No. 3

Difference in favor of making (Exhibit 12-2)	$40,000
Opportunity costs—contribution margin foregone on a potential new product	70,000
Difference in favor of buying	$30,000

ADDING OR DROPPING PRODUCTS

Another problem is to determine if a firm should retain or drop a product. We are assuming that there are no complementary effects, meaning that the deletion of one product will not affect the sales of other products being carried. The technique used here is also appropriate for deciding if a department or division should be eliminated or retained. Study Exhibit 12-5.

Would the firm be more profitable if it deletes products B and C? The answer is "no." As a matter of fact it would be less profitable by $1,000, the amount of B's differential margin. If it deletes only product C, the total profit would increase by $2,000, the amount of C's differential margin. These findings can be proved by preparing income statements under the two alternatives (see Exhibit 12-6).

Exhibit 12-5

Retaining or Eliminating a Product

			PRODUCT	
	TOTAL	A	B	C
Sales	$100,000	$40,000	$35,000	$25,000
Variable costs	88,000	30,000	32,000	26,000
Contribution margin	12,000	10,000	3,000	(1,000)
Fixed costs which would be eliminated if product were dropped	6,000	3,000	2,000	1,000
Differential margin	6,000	7,000	1,000	(2,000)
Fixed costs which would continue if product were dropped	4,000	2,000	1,500	500
Net income (loss)	$ 2,000	$ 5,000	$ (500)	$ (2,500)

Exhibit 12-6
Income Statements for Product A
and Products A and B

	A	A & B
Sales	$40,000	$75,000
Variable costs	30,000	62,000
Contribution margin	$10,000	$13,000
Fixed costs which would be eliminated if product were dropped	3,000	5,000
Differential margin	$7,000	$ 8,000
Fixed costs which would continue if product were dropped	4,000	4,000
Net income	$3,000	$ 4,000

Thus, the results show net income of:

A, B, C (Exhibit 12-5)	$2,000
A, B (Exhibit 12-6)	$4,000
A only (Exhibit 12-6)	$3,000

Clearly, producing products A and B is the most profitable alternative.

ADDITIONAL PROCESSING

Many products that are processed jointly to a certain point are then split into separate products. A frequent problem is whether it is more profitable to sell the product at the split-off point or process it further after the point of separation. Joint costs to the split-off point are always irrelevant, regardless of the method by which these costs are allocated to the products. Relevant data are future revenue and future cost. For example, assume that there are four feasible alternatives as to how to handle product A after the split-off point. They are:

1. Dump the product as waste
2. Sell as scrap for $20 a ton
3. Expend an additional $10 a ton and sell it for $35 a ton
4. Expend an additional $24 a ton and sell it at $46 a ton

The key to deciding among these alternatives is to continue processing so long as incremental revenue exceeds incremental cost. Therefore, alternative 1

Exhibit 12-7
Analysis of Additional Processing
Problem

	ALTERNATIVES			
	1	2	3	4
Incremental revenue	0	$20	$35	$46
Incremental costs	0	0	10	24
Incremental profit	0	$20	$25	$22

is clearly undesirable. Because we are interested in profit maximization, we are seeking the alternative with the largest spread between incremental revenue and incremental cost. This is alternative 3, as proved in Exhibit 12-7. Do not be fooled into believing that the alternative with the highest revenue is the most desirable.

OBSOLETE INVENTORY

Suppose a firm has 100 obsolete aircraft parts with a carrying value on the books of $500,000. Assume that these parts can be:

1. Remachined for $60,000 and sold for $75,000
2. Scrapped for $15,000 revenue

Again, the carrying value of $500,000 is a sunk cost and irrelevant to the decision to remachine. Both alternatives result in an incremental profit of $15,000; therefore, the firm is indifferent as to the two alternatives. Incidently, the net overall loss on the obsolete inventory reportable on the income statement is $485,000 ($500,000 − $15,000).

USE OF FACILITIES

Suppose a firm has fixed cost of $10,000 applicable to excess facilities. Assume the following alternatives are feasible.

1. Leave the facilities idle
2. Lease the facilities at $12,000 a year
3. Make product X which will result in a differential profit of $15,000 a year
4. Use part of the facilities to make product Y, which will result in a differential profit of $7,000, and lease the remaining facilities for $9,000

Again, the $10,000 fixed cost is irrelevant because it applies to all four alternatives. An analysis of future revenue with future expenses shows that alternative 4 is the most desirable.

Alternative	Differential Income
1	0
2	$12,000
3	$15,000
4	$16,000

PLANT SHUTDOWN

If a plant is operating at a loss, the firm must decide whether to

1. Continue operations
2. Close the plant temporarily
3. Permanently close the plant

If the contribution margin is positive, the plant should continue operations temporarily because the positive contribution margin contributes toward fixed cost. Assume the following data.

Sales (500 units at $300)	$150,000
Variable cost (500 units at $200)	(100,000)
Fixed cost	(80,000)
Net loss	($ 30,000)

The plant should be kept open temporarily since it is yielding a positive contribution margin of $50,000 ($150,000 − $100,000). To determine if the plant should be sold permanently, the firm must judge whether the cash inflow from the sale price of the plant exceeds the cash inflow in excess of contribution margin over the life of the asset. Keep in mind that much of fixed cost is likely to be depreciation expense and therefore does not cause cash outflow. Assuming depreciation of $45,000 a year, for ten years and a current market value of the plant of $290,000, the calculations are:

Contribution to fixed cost	$50,000
Less other fixed cost ($80,000 − $45,000)	35,000
Contribution toward depreciation per year	$ 15,000
Total for 10 years	$150,000

Since the $290,000 present market value is higher than the $150,000 contribution toward depreciation, the firm should sell the plant.

DECISION TREES

A highly practical technique for visually displaying the profitability of various alternatives is a decision tree. Ideally, probabilities are assigned to the various events so that the expected value of the various alternatives can be computed and compared with one another. The highest expected value depicts the most profitable alternative.

Assume that a firm is considering developing and marketing a new product. The pertinent data are:

Development cost	$50,000
Probability of:	
High success	.10
Medium success	.40
Low success	.30
Failure	.20
Profit (loss):	
High success	$100,000
Failure	($180,000)
Medium success	$ 60,000
Low success	$ 10,000

The decision tree is shown as Exhibit 12-8.

The expected value of developing the product is $1,000 as compared to zero profit from not developing it. Keep in mind, however, that this very simplified example does not consider all possible degrees of success and failure. In addition, a typical problem would have many more alternatives than the one illustrated here, whose magnitude and degrees of complexity could soon render the decision tree unfeasible.

Exhibit 12-8
Decision Tree

	INCOME	PROBABILITY	EXPECTED VALUE
High success	$100,000	.10	$10,000
Medium success	60,000	.40	24,000
Low success	10,000	.30	3,000
Failure	(180,000)	.20	(36,000)
		1.00	$ 1,000
develop product	0	1.00	0

Develop product

Do not

CRITICAL PATH METHOD (PERT)

Critical path focuses not only on the costs relevant to perform a task, but also on the element of time. The critical path is a calculation of the shortest time it takes to make an item. Time is valuable: The sooner a project is finished, the sooner a firm has the capacity and resources available for another profitable activity. One of the values of critical path is that it forces management to preanalyze project problems and identify bottlenecks.

Critical path is especially applicable to well-defined projects that go through a series of distinct activities. The activities are distinct in that they can be started and stopped independently of each other. Frequently, certain activities must precede others; therefore, knowledge of sequencing is essential before the activities can be diagrammed.

Consider the following illustration for a construction business. The problem is to determine the shortest period of time possible to build a custom-made house. The first thing to do is to identify the activities required, the period of time required for each activity, and their sequences. Obviously, it is not possible to schedule roofing before pouring the foundation.

Activity Time

Based on past experience the firm identifies the time required for each activity (see Exhibit 12-9).

Exhibit 12-9
Assumed Data For House Construction

ACTIVITY NO.	ACTIVITY DESCRIPTION	EST. DAYS REQ'D	IMMEDIATE PREDECESSOR
1	Grade lot	1	
2	Blueprints	3	
3	Obtain permits	1	2
4	Pour foundation	3	1,2,3
5	Framing	4	4
6	Roofing	2	5
7	Electrical	1	6
8	Plumbing	3	6
9	Flooring	2	6
10	Windows & doors	1	6
11	Siding & drywall	4	7,8,9,10
12	Painting	2	11
13	Cabinets & appliances	1	11
Finish		0	12,13

Schematic

The next step is to draw a schematic depicting all possible alternatives (see Exhibit 12-10).

Critical Path

The critical path, shown by the double parallel lines, is determined by computing the time required for all possible alternatives (see Exhibit 12-11). The critical path is 22 days because this is the shortest period of time from the start to the completion of the project. The shortest period is ironically the highest number in the Total Days column.

Slack

Knowing the amount of slack available for each activity is helpful for scheduling and time-reduction decisions. Slack is computed by comparing the latest starting day with the earliest starting day. The first number in parenthesis is the latest starting date. The latest starting date is the latest time an activity can be started without causing a delay in the total project. The earliest starting date is the earliest time an activity can be started. Slack gives an idea of how much "breathing room" there is at each activity level. The following chart, Exhibit 12-12, displays how much slack there is in each activity. Note that along the critical path, slack is zero.

Varying Activity Time

Once the critical path is known, a firm can compute what would happen if it tries to build a house in less than 22 days. In some cases, the time for certain activities can be condensed if the firm is willing to incur additional cost, such as overtime. Suppose the time for various activities can be reduced as follows:

ACTIVITY NO.		FROM	TO	ADDITIONAL DIRECT COST
2	Blueprints	3	2	$ 200
5	Framing	4	3	$ 500
8	Plumbing	3	1	$1000

Suppose that the buyer is willing to pay a $1,000 premium if he could obtain delivery in 21 days. Now, compare the $1,000 premium to the cost of com-

Exhibit 12-10
Critical Path for House Construction

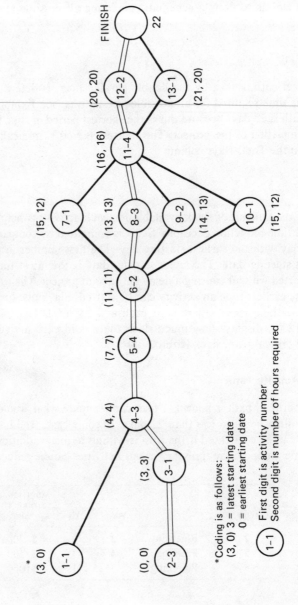

*Coding is as follows:
(3, 0) 3 = latest starting date
       0 = earliest starting date

1-1 First digit is activity number
     Second digit is number of hours required

Exhibit 12-11
Calculation of Critical Path

ACTIVITIES	ACTIVITY DAYS	TOTAL DAYS
1,4,5,6,7,11,12	(1 + 3 + 4 + 2 + 1 + 4 + 2)	17
1,4,5,6,8,11,12	(1 + 3 + 4 + 2 + 3 + 4 + 2)	19
1,4,5,6,9,11,12	(1 + 3 + 4 + 2 + 2 + 4 + 2)	18
1,4,5,6,10,11,12	(1 + 3 + 4 + 2 + 1 + 4 + 2)	17
1,4,5,6,7,11,13	(1 + 3 + 4 + 2 + 1 + 4 + 1)	16
1,4,5,6,8,11,13	(1 + 3 + 4 + 2 + 3 + 4 + 1)	18
1,4,5,6,9,11,13	(1 + 3 + 4 + 2 + 2 + 4 + 1)	17
1,4,5,6,10,11,13	(1 + 3 + 4 + 2 + 1 + 4 + 1)	16
2,3,4,5,6,7,11,12	(3 + 1 + 3 + 4 + 2 + 1 + 4 + 2)	20
*2,3,4,5,6,8,11,12	(3 + 1 + 3 + 4 + 2 + 3 + 4 + 2)	22
2,3,4,5,6,9,11,12	(3 + 1 + 3 + 4 + 2 + 2 + 4 + 2)	21
2,3,4,5,6,10,11,12	(3 + 1 + 3 + 4 + 2 + 1 + 4 + 2)	20
2,3,4,5,6,7,11,13	(3 + 1 + 3 + 4 + 2 + 1 + 4 + 1)	19
2,3,4,5,6,8,11,13	(3 + 1 + 3 + 4 + 2 + 3 + 4 + 1)	21
2,3,4,5,6,9,11,13	(3 + 1 + 3 + 4 + 2 + 2 + 4 + 1)	20
2,3,4,5,6,10,11,13	(3 + 1 + 3 + 4 + 2 + 1 + 4 + 1)	19

*Critical path because 22 is the shortest period of time from start to completion.

Exhibit 12-12
Slack by Activity

ACTIVITY	LATE START	EARLY START	SLACK
1	3	0	3
2	0	0	0
3	3	3	0
4	4	4	0
5	7	7	0
6	11	11	0
7	15	12	3
8	13	13	0
9	14	13	1
10	15	12	3
11	16	16	0
12	20	20	0
13	21	20	1
Finish			0

pressing activity along the critical path. Activities 2, 5, and 8 are all on the critical path; therefore, cost of each is relevant. Reducing activity 2 is the cheapest way to gain a day. The firm would incur an additional $200 of cost. Is it worth it? Yes. The additional profit is $800.

Premium received	$1,000
Additional cost	200
Incremental profit	$ 800

What if the buyer is willing to pay $1,000 extra for delivery in 19 days? In this case, the firm would incur $1,700 additional cost or an overall loss of $700.

Premium received		$1,000
Additional cost		
Activity 2	$ 200	
Activity 5	500	
Activity 8	1000	1,700
Incremental loss		($ 700)

The offer should be rejected. Whenever time is reduced, it is necessary to recalculate the critical path to know what costs are relevant. As a result of the last calculation, there are now two critical paths. See Exhibit 12-13.

Program Evaluation Review Technique (PERT)

PERT is an extension of critical path. Probabilities are assigned to the uncertainty of activity times. Hence, PERT is more suitable for new projects where there is considerable uncertainty as to the time required to complete an activity, whereas critical path is more applicable to projects for which activity times are known. Use of such statistics as the mean and variance is necessary to compute earliest and latest start times for PERT.

Both PERT and critical path can be expanded to include cost too. A computer is essential for most projects because the calculations become unwieldly very quickly as the complexities increase; for this reason we will not demonstrate PERT. Please remember that errors made in establishing the probabilities will quickly distort the critical path. PERT is not frequently utilized in practice.

COST INDIFFERENT POINT

Decisions involving two alternate courses of action can often be solved by computing the cost indifferent point, the activity level where the cost is identical for two alternatives. The formula is:

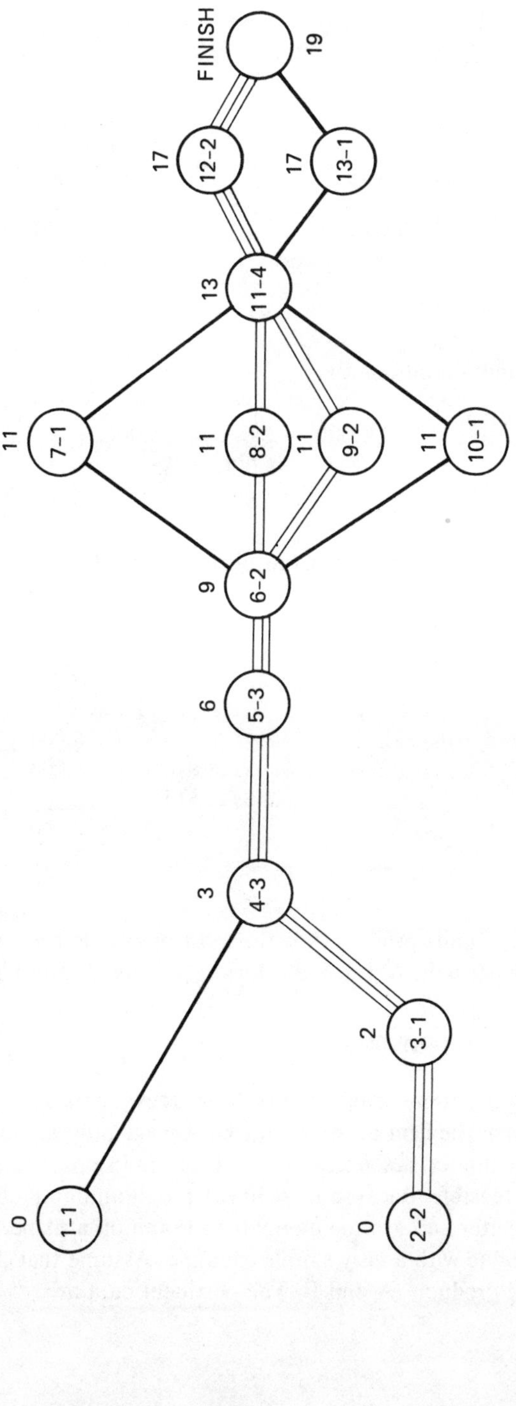

Exhibit 12-13
Critical Path

Total cost of alternative A = total cost of alternative B

Assume the following data:

| | ALTERNATIVE | |
	A	B
Fixed cost	$8,000	$5,000
Variable cost	$10	$15

The cost indifferent point is

$$\$8,000 + \$10x = \$5,000 + \$15x$$
$$\$3,000 = \$5x$$
$$600 = x$$

At 600 units both alternatives result in the same cost.

| | | ALTERNATIVE | |
		A	B
Fixed cost		$ 8,000	$ 5,000
Variable cost	600 units at $10	6,000	
	600 units at $15		9,000
		$14,000	$14,000

Beyond 600 units product A is the most profitable because it has a lower variable cost per unit. A graph displays this conclusion in Figure 12-14.

LINEAR PROGRAMMING

Since organizations have limited resources, some means of optimizing the objectives of the firm must be utilized. Linear programming is a technique for allocating limited resources among projects in order to determine which are the most feasible. Because most linear programming problems require the use of a computer and are too complex to graph on a plane, we will demonstrate the technique with a very simple example. Assume that Bandy Company produces two products, A and B. The pertinent data are:

	A	B	MAXIMUM TIME
Profit	$3	$4	
Machining time	8 hours	15 hours	90 hours
Planing time	4 hours	10 hours	50 hours

The question is how many units of each product should the firm produce to optimize profits. If there were no constraints, the answer would be to produce all of product B, the product with the highest profit. For most problems in the real world, there are constraints, so a profit objective must be defined. The profit objective is:

Maximize: $3A + $4B

Subject to these constraints:

$$8A + 15B \leq 90 \text{ machining resource}$$
$$4A + 10B \leq 50 \text{ planing resource}$$
$$A, B \geq 0$$

Exhibit 12-14
Indifferent Point Between Two Alternatives

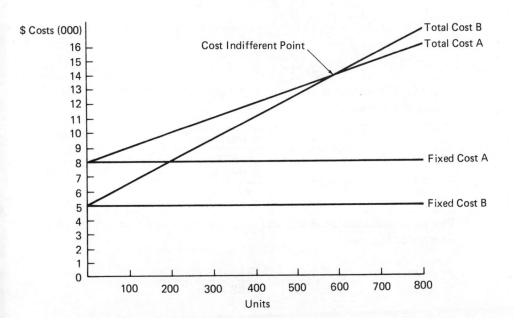

Exhibit 12-15
Linear Programming

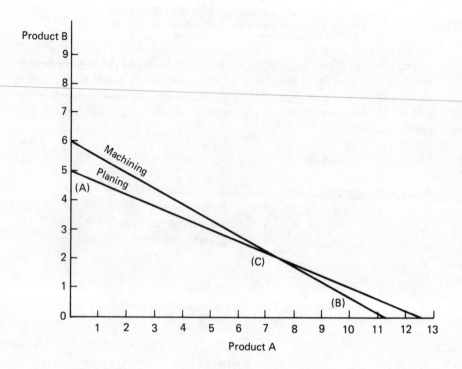

A graph of the solution is shown as Exhibit 12-15. The machining line is arrived as follows:

$$\text{Set A at zero} \quad \frac{90 \text{ total hours}}{15B \text{ hours}} = 6$$

$$\text{Set B at zero} \quad \frac{90 \text{ total hours}}{8A \text{ hours}} = 11.25$$

Plot points are 6 for the B axis and 11.25 for the A axis. The planing line is determined by:

$$\text{Set A at zero} \quad \frac{50 \text{ total hours}}{10B \text{ hours}} = 5$$

$$\text{Set B at zero} \quad \frac{50 \text{ total hours}}{4A \text{ hours}} = 12.5$$

Plot points are 5 for B axis and 12.5 for A axis.

All points on the inside area of Exhibit 12-15 are feasible. The answer must be one of the 3 intersections on the graph: (A), (B) or (C). The intersection with the highest profit is the level at which the firm should manufacture if it wishes to maximize profits. Hence, we must compute the profit at each itersection.

Recall the basic formula is:

$$\$3A + \$4B$$

Therefore:

(A) $3(0) + $4(5) = $20
(B) $3(11.25) + $4(0) = $33.75
(C) $3(7.5) + $4(2) = $30.50

Alternative B is the most profitable. The firm should make 11.25 units of B per period and none of A.

In order to calculate the number of units at the C point, two simultaneous equations must be solved.

$$8A + 15B = 90$$
$$4A + 10B = 50$$

Solving the equations yields A = 7.5, and B = 2.

You might be thinking that to make all of B and none of A is the obvious answer since B is the most profitable. If we change B's planing time to 20 instead of 10, we will find that the firm should make only A. Seldom is the answer to linear programming problems obvious.

Linear programming can also be used for minimization problems. For example, the firm might want to know which combination of alternatives minimizes cost.

Before leaving linear programming, there are several rigid assumptions we should mention. Linear programming assumes that:

1. Reliable raw data is known or can be collected.
2. Unit cost is constant over the entire range of the problem; in other words, it assumes a straight-line relationship.

3. Partial units are feasible. For example, in our illustration the most profitable level for product B was 11.25 units. Keep in mind, however, that for some products or alternatives a partial unit cannot be made. The simplex method can be used to solve complicated problems where partial units are not feasible.

SUMMARY

In this chapter we discussed a variety of problems concerned with how to make choices among alternatives. The key to the solution of most of these problems is to identify the relevant cost. The emphasis must be on incremental cost. Book value is irrelevant but disposal value of existing assets is relevant. Usually, it is preferable to use total cost in analyses rather than unit cost.

We explained and demonstrated critical path and linear programming. We intentionally did not include pricing problems because pricing decisions is the subject of the next chapter.

13. Pricing

Sound pricing models are crucial for profit making. A simple definition of profit is the difference between cost and revenue. Revenue is the number of units sold multiplied by the selling price, and the selling price is determined by a firm's pricing policy. Cost is a much more nebulous concept, however. A firm's profit as reported on the income statement will increase in direct proportion to the amount that the selling price exceeds variable cost—not total cost.

SUPPLY/DEMAND FUNCTIONS

Let us start out by reviewing supply/demand functions from economics. Consider a graph whose x axis denotes units and y axis, price. The supply function slopes upward to the right because the line represents the total number of units suppliers would be willing to sell at a particular price. A typical supply curve is shown in Exhibit 13-1.

As price increases, suppliers are willing to manufacture more and more units.

The demand curve is the opposite of the supply curve. As prices increase, buyers are willing to purchase less and less units. Hence, the demand curve consists of the number of units buyers are willing to buy at a particular price. The demand curve slopes downward to the right as illustrated in Exhibit 13-2.

The intersection of the supply and demand curves establishes the price and the quantity sold. Exhibit 13-3 shows that the equilibrium point is a demand for 40,000 units at $5.00 a unit. If the price is set higher than $5.00, some units will remain unsold. On the other hand, if the price is set below $5.00, there will be excess demand, which will cause the price to rise until it reaches equilibrium.

Frequently, supply and demand curves shift. Demand curves may shift because of changes in consumer taste, consumer income, or the prices of substitute goods. Similarly, changes in the factors of production or the cost of inputs could cause a shift in supply. Consider just one such change; say, producers decrease the supply of the available product. Demand has not changed, The supply/demand curves would look like those in Exhibit 13-4.

The equilibrium has moved from 40,000 units at $5.00 to 30,000 units at $6.50.

Exhibit 13-1
Supply Function

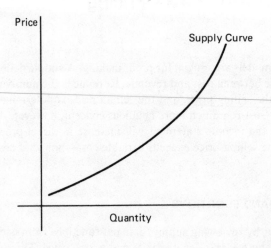

Exhibit 13-2
Demand Function

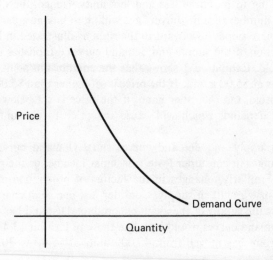

Exhibit 13-3
Supply/Demand Equilibrium

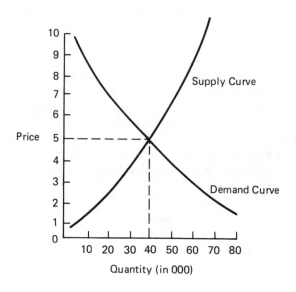

Exhibit 13-4
Shift in Supply Curve

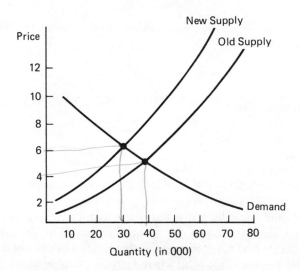

ELASTICITY

Because certain factors constantly at play press for changes in the supply and demand curves, supply/demand curves are not static over a long period of time for a firm or industry. Price elasticity measures the degree to which sales volume is affected by a change in per unit price. The demand is said to be price inelastic if a change in price has little or no effect on volume sold. For example, doubling the price of salt may only slightly decrease the demand. Hence, salt is price inelastic. On the other hand, if we increase the price and demand drops dramatically, the product is price elastic. Knowing the degree of elasticity can be very valuable in setting prices. Unfortunately, many times we do not know the degree of elasticity nor the degree of crosselasticity. If coffee prices are too high, consumers may switch to tea. If meat is too high, consumers may switch to nonmeat products. Coffee and tea have crosselasticity; so have meat and nonmeat products.

MARKETS

The way prices are set depends upon the type of market in which a firm operates. There are basically four kinds:

1. Perfect competition
2. Monopolistic competition
3. Oligopoly
4. Monopoly

Keep in mind that these are general models and that no firm is likely to fit any of them perfectly.

Perfect Competition

Perfect competition assumes:

1. A homogeneous product
2. Perfect knowledge
3. Easy entrance into and exit from the market
4. No one buyer or seller capable of individually influencing the price

The supply/demand curve for the industry will look very much like the one illustrated in Exhibit 13-3. Since no one supplier can affect the price, each supplier must decide how much to produce, that is, the amount where profit is maximized. This amount is the point where marginal revenue equals marginal cost. Recall that marginal revenue is the increase in revenue from selling one

Exhibit 13-5
Supply/Demand Curves for Firm Perfect Competition

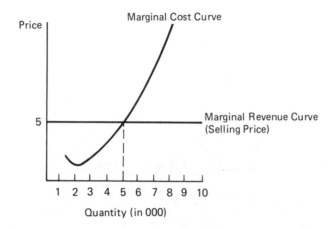

additional unit of a product, whereas marginal cost is the increase in cost from producing one additional unit.

Exhibit 13-5 is a graph of the marginal cost and revenue curves for the firm. Note that the marginal revenue curve is the industry's price and that it is a straight line for the firm because no supplier can individually affect the market price. After a low point, marginal cost will increase because of factors such as the firm's exceeding its normal capacity. In this case the supplier will strive to make 5,000 units because that is the most profitable level of production.

Monopolistic Competition

Monopolistic competition is when many sellers offer similar but not identical units for sale. Product substitution is a key factor. For example, Fords may be substituted for Chevrolets; Cheerios for Corn Flakes. Suppliers strive to make their products unique or market them more aggressively. Every effort is made to build up brand-name loyalty, which creates a limited price range within which consumers are not likely to switch to another brand.

Again, the supplier will produce to the point where marginal revenue equals marginal costs, as depicted by Exhibit 13-6.

Net income will be maximized if 3,000 units are sold at $5.00 each.

Oligopoly

Oligopoly occurs when there are several large sellers that dominate the market. Prior to the introduction of foreign competition, American automobiles consti-

Exhibit 13-6
Monopolistic Competition

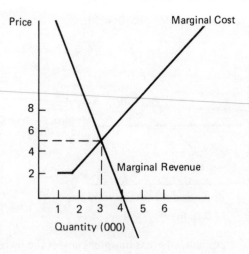

tuted an oligopolistic market. Oligopolies frequently have a price leader; if the leader changes the price, all other firms will quickly follow. Therefore, the demand curve can undergo a sharp change when going from one price to another and is likely to show a kink, as for example in Exhibit 13-7.

Monopoly

Monopoly exists when one firm is the sole supplier of a product, as when, for example, a utility company is the sole supplier of electricity in a given region. A patent may allow a manufacturer to be the sole producer of a product, at least until a creative individual discovers ways of circumventing the patent.

The monopolist also maximizes profit where marginal cost equals marginal revenue. As shown by Exhibit 13-8, the dotted line must be extended to the demand curve. The most profitable point is 4,000 units at $8.50.

Unfortunately, the use of economic theory in price setting is limited because we do not always know the demand function and degree of elasticity.

PRICING PHILOSOPHIES

In many segments of the United States population, there are strong sentiments against profit maximization. Many Americans see big business as "bad" and guilty of taking advantage of consumers. To counter this prejudice, firms often

Exhibit 13-7
Oligopoly

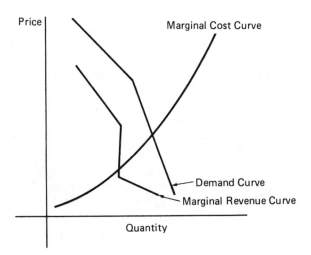

Exhibit 13-8
Monopoly

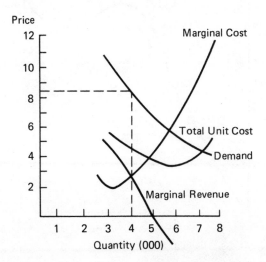

operate at a level of satisfactory profit or target profit. There are two basic philosophies that govern the pricing of new products: (1) skimming and (2) penetration.

Skimming is a short-run profit-maximizing strategy. Prices are set very high, especially if the market proves to be relatively insensitive to price. Pricing of hand calculators in the early 1970s is an illustration of skimming.

Penetration pricing is a strategy of mass marketing. Prices are set sufficiently low so as to encourage mass acceptance by consumers. It is a long-term strategy with the emphasis on long-run profitability, rather than a "quick kill" approach.

PRICE–COST–PROFIT GRAPH

Sometimes it is helpful to draw a price–cost–profit graph which gives at a glance the relative profitability of several feasible prices and the range of prices that will result in a profit. Consider this graph in Exhibit 13-9.

We can easily see that a selling price around $5.00 would generate the largest amount of profit. Below $1.50 and above $7.50 the firm would operate at a loss. This type of graph is especially suitable for committee meetings. Profit is not the sole criterion for price determination, but once the profit range has been

Exhibit 13-9
Price — Cost — Profit Graph

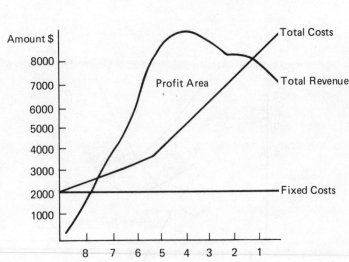

Selling Price per Unit

established, consideration can be given to other factors crucial to the firm, such as corporate image, consumer satisfaction, share of market, price leader, and so forth.

Our proposition that the largest difference between total revenue and total costs maximizes profit is theoretically sound, but in practice the trouble is: (1) We never really know how many units will sell at each price, that is, we do not know the demand curve, and (2) if sales are erroneously forecast, production costs are estimated wrong because fixed cost is spread over the wrong volume.

To determine the total cost of an item, recall that full cost is (1) the allocation of fixed cost plus (2) the variable cost. Over the long run, the company must cover all of its fixed costs. The difficulties are:

1. Determining volume of sales
2. Determining a fair allocation base in which to spread fixed overhead.

Also, recall from preceding chapters that the more units produced, the lower is the fixed cost per unit and therefore the lower is the total cost per unit. The point where total costs equal total revenue is breakeven. Below breakeven, the firm operates at a loss, and above breakeven, the firm operates at a profit.

IMPACT OF CHANGE IN SELLING PRICE

How can a manager estimate the impact of a change in price on sales volume? For many products the marketing personnel should be sufficiently familiar with their customers and with the prices and products of their competitors to give good advice. Such knowledge should give them a good feel for the range of price changes which would have a material effect on volume. This is called the "informed judgement" approach. Obviously, the informed judgment approach is not likely to be as suitable for new products as for existing products.

A statistical analysis of the past relationship between price and volume can sometimes be helpful. Unfortunately, there are many factors other than price that have a major impact on the demand for a product. Use of test regions can be very effective. For example, if an item is introduced into three separate cities with materially different prices, the effect on volume can be measured. Care must be exercised that the cities are comparable in terms of product taste, consumer spending power, and sales promotion.

For some products it is possible to calculate the value of an item to the consumer. This will give the seller a notion of how much the consumer would be willing to pay for it. For example, if an attachment to a machine saves the firm one hour of labor, the total number of hours saved times the total hourly labor costs would give an indication of the value of the attachment.

Market studies asking the consumer what price he or she would be willing to pay are generally not very reliable. There appears to be a substantial gap between what people say and what they do.

PRICE INDIFFERENT POINT

Knowing the price indifferent point can be immensely helpful if a firm is considering product improvement. A firm might raise its selling price because of the increased cost of manufacturing a superior product. For example, assume that the number of units that must be sold to generate a $10,000 profit is as follows:

$$(\text{Selling price})(\text{number of units}) = (\text{variable cost})(\text{number of units})$$
$$+ \text{ fixed cost} + \text{profit}$$
$$\$10x = \$6x + \$20,000 + \$10,000$$
$$\$4x = \$30,000$$
$$x = 7,500 \text{ units}$$

Now, assume as a result of product improvement the selling price is set at $12 a unit, variable cost increases $1 a unit, and fixed cost increases $2,000. The solution is found by inserting the new data in the above formula.

$$\$12x = \$7x + \$22,000 + \$10,000$$
$$\$5x = \$32,000$$
$$x = 6,400 \text{ units}$$

The price indifference point is 6,400 units. If management cannot sell 6,400 units at $12 per unit, the modification should not be made. On the other hand, if the firm call sell more than 6,400 units at the new price of $12 a unit, but can only sell 7,500 units at $10 a unit, it is to the firm's advantage to improve the product. Keep in mind, however, that many other factors affect this decision, such as competitors, employee job security, and the firm's public image.

JOINT COST

Before we talk about specific pricing models a word of caution concerning use of full cost as a basis for pricing when there are joint costs. Recall in Chapter 7 where we discussed methods of allocating joint costs, we demonstrated the relative sales value method in detail.

We now take a very elementary example to review the sales value method (which is the same as the relative sales value method except there is no additional processing after the split-off point.) Assume we have a joint cost of

Exhibit 13-10
Allocation of Joint Cost
Sales Value Method

	TOTAL UNITS	UNIT SELLING PRICE	SALES VALUE	RATIO	JOINT COSTS
A	600	$8	$4800	$4800/6000	$800
B	400	$3	1200	$1200/6000	200
			$6000		$1000

$1,000 to be allocated between products A and B. The $1,000 is allocated on the basis of sales value, as calculated in Exhibit 13-10.

Although this method is useful for inventory purposes, it is not a good pricing method. Actually, we are chasing ourselves around in a circle because sales determine costs and costs determine selling price. Another weakness is that the sales value method and the relative sales value method result in a constant gross profit percentage for each product at the point of split-off. Exhibit 13-11 easily proves this:

Exhibit 13-11
Gross Profit Calculations

	PRODUCTS			
	A		B	
Sales value	$4,800	100%	$1,200	100%
Apportioned joint cost	800	17	200	17
Gross profit	$4,000	83%	$1,000	83%

Frequently, joint cost contains a high amount of fixed cost; therefore, let us caution against treating allocated joint cost as variable cost after the point of separation in decision models.

PRICING POLICIES

The company's pricing policy should cover all products and be based on sound pricing objectives. Each firm must decide for itself what its price objective is. Some of the *more* common ones are:

1. Profit—which can be defined as maximization or profits or satisfactory amount of profit
2. Steady profit rate of growth, expressed as a percentage or in absolute dollars
3. Share of the market, expressed as a percentage
4. Reasonable price that consumers can afford
5. National welfare
6. Steady employment for employees
7. Good citizen—compliance with government regulations

PRICING MODELS

We now turn our attention to some specific pricing models. It is extremely important that you understand that there is no one best pricing model because the way prices should be set is dependent on the circumstances. Consider the following data for 10,000 units.

	PER UNIT
Direct material	$ 5.00
Direct labor	8.00
Variable manufacturing overhead	4.00
Variable selling, G&A expenses	1.00
Total variable cost	$18.00
Fixed manufacturing overhead	3.00
Fixed selling, G&A expenses	2.00
Full Cost	$23.00

There are various ways we can utilize these data in setting prices.

Full Costing

Full costing is really a cost-plus pricing formula. Starting with a full cost of $23.00, we can arrive at a selling price by adding:

1. A flat per unit profit—$23.00 + $5.00 profit = $28.00 selling price
2. Profit as a percentage of cost—$23.00 + 20% ($23.00) = $27.60 selling price
3. Profit based on the return on investment

$$\$23.00 + \frac{.10(\$600,000)}{10,000} = \$29.00 \text{ selling price}$$

Many other variations are possible.

Cost-based pricing formulas are popular. Why? Because managers think they protect them against loss. By adopting full cost as the pricing formula, these managers reason that any amount received beyond cost has to be profit. The error in this logic is that a high price may drive customers away; thus sales volume will drop and not all fixed cost will be covered. Hence, the firm can easily operate at a loss in spite of a full cost pricing model.

The cost-based model allows managers freedom to ignore the multitude of uncertainties affecting the success of a product. It is also used to estimate competitors' cost and therefore their selling prices. In some situations managers set the price at a certain volume to breakeven. If the breakeven volume is not met, the product is dropped; otherwise, it is retained. Cost-based models are not a panacea for all pricing problems; hence managers should be aware of their weaknesses.

Standard Cost

Under this method the price is based on standards. A major weakness of full cost models is that the more inefficient the manufacturing, the higher the selling price and profit (assuming profit is set as a percentage of cost). If standards are properly set, the standard cost model should eliminate the inefficiencies of full cost models.

Loss Leader Pricing

This type of pricing is commonly used in retailing such as grocery stores. In order to entice customers into the store, a limited number of desirable products are temporarily priced well below normal prices. These items are called *loss leaders*. While some customers will buy only the loss leaders, experience shows that generally customers will buy enough regularly priced items to offset the low prices of the loss leaders. Care must be taken that a sufficient quantity of the loss leader is stocked, or customers are likely to be disgruntled. "Rain checks" are hardly the answer as they create additional cost to the seller and inconvenience to the buyer. Customers want the desired product immediately, not at an undetermined future date.

Contribution Approach

This is also a long-run approach that focuses on variable cost. To the variable cost is added a factor for fixed cost and profit, for instance:

$$\$18.00 \text{ variable cost} + .50(\$18.00) = \$27.00 \text{ selling price}$$

The contribution margin approach eliminates the difficulty of allocating fixed cost to products, but it creates a problem of determining the fixed cost and profit factor.

Variable Pricing

Variable pricing is frequently used for special orders. According to variable-pricing theory, orders should be accepted as long as the price exceeds the variable cost. In our illustration any price over $18.00 would increase income. Note that variable pricing is a short-run concept. Over the long run all cost must be covered. Pricing theorists argue that variable pricing should be limited to the following three circumstances.

1. *When idle capacity exists.* If idle capacity cannot be used to expand regular sales, net profit can be increases so long as the capacity is used for products generating more revenue than their incremental cost.

2. *Distress conditions.* Obviously, such conditions should be temporary. Still, it is preferable to liquidate a slow-moving item at less than full cost than not to sell it at all.

3. *Competitive bidding.* Variable pricing can be very useful in stiff competitive bidding. In such a situation, if a firm refuses to sell at less than full cost, it will receive few or no orders.

Some theorists expand this list to include two additional factors for special orders.

4. A firm that does not want to accept special orders from normal customers should not sell at less than regular prices if regular prices can be obtained. Why sell for $20.00 when $28.00 is obtainable? Lowering prices will start a price war in which all suppliers will suffer. Such arguments may be only partially true as they presuppose that the demand curve is known.

5. A firm does not want to violate governmental pricing laws, the most well known of which is the Robinson-Paton Act. This act prohibits quoting different prices to different customers who compete with each other for the same goods, unless the difference can be directly traced to differences in the cost of manufacturing, marketing, or delivery. Cost has been defined by the Federal Trade Commission and the courts to be full cost, rather than variable cost. Note that

the key words are *competing* customers and *same* goods. Hence, the Robinson-Paton Act does not apply to many competitive bidding situations and noncompeting products.

Return-on-Asset Pricing

The return-on-asset method recognizes a satisfactory return on the assets required to produce, finance, and market a product. If selling prices do not reflect the effect of capital, management might be misled on dividend and capital maintenance policies.

Assume the following:

	PRODUCTS	
	A	B
Sales	$300,000	$400,000
Costs	200,000	320,000
Net profit	$100,000	$ 80,000
Profit as a percentage of sales	33%	20%

We might conclude that A should be promoted over B because A has the largest profit percentage. But what happens when investment is considered? Investment is defined here as the total dollar amount of assets to produce the product (e.g., cash, receivables, inventories, fixed assets, etc.), although many other definitions could be used.

	PRODUCT	
	A	B
Total assets	$800,000	$500,000
Net profit	$100,000	$ 80,000
Return on assets	12.5%	16%

Now it is more apparent that product B should be emphasized over product A.

In the above illustration we assumed we knew the selling price and volume of sales. By using the following formula, we can work backwards to compute sales and profit.

$$\% \text{ mark-up on cost } = \frac{\text{assets}}{\text{total annual cost}} \times \text{desired rate of return on assets}$$

Substituting B's figures, we have

$$25\% = \frac{\$500,000}{\$320,000} \times 16\%$$

The application of the 25% to the cost of $320,000 gives the desired sales of $400,000, profit of $80,000 and a 20% return on sales of $400,000. The main value of this return-on-asset model is its ability to assess which selling price will give the desired rate of return. Conversely, given certain selling prices, the rate of return for each can be calculated.

Cost-plus-fixed-fee

This is a common model for goverment contracts where costs are difficult to estimate, such as research and development projects. Sometimes it is used in commercial sales, especially for special orders. The customer is charged the actual cost of producing the product plus a predetermined profit. The profit, called *fixed fee,* has been agreed on by the contracting parties in advance. Variations of this model include putting a ceiling on the amount of cost to be incurred.

This pricing model provides a great deal of protection for the seller because both the cost and profit are guaranteed. Generally, the profit is lower than other pricing models, and, unfortunately, the seller has little incentive to control cost. Unless the seller's books are open to audit by the buyer, the buyer has no way of validating actual cost. It is also important that both the buyer and seller are in agreement as to what constitutes allowable costs. For government contracts, the Defense Acquisition Regulations (DAR) serve as a guide. In addition, government suppliers must conform to cost standards issued by the Cost Accounting Standards Board (CASB). Keep in mind, however, that the intent of the CASB's standards is to simplify pricing and auditing problems of the government, not to develop cost data for managerial decision making.

If the buyer reimburses full cost, that is, the full overhead rate, it is generally to the seller's benefit to maximize cost because the fixed portion of the overhead rate is not increasing. Therefore, the seller is really increasing profit from the fixed portion of the predetermined overhead rate. For example, assume a cost plus fixed fee contract allows cost up to $10,000 plus a fixed fee of $1,000. Assume the supplier's costs are as follows:

	PER HOUR
Variable:	
Direct material	$ 2.00
Direct labor	25.00
Variable overhead	13.00
Total variable cost	$40.00
Fixed:	
Overhead—25% of total variable cost	10.00
Billable cost per hour	$50.00

The firm would maximize profit if it incurs 200 hours, the maximum number of hours possible ($10,000/$50) because it will incur the fixed cost of $2,000 ($10 × 200) anyway. We can easily prove this by considering the effect on the profit and loss statement if the firm incurs a lower number, say, 150 hours rather than 200. The difference in profit is $500.

NUMBER OF HOURS	150	200
Amount reimbursed		
Total variable costs		
150 × $40	$6,000	
200 × $40		$8,000
Fixed overhead		
$6,000 × 25%	1,500	
$8,000 × 25%		2,000
Fixed fee	1,000	1,000
Total received	$8,500	$11,000
Incremental cost—variable only	6,000	8,000
Increase in profits per income statement	$2,500	$3,000

Some managers utilize a rate of return on sales as a guide to determine whether a contract generates an acceptable return. If a ceiling is not provided in a contract or if the ceiling is higher than contract cost, managers may reason that the firm's overall rate of return on sales is insufficient to maintain the investment. For example, suppose a firm negotiated a CPFF contract for $1,150,000.

Estimated cost	$1,000,000
Fixed fee—15%	150,000
Contract price	$1,150,000

Assume actual allowable costs incurred are $1,200,000. The firm would receive $1,350,000 ($1,200,000 + $150,000), but its rate of return on sales is only 12.5% ($150,000/$1,200,000) instead of 15%. Management may consider 12.5% unacceptable. However, returning to the point we made previously, that the fixed-cost portion of the $200,000 cost increase would have been incurred anyway; hence one must be careful in utilizing a return-on-sales model.

Cost-plus-incentive-fee

Under this pricing model, the buyer reimburses the seller for actual cost if equal to estimated cost when negotiating the contract. If actual costs are less than projected costs, the buyer and seller share the increased profit. Incentive fee can also be paid for advance delivery or some element of superior performance.

Although the purpose of these incentive models is to encourage the sellers to be more efficient, they do not always work. Since development contracts tend to precede production contracts, sellers soon learn to pad actual costs for developmental work, which is usually performed under cost-plus-fixed-fee contracts. Such practices result in a high cost base to negotiate an incentive formula. Once the cost-plus-incentive-fee contract is agreed on, sellers have ample slack to reduce actual costs and thus obtain fatter profits.

If an incentive profit is paid for advance delivery, a contractor must look beyond the cost reimbursable per DAR and assess the net advantage to the firm. For example, it may be to the contractor's advantage to ship by air freight even though the additional cost over rail is disallowable per the Defense Acquisition Regulations. Assume:

Incentive fee per day for advance delivery	$200
Normal freight cost allowed by Defense Acquisition Regulations	
Rail—3 days delivery time	$ 50
Air freight—one day delivery time	$120

It is the contractor's advantage to "eat" part of the air freight cost in order to obtain the incentive fee.

Additional incentive fee received (2 day × $200)		$400
Additional cost incurred—air freight	$120	
Cost allowed per DAR—rail	50	70
Additional profit from shipping air freight		$330

Obviously if there is no incentive fee for advance delivery, the contractor should ship by rail.

The many other sophisticated pricing models applicable to complex government contracting are beyond the scope of this chapter.

SUMMARY

A knowledge of the economic concepts of supply and demand is crucial to price setting; hence we reviewed supply and demand for the four primary types of industries:

1. Perfect competition
2. Monoplistic competition
3. Oligopoly
4. Monopoly

Price elasticity is the effect of a change in per unit selling price on sales volume.

Pricing philosophies include skimming and penetration. A firm must establish its pricing objectives before determining its pricing formula. Each of the many pricing formulas we discussed has its strengths and weaknesses.

We want to leave you with two final thoughts on pricing:

1. There is no perfect pricing model. A good manager selects the one more suitable to the firm's environment.
2. Price setting must include *quantity* as well as cost. To ignore volume is to ignore one of the most crucial elements in cost-volume-profit analysis theory. This theory forms the foundation of pricing.

14. The Time Value of Money

In order to make financial decisions of a long-term nature one must understand the time value of money. A decrease in the value of money (reduction of purchasing power) is known as inflation, which we will discuss in Chapter 18. In this chapter we are concerned with the cost of money, commonly referred to as interest. The higher the interest rate and the longer the time period, the more crucial it is to measure future cash inflows and outflows at present value.

A dollar to be received in 10 years is not worth the same as a dollar right now because the present dollar can be invested. If invested wisely, it would grow to considerably more than one dollar after 10 years. To understand interest it is essential that you comprehend present-value and future-value theory. In this chapter we explain these concepts and provide several business applications. In the next chapter we will apply present- and future-value theory to capital acquisition decisions.

INTEREST

Interest is payment for the use of money. If an individual borrows $10,000 from a bank at 12% interest for six months, the borrower would return to the bank (the lender) $10,600.

Amount borrowed	$10,000
Interest ($10,000 × 12% × %12)	600
	$10,600

The $10,000 is the present value (also called principal) and the $10,600 is the future value. The difference between $10,600 and $10,000 is interest and is an expense for the six months.

Interest rates are normally quoted as annual rates; therefore, to compute the amount of interest dollars for a period other than a year the following formula can be used:

Principal × rate × time

In the above illustration:

$$\$10,000 \times 12\% \times \%_{12} = \$600$$

where:

$10,000 is the principal.

12% is the annual rate of interest.

$\frac{6}{12}$ is the time period—6 months of 12 months in a year

Interest for a two-year period is:

$$\$10,000 \times 12\% \times 2 = \$2,400$$

Sometimes a financial institution will discount a loan, that is, take the interest out before giving the proceeds to the borrower. If the bank discounted the note in the above illustration the borrower would receive $9,400 ($10,000 principal less $600 interest). The amount to be repaid to the bank after six months is $10,000. It is important that you realize that the effective rate of interest is higher than the face rate when a note is discounted because the borrower receives less than $10,000.

$$\frac{\$600}{\$9,400} = 6.38\% \text{ for six months}$$
$$6.38\% \times 2 = 12.76\% \text{ annual rate}$$

Thus, the effective rate is 12.76% if the note is discounted and 12% if it is not.

For determining the interest period it is common practice to use 30 days in a month regardless of the actual number of days in a month and 360 days for a year in lieu of 365. Another common practice is to treat each month as $\frac{1}{12}$ of a year, regardless of the number of days in the month. If the exact number of days are used we count the last day but not the first day. For example, for a loan taken out on March 15 and payable on May 5, the exact number of days is 51.

March	16
April	30
May	5
	51

NONINTEREST-BEARING NOTES

In the business world there is no such thing as "true" noninterest-bearing notes. So called noninterest-bearing notes have interest buried in them. For example, if the market rate of interest is 15%, a three-year note of $10,000 really consists of:

Principal	$6,575.20
Interest	3,424.80
	$10,000.00

The $6,575.20 is the present value of the note. Let us prove the accuracy of this figure. If we put $6,575.20 in an investment for three years the data would look like this:

Year 1 principal	$6,575.20
Interest for year 1 ($6,575.20 × 15%)	986.28
Balance at end of year 1	$7,561.48
Interest for year 2 ($7,561.48 × 15%)	1,134.22
Balance at end of year 2	$8,695.70
Interest for year 3 ($8,695.70 × 15%)	1,304.30
Balance at end of year 3	$10,000.00

COMPOUND AND SIMPLE INTEREST

Present- and future-value theory is based on the concept of compound interest. Compound interest is computed on principal and interest. In the previous illustration you can see that we computed interest on the total of the principal and interest to date. Note that the amount of compound interest increases each period.

Simple interest is applied to the principal only. In our example, each year's simple interest would be based on the principal of $6,575.20. The amount is a constant $986.28 ($6,575.20 × 15%). Compound interest causes the balance to increase more rapidly than simple interest, which can be proved by the following calculation.

Simple interest	
Principal	$6,575.20
Interest ($986.28 × 3 years)	2,958.84
Total in 3 years	$9,534.04
Compound interest	10,000.00
Difference	$465.96

In this example compounding interest results in $465.96 more interest income to the lender (interest expense to the borrower) than simple interest because the interest rate is applied to the unpaid interest and the principal.

METHODS OF COMPUTING COMPOUND INTEREST

How did we know that the $10,000 noninterest-bearing note really consisted of principal of only $6,575.20? We could compute it long hand like this:

Present value of $1 discounted for:

1 period at 15%	$1.00/1.15 = .86957$
2 periods at 15%	$.86957/1.15 = .75614$
3 periods at 15%	$.75614/1.15 = .65752$

where 1.15 is one plus 15% interest rate. The final factor of .65752 is the present value of $1. To obtain the present value of $10,000 we multiply .65752 by $10,000:

$$\$10,000 \times .65752 = \$6,575.20$$

Visually, this theory appears as:

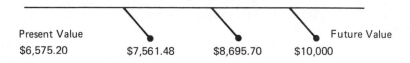

Present Value			Future Value
$6,575.20	$7,561.48	$8,695.70	$10,000

If we want to know the present value of $10,000 for one or two years rather than three, we multiply the $10,000 by the applicable factor shown above.

$$1 \text{ year } \$10,000 \times .86957 = \$8,695.70$$
$$2 \text{ years } \$10,000 \times .75614 = \$7,561.40$$

We could also use the following formula to compute present value.

$$PV = \frac{1}{(1 + i)^n}$$

where:

i = interest rate
n = number of periods

Tables have been developed to simplify calculations of the time value of money. There are four common tables that you should be familiar with. We now explain each of these tables and demonstrate applications of them.

PRESENT VALUE

The table we are interested in for the above illustration is the present-value table (Exhibit 14-1).

The mechanics of utilizing each of the four tables is identical; therefore, we

Exhibit 14-1
Present Value of 1

(n) PERIODS	2 %	2½%	3 %	4 %	5 %	6 %
1	.98039	.97561	.97087	.96154	.95238	.94340
2	.96117	.95181	.94260	.92456	.90703	.89000
3	.94232	.92860	.91514	.88900	.86384	.83962
4	.92385	.90595	.88849	.85480	.82270	.79209
5	.90573	.88385	.86261	.82193	.78353	.74726
6	.88797	.86230	.83748	.79031	.74622	.70496
7	.87056	.84127	.81309	.75992	.71068	.66506
8	.85349	.82075	.78941	.73069	.67684	.62741
9	.83676	.80073	.76642	.70259	.64461	.59190
10	.82035	.78120	.74409	.67556	.61391	.55839
11	.80426	.76214	.72242	.64958	.58468	.52679
12	.78849	.74356	.70138	.62460	.55684	.49697
13	.77303	.72542	.68095	.60057	.53032	.46884
14	.75788	.70773	.66112	.57748	.50507	.44230
15	.74301	.69047	.64186	.55526	.48102	.41727
16	.72845	.67362	.62317	.53391	.45811	.39365
17	.71416	.65720	.60502	.51337	.43630	.37136
18	.70016	.64117	.58739	.49363	.41552	.35034
19	.68643	.62553	.57029	.47464	.39573	.33051
20	.67297	.61027	.55368	.45639	.37689	.31180
21	.65978	.59539	.53755	.43883	.35894	.29416
22	.64684	.58086	.52189	.42196	.34185	.27751
23	.63416	.56670	.50669	.40573	.32557	.26180
24	.62172	.55288	.49193	.39012	.31007	.24698
25	.60953	.53939	.47761	.37512	.29530	.23300
26	.59758	.52623	.46369	.36069	.28124	.21981
27	.58586	.51340	.45019	.34682	.26785	.20737
28	.57437	.50088	.43708	.33348	.25509	.19563
29	.56311	.48866	.42435	.32065	.24295	.18456
30	.55207	.47674	.41199	.30832	.23138	.17411
31	.54125	.46511	.39999	.29646	.22036	.16425
32	.53063	.45377	.38834	.28506	.20987	.15496
33	.52023	.44270	.37703	.27409	.19987	.14619
34	.51003	.43191	.36604	.26355	.19035	.13791
35	.50003	.42137	.35538	.25342	.18129	.13011
36	.49022	.41109	.34503	.24367	.17266	.12274
37	.48061	.40107	.33498	.23430	.16444	.11579
38	.47119	.39128	.32523	.22529	.15661	.10924
39	.46195	.38174	.31575	.21662	.14915	.10306
40	.45289	.37243	.30656	.20829	.14205	.09722

8 %	9 %	10 %	12 %	15 %	(n) PERIODS
.92593	.91743	.90909	.89286	.86957	1
.85734	.84168	.82645	.79719	.75614	2
.79383	.77218	.75132	.71178	.65752	3
.73503	.70843	.68301	.63552	.57175	4
.68058	.64993	.62092	.56743	.49718	5
.63017	.59627	.56447	.50663	.43233	6
.58349	.54703	.51316	.45235	.37594	7
.54027	.50187	.46651	.40388	.32690	8
.50025	.46043	.42410	.36061	.28426	9
.46319	.42241	.38554	.32197	.24719	10
.42888	.38753	.35049	.28748	.21494	11
.39711	.35554	.31863	.25668	.18691	12
.36770	.32618	.28966	.22917	.16253	13
.34046	.29925	.26333	.20462	.14133	14
.31524	.27454	.23939	.18270	.12289	15
.29189	.25187	.21763	.16312	.10687	16
.27027	.23107	.19785	.14564	.09293	17
.25025	.21199	.17986	.13004	.08081	18
.23171	.19449	.16351	.11611	.07027	19
.21455	.17843	.14864	.10367	.06110	20
.19866	.16370	.13513	.09256	.05313	21
.18394	.15018	.12285	.08264	.04620	22
.17032	.13778	.11168	.07379	.04017	23
.15770	.12641	.10153	.06588	.03493	24
.14602	.11597	.09230	.05882	.03038	25
.13520	.10639	.08391	.05252	.02642	26
.12519	.09761	.07628	.04689	.02297	27
.11591	.08955	.06934	.04187	.01997	28
.10733	.08216	.06304	.03738	.01737	29
.09938	.07537	.05731	.03338	.01510	30
.09202	.06915	.05210	.02980	.01313	31
.08520	.06344	.04736	.02661	.01142	32
.07889	.05820	.04306	.02376	.00993	33
.07305	.05340	.03914	.02121	.00864	34
.06763	.04899	.03558	.01894	.00751	35
.06262	.04494	.03235	.01691	.00653	36
.05799	.04123	.02941	.01510	.00568	37
.05369	.03783	.02674	.01348	.00494	38
.04971	.03470	.02430	.01204	.00429	39
.04603	.03184	.02210	.01075	.00373	40

will explain the composition of the tables only once. Columnar headings reflect various interest rates (i). Of course, tables have been developed with finer gradations of interest rates than shown here and are available in books devoted to mathematical tables. The number of periods (n) is provided in the margin.

To utilize the present-value table, all we have to do is select the column headed 15% (because the interest rate is 15%) and look down this column until we get to n = 3 (for three years). The corresponding factor of .65752 is for $1, so we multiply it by the number of dollars:

$$\$10,000 \times .65752 = \$6,575.20$$

Note that this is exactly the same answer we arrived at previously. Now we solve two problems utilizing present value theory.

Problem A

Suppose your daughter, Susie, is lucky enough to have a rich aunt who is willing to finance her college education. Aunt Martha would like to know how much she should invest the day Susie is age one to have $50,000 when Susie is age 18. Assuming a constant rate of return of 15%, we look at the present value table for n = 18 and i = 15%. The factor is .08081. Since the factor is for $1, we multiply it by $50,000 and find that Aunt Martha will have to invest $4,040.50 for Susie to have $50,000 at age 18.

$$\$50,000 \times .08081 = \$4,040.50$$

Were you surprised that the amount is so low?

Problem B

Continuing with the above illustration, what if Aunt Martha estimates that interest rates will be 12% for the next five years and 15% for the remaining 13 years. This creates no problem. We just need to obtain two present-value factors from the present-value table:

n = 5, i = 12% .56743
n = 13, i = 15% .16253
$50,000 × .56743 × .16253 = $4,611.22

The answer is $4,611.22. It does not matter which factor is listed first. For example:

$$\$50,000 \times .16253 \times .56743 = \$4,611.22$$

will give exactly the same answer. Aunt Martha will have to invest $570.72 more than in problem A because a lower interest rate is earned for 5 of the 18 years.

FUTURE VALUE

The opposite of present value is future value. Here, the question is, How much money would we have at the end of *n* periods at *x* rate of interest? You already know that $6,575.20 invested at 15% for three years will result in $10,000 at the end of the three years. But let us consider a new illustration so you can practice using a future-value table.

Problem C

Aunt Martha puts $5,000 in Susie's college fund the day Susie is one and expects the investment to earn an average of 12%. How much money will Susie have at age 18?

Note that we are trying to determine a future amount. $5,000 is the present value, but we want to know the future value, that is, the amount in 18 years. Hence, we need to consult a future-value table, which is based on the following formula:

$$FV = (1 + i)^n$$

where:

FV = future value
i = interest rate
n = number of periods

A future-value table is provided as Exhibit 14-2.

We read down the interest column of 12% to 18 periods to select the factor of 7.68997. Since this is for $1 we multiply it by $5,000.

$$\$5,000 \times 7.68997 = \$38,450$$

Were you surprised that the amount is so high?

As we mentioned before, increasing the interest rate and the number of periods can substantially increase the future value (or, conversely, decrease the present value). For example, if Susie's fund were invested at an annual rate of 15% instead of 12%, she would have $61,877 at age 18.

$$\$5,000 \times 12.37545 = \$61,877$$

Exhibit 14-2
Future Value of 1

(n) PERIODS	2%	2½%	3%	4%	5%	6%
1	1.02000	1.02500	1.03000	1.04000	1.05000	1.06000
2	1.04040	1.05063	1.06090	1.08160	1.10250	1.12360
3	1.06121	1.07689	1.09273	1.12486	1.15763	1.19102
4	1.08243	1.10381	1.12551	1.16986	1.21551	1.26248
5	1.10408	1.13141	1.15927	1.21665	1.27628	1.33823
6	1.12616	1.15969	1.19405	1.26532	1.34010	1.41852
7	1.14869	1.18869	1.22987	1.31593	1.40710	1.50363
8	1.17166	1.21840	1.26677	1.36857	1.47746	1.59385
9	1.19509	1.24886	1.30477	1.42331	1.55133	1.68948
10	1.21899	1.28008	1.34392	1.48024	1.62889	1.79085
11	1.24337	1.31209	1.38423	1.53945	1.71034	1.89830
12	1.26824	1.34489	1.42576	1.60103	1.79586	2.01220
13	1.29361	1.37851	1.46853	1.66507	1.88565	2.13293
14	1.31948	1.41297	1.51259	1.73168	1.97993	2.26090
15	1.34587	1.44830	1.55797	1.80094	2.07893	2.39656
16	1.37279	1.48451	1.60471	1.87298	2.18287	2.54035
17	1.40024	1.52162	1.65285	1.94790	2.29202	2.69277
18	1.42825	1.55966	1.70243	2.02582	2.40662	2.85434
19	1.45681	1.59865	1.75351	2.10685	2.52695	3.02560
20	1.48595	1.63862	1.80611	2.19112	2.65330	3.20714
21	1.51567	1.67958	1.86029	2.27877	2.78596	3.39956
22	1.54598	1.72157	1.91610	2.36992	2.92526	3.60354
23	1.57690	1.76461	1.97359	2.46472	3.07152	3.81975
24	1.60844	1.80873	2.03279	2.56330	3.22510	4.04893
25	1.64061	1.85394	2.09378	2.66584	3.38635	4.29187
26	1.67342	1.90029	2.15659	2.77247	3.55567	4.54938
27	1.70689	1.94780	2.22129	2.88337	3.73346	4.82235
28	1.74102	1.99650	2.28793	2.99870	3.92013	5.11169
29	1.77584	2.04641	2.35657	3.11865	4.11614	5.41839
30	1.81136	2.09757	2.42726	3.24340	4.32194	5.74349
31	1.84759	2.15001	2.50008	3.37313	4.53804	6.08810
32	1.88454	2.20376	2.57508	3.50806	4.76494	6.45339
33	1.92223	2.25885	2.65234	3.64838	5.00319	6.84059
34	1.96068	2.31532	2.73191	3.79432	5.25335	7.25103
35	1.99989	2.37321	2.81386	3.94609	5.51602	7.68609
36	2.03989	2.43254	2.89828	4.10393	5.79182	8.14725
37	2.08069	2.49335	2.98523	4.26809	6.08141	8.63609
38	2.12230	2.55568	3.07478	4.43881	6.38548	9.15425
39	2.16474	2.61957	3.16703	4.61637	6.70475	9.70351
40	2.20804	2.68506	3.26204	4.80102	7.03999	10.28572

8%	9%	10%	12%	15%	(n) PERIODS
1.08000	1.09000	1.10000	1.12000	1.15000	1
1.16640	1.18810	1.21000	1.25440	1.32250	2
1.25971	1.29503	1.33100	1.40493	1.52088	3
1.36049	1.41158	1.46410	1.57352	1.74901	4
1.46933	1.53862	1.61051	1.76234	2.01136	5
1.58687	1.67710	1.77156	1.97382	2.31306	6
1.71382	1.82804	1.94872	2.21068	2.66002	7
1.85093	1.99256	2.14359	2.47596	3.05902	8
1.99900	2.17189	2.35795	2.77308	3.51788	9
2.15892	2.36736	2.59374	3.10585	4.04556	10
2.33164	2.58043	2.85312	3.47855	4.65239	11
2.51817	2.81267	3.13843	3.89598	5.35025	12
2.71962	3.06581	3.45227	4.36349	6.15279	13
2.93719	3.34173	3.79750	4.88711	7.07571	14
3.17217	3.64248	4.17725	5.47357	8.13706	15
3.42594	3.97031	4.59497	6.13039	9.35762	16
3.70002	4.32763	5.05447	6.86604	10.76126	17
3.99602	4.71712	5.55992	7.68997	12.37545	18
4.31570	5.14166	6.11591	8.61276	14.23177	19
4.66096	5.60441	6.72750	9.64629	16.36654	20
5.03383	6.10881	7.40025	10.80385	18.82152	21
5.43654	6.65860	8.14028	12.10031	21.64475	22
5.87146	7.25787	8.95430	13.55235	24.89146	23
6.34118	7.91108	9.84973	15.17863	28.62518	24
6.84847	8.62308	10.83471	17.00006	32.91895	25
7.39635	9.39916	11.91818	19.04007	37.85680	26
7.98806	10.24508	13.10999	21.32488	43.53532	27
8.62711	11.16714	14.42099	23.88387	50.06561	28
9.31727	12.17218	15.86309	26.74993	57.57545	29
10.06266	13.26768	17.44940	29.95992	66.21177	30
10.86767	14.46177	19.19434	35.55511	76.14354	31
11.73708	15.76333	21.11378	37.58173	87.56507	32
12.67605	17.18203	23.22515	42.09153	100.69983	33
13.69013	18.72841	25.54767	47.14252	115.80480	34
14.78534	20.41397	28.10244	52.79962	133.17552	35
15.96817	22.25123	30.91268	59.13557	153.15185	36
17.24563	24.25384	34.00395	66.23184	176.12463	37
18.62528	26.43668	37.40434	74.17966	202.54332	38
20.11530	28.81598	41.14479	83.08122	232.92482	39
21.72452	31.40942	45.25926	93.05097	267.86355	40

This is an increase of $23,427 ($61,877 − $38,450). The power of compound interest is truly astonishing.

Problem D

Now let us look at the same situation except that the interest rate is not expected to be constant. Suppose Aunt Martha expects interest to be 10% for six years, 12% for eight years, and 15% for four years. The factors from the future-value table are:

$$n = 6, i = 10\% \quad 1.77156$$
$$n = 8, i = 12\% \quad 2.47596$$
$$n = 4, i = 15\% \quad 1.74901$$

Now the amount Susie would receive is $38,358.

$$\$5,000 \times 1.77156 \times 2.47596 \times 1.74901 = \$38,358.$$

FUTURE-VALUE ANNUITY

Problem E

Instead of putting a lump sum in the college fund when Susie is age one, suppose Aunt Martha puts ⅟₁₈ of $5,000 or $277.78 each year for 18 years in the fund at 12% interest. This represents an annuity because the payments are periodical. Examples include pensions, mortgages, notes, installments, and car payments. The periodic amounts are called *rents*.

In this case we are again projecting into the future, that is, Aunt Martha wants to know how much Susie will have in 18 years. It is hoped that you can see intuitively that the amount will be substantially less than $38,358 because all of the principal contributions do not earn interest for 18 years. In fact the last contribution does not earn interest at all because all four tables assume that payments are made at the *end* of the period.

You should also be able to see intuitively that the amount would be substantially more than $5,000, the sum of the contributions ($277.78 × 18 years) because each contribution earns interest for the number of years it is invested. We could compute the interest on each contribution by year but that is tedious. The future-value annuity table greatly simplifies the calculation. The future-value annuity table, frequently called "Amount of an Ordinary Annuity of 1," is based on the following formula:

$$FVA = \frac{(1 + i)^n - 1}{i}$$

This table is provided as Exhibit 14-3.

At i = 12% and n = 18 the factor is 55.74972. Therefore, the future value is $15,486.

$$\$277.78 \times 55.74972 = \$15,486$$

As you can see the result is substantially less than the future value of a lump amount of $5,000, which is $38,450.

PRESENT-VALUE ANNUITY

The opposite of future-value annuity is the present-value annuity.

Problem F

Assume an individual, age 65, would like to buy an annuity from an insurance company which would return to him $10,000 a year for life. If his life expectancy is 11 years and the interest rate is 12%, how much must he pay for such a policy? Note that we are again dealing with an annuity because we have periodic rents. Since we want to know how much to pay right *now*, we use a present value of an ordinary-annuity-of-$1 table, which is based on the following formula:

$$PVA = \frac{1 - \dfrac{1}{(1 + i)^n}}{i}$$

This table is provided as Exhibit 14-4.

The factor for i = 12% and n = 11 is 5.93770; hence he would pay $59,377 for the policy.

$$\$10,000 \times 5.93770 = \$59,377$$

Again you should have been able to see intuitively that the amount would be substantially less than the total payments to be received in the future which is $110,000 ($10,000 × 11 years) because the insurance company is earning a 12% return on unpaid dollars throughout the 11-year period.

Exhibit 14-3
Future Value Annuity
Amount of an Ordinary Annuity of 1

(n) PERIODS	2%	2½%	3%	4%	5%	6%
1	1.00000	1.00000	1.00000	1.00000	1.00000	1.00000
2	2.02000	2.02500	2.03000	2.04000	2.05000	2.06000
3	3.06040	3.07563	3.09090	3.12160	3.15250	3.18360
4	4.12161	4.15252	4.18363	4.24646	4.31013	4.37462
5	5.20404	5.25633	5.30914	5.41632	5.52563	5.63709
6	6.30812	6.38774	6.46841	6.63298	6.80191	6.97532
7	7.43428	7.54743	7.66246	7.89829	8.14201	8.39384
8	8.58297	8.73612	8.89234	9.21423	9.54911	9.89747
9	9.75463	9.95452	10.15911	10.58280	11.02656	11.49132
10	10.94972	11.20338	11.46338	12.00611	12.57789	13.18079
11	12.16872	12.48347	12.80780	13.48635	14.20679	14.97164
12	13.41209	13.79555	14.19203	15.02581	15.91713	16.86994
13	14.68033	15.14044	15.61779	16.62684	17.71298	18.88214
14	15.97394	16.51895	17.08632	18.29191	19.59863	21.01507
15	17.29342	17.93193	18.59891	20.02359	21.57856	23.27597
16	18.63929	19.38022	20.15688	21.82453	23.65749	25.67253
17	20.01207	20.86473	21.76159	23.69751	25.84037	28.21288
18	21.41231	22.38635	23.41444	25.64541	28.13238	30.90565
19	22.84056	23.94601	25.11687	27.67123	30.53900	33.75999
20	24.29737	25.54466	26.87037	29.77808	33.06595	36.78559
21	25.78332	27.18327	28.67649	31.96920	35.71925	39.99273
22	27.29898	28.86286	30.53678	34.24797	38.50521	43.39229
23	28.84496	30.58443	32.45288	36.61789	41.43048	46.99583
24	30.42186	32.34904	34.42647	39.08260	44.50200	50.81558
25	32.03030	34.15776	36.45926	41.64591	47.72710	54.86451
26	33.67091	36.01171	38.55304	44.31174	51.11345	59.15638
27	35.34432	37.91200	40.70963	47.08421	54.66913	63.70577
28	37.05121	39.85980	42.93092	49.96758	58.40258	68.52811
29	38.79223	41.85630	45.21885	52.96629	62.32271	73.63980
30	40.56808	43.90270	47.57542	56.08494	66.43885	79.05819
31	42.37944	46.00027	50.00268	59.32834	70.76079	84.80168
32	44.22703	48.15028	52.50276	62.70147	75.29883	90.88978
33	46.11157	50.35403	55.07784	66.20953	80.06377	97.34316
34	48.03380	52.61289	57.73018	69.85791	85.06696	104.18376
35	49.99448	54.92821	60.46208	73.65222	90.32031	111.43478
36	51.99437	57.30141	63.27594	77.59831	95.83632	119.12087
37	54.03425	59.73395	66.17422	81.70225	101.62814	127.26812
38	56.11494	62.22730	69.15945	85.97034	107.70955	135.90421
39	58.23724	64.78298	72.23423	90.40915	114.09502	145.05846
40	60.40198	67.40255	75.40126	95.02552	120.79977	154.76197

8 %	9 %	10 %	12 %	15 %	(n) PERIODS
1.00000	1.00000	1.00000	1.00000	1.00000	1
2.08000	2.09000	2.10000	2.12000	2.15000	2
3.24640	3.27810	3.31000	3.37440	3.47250	3
4.50611	4.57313	4.64100	4.77933	4.99338	4
5.86660	5.98471	6.10510	6.35285	6.74238	5
7.33592	7.52334	7.71561	8.11519	8.75374	6
8.92280	9.20044	9.48717	10.08901	11.06680	7
10.63663	11.02847	11.43589	12.29969	13.72682	8
12.48756	13.02104	13.57948	14.77566	16.78584	9
14.48656	15.19293	15.93743	17.54874	20.30372	10
16.64549	17.56029	18.53117	20.65458	24.34928	11
18.97713	20.14072	21.38428	24.13313	29.00167	12
21.49530	22.95339	24.52271	28.02911	34.35192	13
24.21492	26.01919	27.97498	32.39260	40.50471	14
27.15211	29.36092	31.77248	37.27972	47.58041	15
30.32428	33.00340	35.94973	42.75328	55.71747	16
33.75023	36.97371	40.54470	48.88367	65.07509	17
37.45024	41.30134	45.59917	55.74972	75.83636	18
41.44626	46.01846	51.15909	63.43968	88.21181	19
45.76196	51.16012	57.27500	72.05244	102.44358	20
50.42292	56.76453	64.00250	81.69874	118.81012	21
55.45676	62.87334	71.40275	92.50258	137.63164	22
60.89330	69.53194	79.54302	104.60289	159.27638	23
66.76476	76.78981	88.49733	118.15524	184.16784	24
73.10594	84.70090	98.34706	133.33387	212.79302	25
79.95442	93.32398	109.18177	150.33393	245.71197	26
87.35077	102.72314	121.09994	169.37401	283.56877	27
95.33883	112.96822	134.20994	190.69889	327.10408	28
103.96594	124.13536	148.63093	214.58275	377.16969	29
113.28321	136.30754	164.49402	241.33268	434.74515	30
123.34587	149.57522	181.94343	271.29261	500.95692	31
134.21354	164.03699	201.13777	304.84772	577.10046	32
145.95062	179.80032	222.25154	342.42945	644.66553	33
158.62667	196.98234	245.47670	384.52098	765.36535	34
172.31680	215.71076	271.02437	431.66350	881.17016	35
187.10215	236.12472	299.12681	484.46312	1014.34568	36
203.07032	258.37595	330.03949	543.59869	1167.49753	37
220.31595	282.62978	364.04343	609.83053	1343.62216	38
238.94122	309.06646	401.44778	684.01020	1546.16549	39
259.05652	337.88245	442.59256	767.09142	1779.09031	40

Exhibit 14-4
Present Value of an Ordinary Annuity of 1

(n) Periods	2%	2½%	3%	4%	5%	6%
1	.98039	.97561	.97087	.96154	.95238	.94340
2	1.94156	1.92742	1.91347	1.88609	1.85941	1.83339
3	2.88388	2.85602	2.82861	2.77509	2.72325	2.67301
4	3.80773	3.76197	3.71710	3.62990	3.54595	3.46511
5	4.71346	4.64583	4.57971	4.45182	4.32948	4.21236
6	5.60143	5.50813	5.41719	5.24214	5.07569	4.91732
7	6.47199	6.34939	6.23028	6.00205	5.78637	5.58238
8	7.32548	7.17014	7.01969	6.73274	6.46321	6.20979
9	8.16224	7.97087	7.78611	7.43533	7.10782	6.80169
10	8.98259	8.75206	8.53020	8.11090	7.72173	7.36009
11	9.78685	9.51421	9.25262	8.76048	8.30641	7.88687
12	10.57534	10.25776	9.95400	9.38507	8.86325	8.38384
13	11.34837	10.98319	10.63496	9.98565	9.39357	8.85268
14	12.10625	11.69091	11.29607	10.56312	9.89864	9.29498
15	12.84926	12.38138	11.93794	11.11839	10.37966	9.71225
16	13.57771	13.05500	12.56110	11.65230	10.83777	10.10590
17	14.29187	13.71220	13.16612	12.16567	11.27407	10.47726
18	14.99203	14.35336	13.75351	12.65930	11.68959	10.82760
19	15.67846	14.97889	14.32380	13.13394	12.08532	11.15812
20	16.35143	15.58916	14.87747	13.59033	12.46221	11.46992
21	17.01121	16.18455	15.41502	14.02916	12.82115	11.76408
22	17.65805	16.76541	15.93692	14.45112	13.16300	12.04158
23	18.29220	17.33211	16.44361	14.85684	13.48857	12.30338
24	18.91393	17.88499	16.93554	15.24696	13.79864	12.55036
25	19.52346	18.42438	17.41315	15.62208	14.09394	12.78336
26	20.12104	18.95061	17.87684	15.98277	14.37519	13.00317
27	20.70690	19.46401	18.32703	16.32959	14.64303	13.21053
28	21.28127	19.96489	18.76411	16.66306	14.89813	13.40616
29	21.84438	20.45355	19.18845	16.98371	15.14107	13.59072
30	22.39646	20.93029	19.60044	17.29203	15.37245	13.76483
31	22.93770	21.39541	20.00043	17.58849	15.59281	13.92909
32	23.46833	21.84918	20.38877	17.87355	15.80268	14.08404
33	23.98856	22.29188	20.76579	18.14765	16.00255	14.23023
34	24.49859	22.72379	21.13184	18.41120	16.19290	14.36814
35	24.99862	23.14516	21.48722	18.66461	16.37419	14.49825
36	25.48884	23.55625	21.83225	18.90828	16.54685	14.62099
37	25.96945	23.95732	22.16724	19.14258	16.71129	14.73678
38	26.44064	24.34860	22.49246	19.36786	16.86789	14.84602
39	26.90259	24.73034	22.80822	19.58448	17.01704	14.94907
40	27.35548	25.10278	23.11477	19.79277	17.15909	15.04630

8%	9%	10%	12%	15%	(n) Periods
.92593	.91743	.90909	.89286	.86957	1
1.78326	1.75911	1.73554	1.69005	1.62571	2
2.57710	2.53130	2.48685	2.40183	2.28323	3
3.31213	3.23972	3.16986	3.03735	2.85498	4
3.99271	3.88965	3.79079	3.60478	3.35216	5
4.62288	4.48592	4.35526	4.11141	3.78448	6
5.20637	5.03295	4.86842	4.56376	4.16042	7
5.74664	5.53482	5.33493	4.96764	4.48732	8
6.24689	5.99525	5.75902	5.32825	4.77158	9
6.71008	6.41766	6.14457	5.65022	5.01877	10
7.13896	6.80519	6.49506	5.93770	5.23371	11
7.53608	7.16073	6.81369	6.19437	5.42062	12
7.90378	7.48690	7.10336	6.42355	5.58315	13
8.24424	7.78615	7.36669	6.62817	5.72448	14
8.55948	8.06069	7.60608	6.81086	5.84737	15
8.85137	8.31256	7.82371	6.97399	5.95424	16
9.12164	8.54363	8.02155	7.11963	6.04716	17
9.37189	8.75563	8.20141	7.24967	6.12797	18
9.60360	8.95012	8.36492	7.36578	6.19823	19
9.81815	9.12855	8.51356	7.46944	6.25933	20
10.01680	9.29224	8.64869	7.56200	6.31246	21
10.20074	9.44243	8.77154	7.64465	6.35866	22
10.37106	9.58021	8.88322	7.71843	6.39884	23
10.52876	9.70661	8.98474	7.78432	6.43377	24
10.67478	9.82258	9.07704	7.84314	6.46415	25
10.80998	9.92897	9.16095	7.89566	6.49056	26
10.93516	10.02658	9.23722	7.94255	6.51353	27
11.05108	10.11613	9.30657	7.98442	6.53351	28
11.15841	10.19828	9.36961	8.02181	6.55088	29
11.25778	10.27365	9.42691	8.05518	6.56598	30
11.34980	10.34280	9.47901	8.08499	6.57911	31
11.43500	10.40624	9.52638	8.11159	6.59053	32
11.51389	10.46444	9.56943	8.13535	6.60046	33
11.58693	10.51784	9.60858	8.15656	6.60910	34
11.65457	10.56682	9.64416	8.17550	6.61661	35
11.71719	10.61176	9.67651	8.19241	6.62314	36
11.77518	10.65299	9.70592	8.20751	6.62882	37
11.82887	10.69082	9.73265	8.22099	6.63375	38
11.87858	10.72552	9.75697	8.23303	6.63805	39
11.92461	10.75736	9.77905	8.24378	6.64178	40

SELECTION OF A TABLE

How do you know which table to use to solve a problem? If there is periodic rents, it is one of the annuity tables. Similarly if only a lump sum is involved, it is one of the nonannuity tables. In determining whether to use a present-value or future-value table, the key is what date you are interested in knowing an amount for. Sometimes a time diagram can be helpful. If you want to know the value as of a current date, you would use a present-value table. Conversely, if you are interested in knowing a future amount, you would select a future-value table.

NONANNUAL PAYMENTS

Now we discuss how payments made more frequently than once a year are handled. Recall that the interest rate is an annual interest rate. If the interest rate is 12% and payments made twice a year, we divide the rate by two and multiply the number of periods by two. Thus the revised data for problem F are:

$$i = 12\%/2 = 6\%$$
$$n = 11 \times 2 = 22$$
Amount to be received $\$10,000/2 = \$5,000$
Total payments $\$5,000 \times 12.0416 = \$60,208$

If payments of $2,500 are to be received quarterly, i is 3% (12%/4) and n is 44 (11 × 4). If the interest rate is a number more refined than any in Exhibits 14-1 through 14-4, say, 8.47%, we can consult a book of tables or estimate the factor by interpolation. We will demonstrate interpolation in the next chapter.

PAYMENTS AT BEGINNING OF PERIOD

We mentioned earlier that annuity tables assume payments at the end of the period. If payments are made at the beginning of the period, the situation is called an annuity due. The tables can be easily converted with the following formulas:

Future amount of an annuity due = n + rents − 1 payment
Present value of an annuity due = n − 1 rents + 1 payment

Problem G

Let us consider as an example an annuity involving, of course, periodic payments. Walter intends to make annual deposits of $1,000 into a retirement fund starting January 1, 19X1. The fund will earn interest at 12%. How much money will Walter have in his fund when he retires in twenty years? Walter is interested in a future amount. Annuity payments are made at the beginning of the period; therefore we are dealing with a future-value annuity due problem. The formula is:

$$n + 1 \text{ rents} = 20 \text{ years} + 1 = 21$$

From the future-value table the factor for n = 21, i = 12% is 81.69874. Multiplying the factor by $1,000 and deducting one payment, we find that Walter will have $80,698.74 in his retirement fund.

$1,000 × 81.69874	$81,698.74
Less one payment	1,000.00
	$80,698.74

USE OF TWO OR MORE TABLES

Sometimes problems are sufficiently complex—such as problem H—that two or more tables are needed to solve them.

Problem H

How much cash can a treasurer expect to receive from issuing a million dollars of bonds when the face interest is 10% payable quarterly for 10 years, and the market interest is 12%? The buyers of the bonds are purchasing two separate elements:

1. The right to receive the principal of $1,000 per bond at the end of ten years, and
2. The right to receive quarterly interest checks of $25 per bond ($1,000 × 10% × $\frac{1}{12}$).

The latter is an annuity. To solve the problem, it is necessary to calculate the present value of the principal and interest separately and then add the two present-value figures.

Principal $1,000,000 × .30656[a]	$306,560
Interest $25,000[b] × 23.11477[c]	577,869
Amount of cash	$884,429

(a) PV table, n = 40, i = 3%
(b) $1,000,000 × 10% × $\frac{1}{12}$ = $25,000 quarterly
(c) PVA table, n = 40, i = 3%

The treasurer can expect to receive $884,429 cash from the sale of the bonds. The firm is liable for quarterly interest payments of $25,000 and a million dollars principal payment in 10 years.

The entry to record the transaction on the books is:

Cash	$884,429	
Discount on bonds	$115,571	
Bonds payable		$1,000,000

The discount on bonds is, in substance, interest; therefore, the firm would allocate the $115,571 to interest expense over the 10 year period.

Obviously the buyer(s) of the bonds would compute the amount they are willing to pay for the bonds the same way as the treasurer determines the expected cash inflow. Bonds are normally issued in demoninations of $1,000, meaning that $1,000 is the principal and the amount the firm pays at maturity to the holder of the bond. On a per bond basis the purchase price is:

Principal $1,000 × .30656	$306.56
Interest $25 × 23.11477	577.87
Amount of each bond	$884.43

The purchase price multiplied by 1,000 (the number of bonds) is the same amount that the treasurer expects to receive ($1 difference is due to rounding).

PROBLEMS

Now we present several practice problems. Many people have trouble solving time value problems. Because studying the answers to problems is of limited help—especially when the answers appear deceptively simple—we encourage you to work through these problems before looking at the solutions.

Problem 1

When Bob leased an office building for 10 years, he paid a security deposit of $25,000, which is returnable at the expiration of the lease with interest compounded at 12% a year. How much will Bob receive in 10 years from his deposit? This is a future-value problem. The factor for n = 10, i = 12% is 3.10585. The amount Bob will receive is $77,646 ($25,000 × 3.10585).

Problem 2

Mary has an option to receive an immediate bonus of $5,000 or a deferred bonus of $10,000 receivable in 8 years. Assuming an interest rate of 10%, which option should Mary accept? We compare the present value of $10,000, which is $4,665.10, with $5,000.

$$\$10,000 \times .46651^a = \$4,665.10$$
(a) PV table, n = 8, i = 10%

Mary should accept the $5,000 now.

Problem 3

John would like to buy 10 shares of preferred stock that are redeemable for $100 each in 20 years. The stock pays an annual dividend rate of 8% a year. How much should John pay for the stock if he wants a yield of 12%? Note that in substance this is the same problem we demonstrated earlier for bonds. The calculation is identical. John is buying the right to receive $1,000 in 20 years and the right to receive annual dividends of $80 (8% × $100 × 10).

PV of principal $1,000 × .10367[a]	$103.67
PV of dividend $80 × 7.46944[b]	597.55
Purchase price of stock	$701.22

(a) PV table, n = 20, i = 12%
(b) PVA table, n = 20, i = 12%

John should pay $701.22 for the preferred stock.

Problem 4

Karen, in order to retire in five years, wants to create a fund that would enable her to withdraw $10,000 a year for ten years after she retires. She wants to make equal annual contributions during the next 5 years to the fund. Assume interest is 12%.

1. How much must the fund be worth in 5 years to allow her to withdraw $10,000 for 10 years? The answer is $56,502.20.

$$\$10,000 \times 5.65022^a = \$56,502.20$$
(a) PVA table, n = 10, i = 12%

2. How much must Karen invest for each of the next 5 years? The answer is $8,894 ($56,502.20/6.35285). FVA table, n = 5, i = 12%.

Problem 5

Tom borrowed $50,000 on January 1, 19X1 and will make five equal annual payments of $12,854 commencing January 1, 19X2. What interest rate is Tom paying? First we compute a factor and then we locate the factor on the present value annuity table for n = 5.

$$\text{For the factor: } \$50,000/\$12,854 = 3.88984$$

The interest rate is about 9%.

Problem 6

Nancy invested $20,000 at 10% interest for the purpose of paying a debt of $51,800. How many years will it take Nancy to accumulate enough money to liquidate the debt at 10% interest? Again, we first compute a factor and then go to the future-value table and look for the n when i = 10%.

$$\$51,800/\$20,000 = 2.59 \text{ for the factor}$$

It will take Nancy approximately 10 years to obtain $51,800.

Problem 7

Peter invested $10,000 to pay a $30,000 debt, which he owes in eight years. What rate of interest must Peter earn? We compute the factor and consult the future-value table for the interest rate when n = 8.

$$\$30,000/\$10,000 = 3.000 \text{ for the factor}$$

The interest rate is about 15%.

Problem 8

Suppose the city of Timbuctu offered a bond that would pay interest of $40 every six months forever? This kind of a bond is known as a perpetual bond. What amount would an investor pay for the bond if the discount rate were 14% compounded semiannually? The answer is $571.

$14\%/2 = \quad 7\%$ of every six months
$\$40/7\% = \$571$ present value, assuming first interest payment
is six months from now

Problem 9

A lessee signs a lease to acquire the right to use a new piece of equipment for five years. The cost of the equipment is $50,000 to the lessor, who desires a return of 12%. The amount of periodic rent is $13,870 computed as follows:

$$\$50,000/3.60478^a = \$13,870$$
(a) PVA table, n = 5, i = 12%

Conversely, if the lessee did not know the cost of the equipment, but he knew the lease payments, interest rate, and lease period, he could approximate the value of the equipment by determining the present value of the lease payments.

$$\$13,870 \times 3.60478^a = \$50,000$$
(a) PVA table, n = 5, i = 12%

Keep the above concepts in mind when we talk about setting the amount of lease payments in the next chapter.

Problem 10

Betty would like to have $150,000 when she retires 20 years from now. What annual deposit must Betty make if the fund earns interest at 10%? We solve the problem by dividing the $150,000 by a factor obtained from the future-value annuity table for n = 20 and i = 10. The factor is 57.275.

$$\$150,000/57.275 = \$2,619$$

The annual deposit is $2,619.

Problem 11

Laura, who is 60 years old today, wishes to invest starting today an annual amount of $10,000 for 5 years so that on her 65 birthday she can start withdrawing equal annual amounts. Assume her life expectancy is 15 years and her investments will earn 12% a year for five years and 10% thereafter. What is the annual amount she can expect to receive from the fund yearly starting at age 65? First, we compute the future value of the fund to age 65.

$$\$10,000 \times 6.35285^a = \$63,528.50$$
(a) FVA table, n = 5, i = 12%

Then we divide the $63,528.50 by an appropriate factor to determine the annual receipts:

$$\$63,528.50/6.14457^a = \$10,338.96$$
(a) PVA table, n = 10, i = 10%

Annual receipts are $10,338.96 for 10 years.

SUMMARY

This chapter includes the principles of simple and compound interest. We discussed discounting of notes and how to compute the selling prices of securities. We explained the four common time value tables: (1) present value, (2) future value, (3) present-value annuity, and (4) future-value annuity. Finally, we demonstrated the theory through a variety of elementary problems.

Understanding the time value of money is essential for all managers, especially in times of high interest rates and high inflation. In the next chapter we will utilize time value theory to solve capital acquisition problems.

15. Capital Budgeting

Capital budgeting involves questions of capital acquisitions, capital disposals, and leasing. A decision might be made to acquire a new asset or dispose of an existing asset. Asset replacement decisions are of two types:

1. When the old asset can no longer be used, the decision is to either replace the asset or discontinue operations. If the asset is replaced the firm seeks that replacement which will generate the highest return for resources expended.
2. Replace old assets that are still useful. Technological changes cause capital equipment to become obsolete. Many times it is more profitable to replace these items with more modern equipment even if they still have a high book value (undepreciated cost). Computers and jet planes are obvious examples.

Usually, the original cost of the old equipment and its book value are irrelevant; that is, they are sunk costs and have no bearing on the decision other than income taxes applicable to the gain or loss on disposition. Cash inflow from residual value is relevant. The tax impact could be quite valuable if the loss on disposition of old equipment is a tax deductible loss.

Other capital budgeting decisions include cost reductions, plant expansion, and lease versus buy arrangements.

ADMINISTERING A CAPITAL ACQUISITION PROGRAM

Before investigating capital investment models, we will discuss the principles of administering a capital expenditure program. It is important that a firm has written procedures governing capital budgeting decisions. Proposals should be submitted by lower-level managers and approved by higher management, including top management. A separate proposal should be submitted for each project, preferably on standardized forms. A proposal should cover such factors as:

1. Nature of the project
2. Justification
3. Cost

4. Benefit
5. Time phasing
6. Approvals
7. Data required for capital model decision

COST OF CAPITAL

Before a firm can decide if a capital project is desirable, it must first establish its criteria for the cost of capital. Investors who furnish funds must be compensated adequately. When funds are borrowed, the cost of capital is called interest, whereas when they are provided by the stockholders it is called earnings per share or, sometimes, return on shareholder investment. For a firm considering a capital proposal the cost of capital is the cost of acquiring the funds used for the capital project. Since funds can be obtained from many sources, each at a different cost, firms commonly compute a weighted average cost of capital. This weighted average reflects the cost rates of several sources of funds in proportion to the amounts furnished by each source. Exhibit 15-1 displays the mechanics of computing the weighted average cost of capital.

In this illustration 12.6% is the cost of capital, which means that a capital investment return must at least equal the 12.6%. If the return is in excess of this percentage the project will be acceptable; otherwise it will be unacceptable.

Leverage

Before leaving the above illustration, let us comment on leverage. In the illustration above, if the firm could borrow the entire amount it needs at 10%, the cost of capital would be 10%. Obviously, this is a much more favorable situation than having a cost of capital of 12.6%. If the capital project yields a 15% return, the difference between 15% and 10%, which is 5%, would go to the

Exhibit 15-1
Weighted Average Cost of Capital

SOURCE OF CAPITAL	PROPORTION OF TOTAL	CAPITAL COST %	WEIGHTED COST %
Long term dept	20%	10%	2.0%
Preferred stock	30%	12%	3.6
Common stock	15%	14%	2.1
Retained earnings	35%	14%	4.9
Weighted average cost of capital			12.6%

common stockholders and is called leverage or trading on the equity, discussed earlier in Chapter 3 on ratios.

PRESENT VALUE MODELS

We will limit our discussion of the many models available for evaluating capital projects to the most practical and popular ones, starting out with those based on the time value of money. Basically a capital expenditure is the outlay of cash with the expectation that it will produce cash receipts in later years. Of course, the firm expects the cash receipts to exceed the cash expenditure. Since capital acquisitions are long range in nature, the time value of money is a crucial element in the analysis.

In the last chapter, we introduced you to present-value concepts. Now we utilize those concepts in capital acquisition decisions. There are two popular present-value approaches:

1. Minimum acceptable rate of return
2. Internal rate of return

Minimum Acceptable Rate of Return

The minimum acceptable rate of return consists of discounting the expected cash inflow by the discount rate the firm considers to be its minimum acceptable rate of return on investment. Since a firm has many demands on its scarce cash resources, proposals for capital expenditures are analyzed as to which is the most profitable.

We said previously that each proposal must consist of a justification for requesting funds, a calculation of potential profit or cost savings, and an estimate of net cash inflow by years. Cash inflows do not have to be a constant figure. Then the net cash inflows are discounted to present value. Here is an example.

Suppose a firm is considering purchasing a new machine for $78,000. The firm considers a 10% rate of return to be the minimum acceptable rate. The cash flow discounted to present value is shown in Exhibit 15-2.

With the net present value positive, the firm should buy the machine because it meets the requirement of a 10% rate of return. Indeed, the machine will yield a rate of return higher than 10%.

Suppose the cost of the machine were $80,000? Then the firm would have a negative cash flow of $283 ($80,000 cost less $79,717 present value of cash inflow), and the decision would be to not buy the machine. If the firm wanted

Exhibit 15-2
Proposal Evaluated by Minimum
Acceptable Rate of Return — 10%

YRS FROM NOW	CASH FLOW	PRESENT VALUE AT 10% FACTOR	AMOUNT
1	$18,000	.9091	$16,364
2	$22,000	.8264	18,181
3	$25,000	.7513	18,783
4	$25,000	.6830	17,075
5	$15,000	.6209	9,314
			$79,717
Cost of Machine at Present Value			78,000
Net Present Value			$ 1,717

to know its unrecovered investment, a table such as Exhibit 15-3 would provide the information. This exhibit assumes the machine cost $78,000.

By the end of the fifth year the firm has not only recovered its entire investment but also has $2,766 excess, indicating that the firm could have paid more than 10% interest.

Internal Rate of Return

What if a firm wanted to know the exact rate of return that a proposal would generate? Such a calculation is called the internal rate of return approach, a

Exhibit 15-3
Calculation of Unrecovered Investment

(1) YEAR	(2) UNRECOVERED INVESTMENT BEGINNING OF YEAR	(3) INTEREST AT 10%	(4) AMORTIZATION OF INVESTMENT	(5) UNRECOVERED INVESTMENT END OF YEAR
		[(2) × 10%]	(Cash Flow- Col 3)	[(2) — (4)]
1	$78,000	$7,800	$10,200	$67,800
2	$67,800	$6,780	$15,220	$52,580
3	$52,580	$5,258	$19,742	$32,838
4	$32,838	$3,284	$21,716	$11,122
5	$11,122	$1,112	$13,888	$(2,766)

Exhibit 15-4
Proposal Evaluated by Minimum
Acceptable Rate of Return — 11%

| YEARS FROM NOW | CASH FLOW | PRESENT VALUE AT 11% | |
		FACTOR	AMOUNT
1	$18,000	.9009	$16,216
2	$22,000	.8116	17,855
3	$25,000	.7312	18,280
4	$25,000	.6587	16,467
5	$15,000	.5934	8,901
			$77,719
Cost of Machine at Present Value			78,000
Net Present Value			$ (281)

method that proceeds by trial and error. For example, we already know that the interest rate in the preceding example is more than 10%, but we do not know by how much. Suppose we try 11%, as in Exhibit 15-4.

Since the net present value is now negative, we know that the true rate of return is between 10% and 11%, but closer to 11% than 10%. By interpolation we can compute the true rate as 10.8594%.

$$\text{IRR} = 10\% + \frac{1717}{1717^* + 281\dagger} (11\% - 10\%) = 10.8594\%$$

The accuracy of the true rate of return can be double checked by preparing another table with 10.8594% interest. Except for rounding the present value of the cash inflows would be $78,000.

Both present-value models consider the time value of money and income over the life of the project. The internal rate of return has the advantage over minimum rate of return of providing the true rate of return, thus making it easier to assess risk. Proposals can be ranked according to profitability.

The primary weakness of both present-value models is that the amount of cash inflow cannot always be estimated accurately. Nor does a firm always know what discount rate is acceptable, the life expectancy of the capital item, its salvage value, and future income tax rates. Still, the firm must attempt to estimate these variables as closely as possible.

---

*Net present value from Exhibit 15-2
†Net present value from Exhibit 15-4

Exhibit 15-5
Calculation of Cash Inflow by
Expected Value

ALTERNATIVE	NET CASH INFLOW	PROBABILITY	EXPECTED VALUE
A	$10,000	.5	$5,000
B	8,000	.3	2,400
C	7,000	.2	1,400
			$8,800

Risk and Uncertainty

One method of handling risk and uncertainty in estimating cash inflow is through probability theory, which requires a calculation of the expected value. For example a capital investment cash inflow might result in the alternatives shown in Exhibit 15-5. The figure of $8,800 can be used to estimate cash inflow in the capital investment model. If the amounts and probabilities change yearly, a separate calculation of the expected value is made for each year.

Illustration 1: Purchase

We now illustrate two complicated capital acquisition problems. Assume a firm is considering the purchase of a new machine. The pertinent data are:

Minimum desired rate of return	10%
Cost of new machine	$50,000
Annual savings in cash operating expenses for four years	$15,000
Depreciation per year	$12,000
Resale value at end of four years	$5,000
Income tax rate	45%

The conclusion is that the firm should not buy the machine because the net present value is negative. Exhibit 15-6 provides the calculations.

First, the annual cash saving net of tax is discounted to present value. Depreciation is relevant only to the extent of tax savings. Since depreciation expense is an allowable deduction on the tax return, it reduces the amount of income tax payable each year. (In the interest of simplicity we used straight-line depreciation rather than the IRS recovery periods, but the principle is the same). This tax savings must also be brought back to present value. Both cash saving

Exhibit 15-6
Evaluation of Capital Expenditure Proposal

		PRESENT VALUE FACTORS AT 10%	TOTAL PRESENT VALUE
ANNUAL CASH EXPENSE SAVING			
ANNUAL CASH SAVING	$15,000		
LESS TAX @ 45%	6,750		
AFTER TAX CASH SAVING	$ 8,250	3.16986	$26,151
ANNUAL DEPRECIATION TAX SHIELD			
ANNUAL DEPRECIATION DEDUCTION	$12,000		
APPLICABLE TAX RATE	45%		
ANNUAL TAX SHIELD	$ 5,400	3.16986[a]	$17,118
LIQUIDATION PROCEEDS			
SALE PRICE OF MACHINE	$ 5,000		
BOOK VALUE (COST OF 50,000 − 48,000 ACCUMULATED DEPR)	$ 2,000		
GAIN ON SALE	$ 3,000		
TAX ON GAIN 45%	$ 1,350		
AFTER TAX PROCEEDS	$ 5,000		
LESS TAX ON GAIN	$ 1,350		
	$ 3,650	.68301[b]	$ 2,494
TOTAL PRESENT VALUE OF FUTURE CASH INFLOW			$45,763
INVESTMENT REQUIRED IN MACHINE			$50,000
NET NEGATIVE PRESENT VALUE			($4,237)

[a]PVA, n=4, 1 = 10%.
[b]PV, n=4, 1 = 10%.

and the tax shield from depreciation are annual amounts, so it is appropriate to consult the present-value annuity table for the factor.

Residual value after taxes is relevant. Assuming an estimated tax rate of 45% on the gain, the net cash inflow from the residual value is $3,650. The present value of the $3,650 added to the present value of the cash savings and tax shield yields only $45,763. The machine costs $50,000; therefore, the conclusion is that the firm should not buy the machine because it will not yield the desired rate of return of 10%.

Illustration 2: Trade-in

Now we consider a more complicated problem than the purchase of a new machine. Suppose we are considering trading in old equipment under a plant moderization program. In this case we are trying to minimize cost rather than maximize revenue. Cash flow for the new equipment and other pertinent data are:

Cost of equipment	$100,000
Installation	10,000
Testing and training	5,000
	$115,000
Residual value after five years	$10,000

The book value of the old machine is:

Cost	$50,000
Accumulated depreciation	(20,000)
Book value	$30,000
Current residual value	$18,000
Residual value in five years	$2,000
Tax rate	40%

Assume that the new equipment will require an initial $4,000 increase in working capital (items such as increased inventory, receivables, and payables). Suppose further that the present machine could be overhauled at a cost of $40,000.

The new machine will result in a net additional cash inflow of $20,066 or $15,000 after considering taxes and the tax effect of depreciation. The cash saving is computed in Exhibit 15-7.

Exhibit 15-7
Recurring Cash Inflow from Depreciation

DEPRECIABLE BASIS OF NEW MACHINE ($115,000 COST—$10,000 RESIDUAL)	$105,000
DEPRECIABLE BASIS OF OLD MACHINE ($30,000 BOOK VALUE + $40,000 OVERHAUL — $2,000 RESIDUAL)	68,000
TOTAL INCREASE IN DEPRECIABLE BASIS	$ 37,000
YEARLY INCREASE IN DEPRECIABLE BASIS ($37,000/5 YEARS)	$ 7,400
TAX DECREASE FROM DEPRECIATION ($7,400 × 40%)	$ 2,960
YEARLY INCREASE IN NET REVENUE ($20,066 ASSUMED INCREASE — $8.026 TAX)	12,040
RECURRING CASH INFLOW	$ 15,000

Exhibit 15-8
Cash Outflow Before and After Tax

		PRE TAX	TAX SAVING[a]	AFTER TAX
Cost of New Machine (Installed)		$110,000	$(11,000)[a]	$99,000
Testing & Training		5,000	(500)[a]	4,500
Working Capital		4,000	-0-	4,000
Old Equipment Loss				
Book Value	$30,000			
Current Residual Value	18,000	(18,000)		
Loss	$12,000 × 40%		(4,800)	(22,800)
Cash Outflow		$101,000	(16,300)[b]	84,700

[a]Assumed 10% investment credit
[b]Assumed taxed at ordinary rate of 40%

Again, note that the importance of depreciation is solely to compute tax effect. The cash inflow of $15,000 is an annual amount. The next step is to compute the pretax and post-tax cash outflow resulting from the new machine. See Exhibit 15-8.

Now we can compute the total cost effect of procuring a new machine as well as the cost of retaining the old. Exhibit 15-9 shows that the cost to the company for the new machine is $29,450 as compared with $39,006 for the old machine. The company would save $9,556 after income tax by acquiring the new machine.

Exhibit 15-9
Evaluation of Buying a New Machine
Versus Keeping Old Machine

	PRESENT VALUE DISCOUNTED AT 15%	TOTAL PRESENT VALUE
A. BUYING NEW MACHINE		
RECURRING CASH		
INFLOW ($15,000 YEARLY (Exhibit 15-7)	3.352	$50,280
DISPOSAL VALUE END OF YEAR 5 ($10,000)	.497	4,970
INITIAL REQUIRED INVESTMENT AFTER TAX ($84,700 ; Exhibit 15-8)	1.000	(84,700)
		($29,450)
B. KEEPING OLD MACHINE		
OVERHAUL	1.000	$(40,000)
DISPOSAL VALUE END OF YEAR 5 ($2000)	.497	994
		$(39,006)
DIFFERENCE IN FAVOR OF BUYING NEW MACHINE		$ (9,556)

Obviously, the dollar effect of the two alternatives would be different were we to use a rate of return other than 15%.

Additional Complications

Problems such as the above can be further complicated by factors such as:

1. Unequal lives of capital items
2. Changes in tax rates
3. Inconsistent cash inflows or outflows
4. Tax complexities from adjusting depreciable basis because of trade in
5. Inflation

PAYBACK

Although present-value models are theoretically superior, the payback method is far more popular. Payback, widely used and easy to understand, emphasizes liquidity. It consists of dividing the expected cash savings into the initial cash outflow. For example, assume that a $50,000 machine will generate annual cash savings of $10,000. The payback period is five years.

$$\frac{\text{Initial cash outflow } \$50,000}{\text{Annual cash savings } \$10,000} = 5 \text{ years payback}$$

The equipment will have "paid for itself" in five years. If the equipment is used beyond five years, cash savings is profit. If the equipment has an expected life of less than five years, it should not be purchased.

The theory behind the payback method is that the shorter the payback period, the lower the risk and the more desirable the proposal, especially when the danger of obsolescence is high. Note, however, that payback merely measures the period of time it would take to recoup the dollars invested. It ignores income that may be produced beyond the payback period and does not measure profitability. This is a major weakness because a shorter payback period in and of itself does not necessarily mean that one project is preferable to another. Nor does the payback method consider the time value of money. This is another major weakness for long-lived capital items. Still, the longer the life, the more difficult it is to use the present-value models because of possible inaccuracies in projecting cash flow and the appropriate return rate.

Exhibit 15-10 demonstrates how unequal cash saving can be handled in the payback model. How many years will it take for the firm to recover $50,000? Reading down the cumulative column, one discovers that the payback period is 3.5 years.

Exhibit 15-10
Payback with Unequal Cash Flow

YEAR	INITIAL INVESTMENT	NET CASH INFLOWS EACH YEAR	NET CASH INFLOWS ACCUMULATED
0	$50,000		
1		$10,000	$10,000
2		15,000	25,000
3		18,000	43,000
3.5		7,000	50,000
4.		8,000	58,000

ACCOUNTING RATE OF RETURN

Another common model is the accounting rate of return, which gives a rough approximation of the rate of return, as compared with the discounted cash flow method. Its advantage over payback is that it considers income over the entire life of a project. It also facilitates post evaluations in which data available from accounting records can be compared to the original proposal. Its computations parallel the financial accounting model of computing income and recording initial investments in the books of accounts; hence the name, accounting rate of return. The basic formula with assumed figures is:

$$\frac{\text{Increase in future average annual net income}}{\text{Initial increase in required investment}}$$

$$\frac{\overset{\text{Cash}}{\underset{\text{inflow}}{\$20,000}} - \overset{}{\underset{\text{Depreciation}}{\$10,000}}}{\$50,000} = \begin{array}{l} \text{20\% accounting} \\ \text{rate of return} \end{array}$$

Like payback this model ignores the time value of money. Its assumption of constant cash inflows and depreciation implies that it is based on averages. Variations in accounting principles can effect the accounting rate of return. For example, if expenditures are capitalized as assets rather than expensed, the effect is net income. If the life of capital equipment is long and cash inflow not constant, the accounting rate of return can result in substantial error when compared with present-value models.

USE OF SEVERAL MODELS SIMULTANEOUSLY

Sometimes managers will attempt to use various models simultaneously. It is not uncommon for the models to yield conflicting results. Although use of more than one model may be time consuming and costly, still, when the additional

Exhibit 15-11
Analysis of Selling or Keeping a Plant

YEARS FROM NOW	SELL PLANT	CASH INFLOW KEEP PLANT	DIFFERENCE
0	$500,000	0	$500,000
1	0	$250,000	(250,000)
2	0	150,000	(150,000)
3	0	80,000	(80,000)
4	0	60,000	(60,000)
5	0	20,000	(20,000)
	$500,000	$560,000	($60,000)

cost and effort are compared to the magnitude of dollars invested in major capital expenditures and to the infrequency of evaluating capital proposals, the inconveniences of computing several models may be quite trivial.

DISINVESTMENT DECISIONS

Capital investments also include disinvestment decisions such as disposing of a division or plant. Here it is necessary to compare the present value of net cash flow for the various alternatives. For example, what if a plant can be sold for $500,000 immediate cash or can be operated for another five years. Assume that cash flow is as given in Exhibit 15-11.

The firm should not conclude from the data above that it should keep the plant because the cash inflow is $60,000 larger than the selling price. The cash flow must be weighted by the time value of money. Assuming money has a value of 12%, the weighting is calculated in Exhibit 15-12.

Exhibit 15-12
Weighting of Cash Flow

TIME	CASH FLOW	MULTIPLIER	PRESENT VALUE
0	$500,000	1.00000	$500,000
1	(250,000)	.89286	(223,215)
2	(150,000)	.79719	(119,579)
3	(80,000)	.71178	(56,942)
4	(60,000)	.63552	(38,131)
5	(20,000)	.56743	(11,349)
			$50,784

Exhibit 15-13
Investment Proposal Evaluated
by the Present Value Method

ANNUAL CASH INFLOW (5 YRS)	$10,000
PRESENT VALUE OF 5 YRS AT 10%	3.791
PRESENT VALUE OF CASH INFLOW	37,910
PRESENT VALUE OF CASH OUTFLOW	40,000
NET PRESENT VALUE	($2,090)

The decision should be to sell the plant. Again, this example illustrates the importance of considering the time value of money.

INVESTMENT VERSUS FINANCING

A common error in capital budgeting decisions is to confuse investment with financing. Capital budgeting has to do with the use of capital whereas financing has to do with the sources of capital. A poor investment decision is not made profitable by changing the means of financing it; hence, investments and financing should be evaluated separately. For example, consider the following investment proposal (Exhibit 15-13) evaluated by the net present-value method.

This project should not be undertaken because it does not yield the desired 10% rate of return. Actually it yields approximately 8% (internal rate of return). Suppose the investor could finance the $40,000 acquisition with a downpayment of $5,000 and annual installments of $8,500 for five years. An investor might be tempted to combine the investment and financing something like Exhibit 15-14.

Exhibit 15-14
Illustration of Investment
and Financing Combined

ANNUAL CASH RECEIPTS	$10,000
ANNUAL INSTALLMENT PAYMENT	8,500
NET ANNUAL CASH RECEIPTS	1,500
PV OF 5 YEARS AT 10%	3.791
PRESENT VALUE OF CASH RECEIPTS	5,687
PRESENT VALUE OF DOWN PAYMENT	5,000
NET PRESENT VALUE	$ 687

Such an evaluation is erroneous. The analysis of the capital investment must stand by itself, that is, in this case it must be rejected because it does not yield a 10% return. The financing must be separately analyzed. The rate of interest that the installment method requires is computed as:

$8,500 × 5 years	$42,500
Cash immediately ($40,000 less downpayment of $5,000)	35,000
Interest	$ 7,500

The financing rate of interest is approximately 7%.

$$\frac{\$35,000}{\$8,500} = 4.1176 \text{ factor}$$

Looking at a present-value annuity table for five periods, the interest rate is slightly lower than 7%.

FACTORS INFLUENCING CAPITAL INVESTMENTS

Let us now discuss some of the factors influencing capital investments. If a firm had unlimited capital resources, it could simply select those projects that meet the firm's investment standards. This is unrealistic for several reasons. Many low-profit investments or unprofitable investments must be made for reasons of law or social responsibility, such as pollution equipment or safety devices. Other investments are made to improve relations with employees. Company cafeterias and employees' recreation centers are examples. Although these kinds of investments might reduce costs and provide intangible benefits over the long run, such effects are nearly impossible to measure.

Perhaps the most difficult problem of all is that because a firm can seldom obtain all of the resources needed to fund all desired projects, it must resort to capital rationing. The result is that the firm will reject some proposals that otherwise meet its standards of profitability. Projects are ranked with due consideration given for necessary items.

Capital rationing is a function of many variables, some external to the firm and some internal such as restrictions imposed by management. The primary external factors are:

1. Imperfect capital market information
2. Restriction of flow of capital among firms
3. Difference in the firm's borrowing and lending rates of interest

Funds provided by government agencies, such as the Small Business Administration, are limited in amounts.

It is important to realize that capital rationing increases the effective cost of capital relevant to investment decisions. An opportunity cost results when the average cost of capital is raised to the rate of return that must be foregone when a profitable investment proposal is rejected. For example, if the firm's weighted average cost of capital is 10%, its effective rate increases to 16% if because of capital rationing it rejects proposals with a 16% return.

POSTEVALUATIONS

Unfortunately, many firms evaluate a proposal by a present-value model but evaluate performance (after the fact) by the accounting rate of return. Such behavior is inconsistent and likely to lead to confusion, goal incongruence, and resentment. Perhaps a more frequent weakness is that there is little or no evaluation after the fact for capital investment decisions. Granted that determination of incremental cash inflows (or outflows) may not be easy, lack of post evaluation encourages a "squeaky wheel gets the grease" attitude to proposal writing. The firm should carefully monitor the asset's performance and compare actual revenue and cost with the original estimates. Managers should be held responsible for errors and "misrepresentations" in the original proposals. One rather controversial way of forcing managers to generate savings or profit promised in proposals is to adjust their budgets accordingly.

LEASING

Before we leave capital investment problems, a word or two about leasing is in order. Leasing is commonly referred to as "off the balance sheet" financing. However, since the advent of FASB no. 13 in 1976 most long-term leases must be capitalized, that is, leases tend to be treated as purchases on the lessees' books. The present value of the lease payments is set up as an asset, and the present value of the lease payments is recorded as a liability. The asset is amortized to expense and the obligation is reduced as lease payments are made. Lease payments also include an appropriate amount for interest expense.

On the lessors' books, the opposite occurs; a capital lease is treated as a sale even though title has not been transferred. The present value of rents receivable is treated as an asset, the book value of the property is removed from the accounting records, and any difference is recorded as unearned income. As lease payments are received, the asset receivable account is reduced and a portion of the unearned income is transferred to interest income on the income statement.

The FASB requires that a lease be capitalized if it meets one of the following criteria.

Lessee
1. The lease transfers ownership of the property to the lessee by the end of the lease term.
2. The lease contains a bargain purchase option.
3. The lease term is equal to 75% or more of the estimated economic life of the leased property.
4. The present value of the minimum lease payments is 90% or more of the fair value of the leased property.*
   Lessor
   Any one of the four criteria above and both 5 and 6 below.
5. Collectibility of the minimum lease payments is reasonably predictable.
6. No important uncertainty surround the amount of unreimbursable costs yet to be incurred by the lessor under the lease.*

Operating Leases

Leases not meeting the criteria of capital leases are treated as operating leases. For an operating lease the lessor treats rent receipts as revenue and continues to retain the property as an asset on his or her balance sheet. The asset is written off to depreciation expense over its useful life. On the other hand, the lessee treats lease payments as rent expense on his or her income statement.

Obviously, the treatment of a lease as either a capital or operating lease is important for both lessor and lessee as it directly affects the amount of assets, liabilities, and retained earnings reported on the balance sheet and can shift recognition of revenue and expense to different reporting periods, thus distorting net profit and earnings per share. Most of the ratios discussed in Chapter 3 would also be affected.

Basically, leasing proposals should be analyzed much the same as capital acqusitions. The complexities of the calculation depend upon whether it is a capital lease or operating lease and how it is viewed for tax purposes. In the preceding chapter, we demonstrated how lease payments are determined, given a rate of return and the value of the leased property.

Leasing, popular for many reasons:

1. Helps avoid ownership risks
2. May offer some tax advantages
3. Avoids risk of obsolescence in some cases

---

*FASB no. 13, "Accounting for Leases," Financial Accounting Standards Board, 1976.

4. Avoids restrictive covenents or prohibitions against additional debt in certain cases
5. Might be used when conventional means of financing are not available
6. Sometimes provides more flexible terms of payment than might be available through direct borrowing
7. Might be less costly than borrowing funds to purchase an asset
8. May result in "off the balance sheet financing," but footnote disclosure is required

SUMMARY

In this chapter we discussed capital acquisition models, capital disinvestment decisions, and leasing. We reviewed proposal preparation, evaluation, and implementation. Particular attention was given to models incorporating the time value of money.

Capital investment decisions tend to be long-term, incur relatively high risk, and involve substantial sums of money; therefore, the decisions should not be made lightly.

16. Managing Inventories

Inventory control is very important for manufacturing and retail firms because the dollars invested in inventories tend to be large both in an absolute sense and as a percentage of total assets. When inventories are sold, their costs are transferred from the balance sheet to the income statement as cost of goods sold. Cost of goods sold is likely to be the largest expense appearing on the income statement; therefore, the timing of sales and method of valuing cost of goods sold can have a substantial impact on net income during a particular accounting period.

BALANCE SHEET

Inventories are classified as current assets on the balance sheet. They are usually detailed by type of inventory: raw material, work in process and finished goods. An alternate classification is direct labor, direct material, and manufacturing overhead. In addition, the method of valuing the inventory (e.g., cost or lower of cost or market) and the method of cost flow (e.g., last in/first out; first in/first out; average, etc.) are normally disclosed. We explain these cost flow methods later in the chapter.

How current an asset inventories are depends to a large extent on the firm's operating cycle, the period of time it takes the firm to convert resources expended back into cash. Some firms have a long lead time such as the construction industry or shipbuilding. For these firms it may take a couple of years before raw material is converted into work in process, finished goods, accounts receivable, and finally cash. Still, inventories are normally classified as current assets, even if they are not always converted into cash within a one year period.

INCOME STATEMENT

We said that when products are sold, their costs are transferred to cost of goods sold. A condensed version of the cost-of-goods-sold portion of the income statement is as follows:

Sales	$4,000,000	100%

Cost of goods sold:	
Beginning inventory	$60,000

Cost of goods manufactured (purchases)	2,000,000		
Goods available for sale	$2,060,000		
Ending inventory	160,000		
Cost of goods sold		1,900,000	48%
Gross profit		$2,100,000	52%

Every dollar of inefficiency in controlling inventory reduces gross profit and net profit before taxes by one dollar. It is little wonder, then, that control of inventory costs is crucial to the goal of profit maximization. Accounting for inventory cost is complex. One must consider what:

1. Goods are properly classified as inventory.
2. Costs are considered inventoriable.
3. Cost flow assumption is adopted.

We discuss each of these in turn.

ITEMS TO INCLUDE AS INVENTORY

The general rule is to include as inventory only those items to which the firm has legal title; therefore, you need to have an understanding of the term FOB meaning "free on board." FOB shipping point means that title passes to the buyer when the goods have been delivered by the seller to a common carrier who acts as an agent for the buyer. On the other hand, FOB destination means that title does not pass until the buyer receives the goods from the common carrier. A few illustrations make these concepts clear.

1. Seller ships an order to buyer marked FOB Chicago. Title passes to buyer in Chicago regardless of the original shipping point or point of destination.

2. Seller ships FOB destination. Buyer's plant is in Los Angeles. Title passes when the goods are received in Los Angeles.

3. Seller ships FOB shipping point. Seller's shipping point is Philadelphia. Hence, buyer obtains title and assumes risk of ownership in Philadelphia.

All goods to which a firm has title must be included in inventory. A firm would include items in transit that were sold but shipped FOB destination. It would also include goods purchased and shipped FOB shipping point even though they have not yet been physically received. On the other hand, it would not include goods purchased FOB destination that have not yet been received or goods sold FOB shipping point that have already been delivered to the shipping point. In the latter case, title has already been transferred to the buyer.

Goods in the hands of a consignee are included in the consignor's inventory, or stated another way, goods being held for sale by the consignee but where title rests in the consignor can not be included in the consignee's inventory.

INVENTORIABLE COSTS

Under generally accepted accounting principles, inventory is initially recorded on the books at cost. Should cost exceed market, companies generally write down the inventory to market and recognize the writedown as a loss in the current period. This practice is called "lower of cost or market." If market exceeds cost it is usually not permissible to record inventory at market since this would result in recognizing profit prior to the time of sale. Possible exceptions are when firm market prices exist (e.g., agricultural products under government guaranteed programs) or when costs cannot be accurately measured (e.g., cattle raising). However, in the remainder of this chapter we assume that inventory is carried at cost.

Inventoriable costs include all charges directly related to bringing the goods to the buyer's plant and converting them into a salable condition. Some of these costs are:

1. Purchase price of goods
2. Commission paid
3. Freight
4. Setup and installation
5. Testing

For expediency, purchase discounts taken are usually deducted from purchases except when the potential amount of discounts applicable to unpaid inventories (accounts payable) is large. Then, theoretically, the firm should estimate the amount of discounts and reduce inventories and accounts payable accordingly.

Interest cost associated with the purchase or manufacture of inventories is expensed as a period cost and not included as part of inventoriable cost. Examples of other period costs are selling expense, general and administrative expense, purchasing, and storage cost. Storage is excluded from inventory primarily because of the difficulty of measuring the amount applicable to each item.

COST FLOW ASSUMPTIONS

Cost flow assumptions refer to the method of accounting for the flow of costs in the accounting records. It does not refer to the physical movement of a particular item. If goods are purchased or manufactured on varying dates for varying amounts, there must be a way of determining which cost to transfer from inventory accounts. We explain and demonstrate several methods later in the chapter.

INVENTORY CONTROL RATIOS

Of several basic inventory control ratios, perhaps the most well known is the relationship of cost of goods sold to sales, and its complement, the gross profit percentage. In the preceding illustration, it costs the firm $.48 to manufacture each dollar of sales. Stated another way each dollar of sales generated $.52 gross profit. Firms tend to watch cost of goods sold very closely as many of its components are controllable. Cost of goods sold and gross profit should be detailed by major product line for comparison with previous periods and industry ratios.

Inventory turnover and number of days of inventory on hand basically measure the same thing—liquidity of inventory. The formulas with assumed data are:

$$\text{Turnover} = \frac{\text{Cost of Goods Sold}}{\text{Average Inventory}} = \frac{\$1,000,000}{\dfrac{\$300,000 + \$200,000}{2}} = 4 \text{ Times}$$

$$\text{Number of days in a year Inventory Turnover } \frac{365}{4} = 91.2 \text{ Days}$$

Variations in the formula consist of using a 5 or 6 day work week; 260 or 312 days respectively in the numerator.

A common error made in computing the inventory turnover is to divide the average inventory into sales rather than into cost of goods sold. This is wrong because sales include profit, whereas inventories do not.

The above ratios measure how quickly inventory is sold. Generally, firms strive for high turnover and low number of days of inventory on hand. A word of caution—too low an inventory will cause stockouts to occur. Keep in mind that the above ratios are affected by what costs are inventoried, the method of valuing inventory, and cost flow assumptions.

QUANTITY TO ORDER

How does a firm know what quantity to order and the frequency of orders? These are not mutually exclusive problems. A firm does not want to carry too much inventory as holding excess inventory is expensive. Frequent ordering and stockout costs are also high, and the firm must find a way of balancing them. It does this through a mathematical technique called economic order quantity.

Excess inventory costs include:

1. Storage
2. Handling

3. Property taxes
4. Insurance
5. Interest on capital invested in inventory
6. Spoilage, obsolescence, and theft
7. Clerical work of keeping track of inventory
8. Physical security of inventory

Costs of ordering consist of:

1. Acquiring recent price quotations
2. Preparing and approving purchase orders
3. Receiving, counting, and storing merchandise
4. Loss of quantity discounts

Stockout costs include:

1. Assembly line shutdowns
2. Inefficient size production runs
3. Lost sales
4. Penalties for late completion of contracts
5. Substitution of different material

The optimum amount to purchase at one time is the quantity which minimizes the total inventory purchasing and carrying costs. This amount can be computed by the economic order quantity formula (EOQ). Let us look at the diagram in Exhibit 16-1.

The optimum order size occurs at the point where cost of the total annual purchase order intersects with the annual carrying cost. If the line is extended upward, it will touch the total annual relevant cost line at its lowest point. The quantity to be ordered is 4,000 units. Although preparing such a diagram can be tedious, its advantage is that a visual inspection of the slope of the lines gives a notion of how sensitive the data are to changes in any one of the variables.

Economic Order Quantity (EOQ)

Sensitivity can also be measured through simulation utilizing the economic order quantity formula. The EOQ formula mathematically computes the optimum order size. Although it is frequently criticized because of the detailed cost data required, such criticism is unwarranted. A well-managed firm should be

Exhibit 16-1
Optimum Order Size

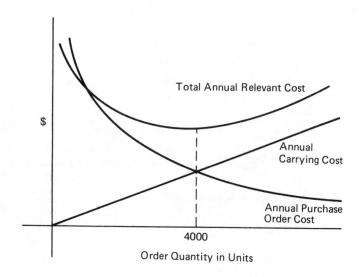

cognizant of these costs anyway. One way of measuring sensitivity to inaccuracies in input is to recompute EOQ under varying assumptions.

The EOQ formula is:

$$EOQ = \sqrt{\frac{2\,AP}{UI}}$$

A = quantity of inventory required for period
P = cost of placing one order
U = cost per unit
I = inventory carrying costs expressed as a
    percentage of unit cost

To illustrate the use of the EOQ formula, assume a firm wants to know what
is the optimum order size of the handles of an electrical appliance. The pertinent data and the solution are:

Yearly demand   A = 20,000 handles
Cost of one order   P = $200

Cost per handle $\qquad$ U = $10
Inventory carrying costs I = 5%

$$EOQ = \sqrt{\frac{2(20,000)\,(200)}{(10)\,(.05)}}$$

$$= \sqrt{\frac{8,000,000}{.50}}$$

$$= \sqrt{16,000,000}$$

$$= 4,000 \text{ handles}$$

The firm should order 4,000 handles at a time and place five (20,000 demand/4,000 per order) orders a year. If the EOQ results in an odd number and the firm cannot place an odd-lot order, the quantity is adjusted to the nearest lot size.

The EOQ is based on several assumptions:

1. A known constant demand
2. Known constant ordering costs
3. Known constant carrying costs
4. Unlimited production and inventory capacity

TIMING OF ORDERS

How does a firm know when to place an order? First, it is necessary to know the lead time, that is, the number of days between the date of placing the purchase order and the date of receiving the goods. If the firm in the preceding example uses 100 handles a day and it takes six days to receive an order, the lead time demand is 600 (100 × 6) handles.

Most manufacturing firms carry safety stock because, as mentioned previously, the cost of stockouts can be high. Past experience tempered by judgment can be used to estimate the amount of safety stock. Keep in mind though that the cost of carrying safety stock is included in the EOQ. Assuming safety stock is 1,000 handles or ten days of sales, a graph showing the flow of events looks like Exhibit 16-2.

Note that the safety stock is a constant 1,000 units or 10 days. If it takes 6 days to receive an order the firm places an order when the stock falls to 16 (10 + 6) days of inventory, which is 1,600 units. The quantity ordered is 4,000 units as determined by the EOQ formula. On the 40th day (5000 units − 1000 safety stock/100 units a day), the 4,000 units are received and thus added to the 1,000 units of safety stock to bring the total inventory back to 5,000 units.

Exhibit 16-2
Timing of Orders

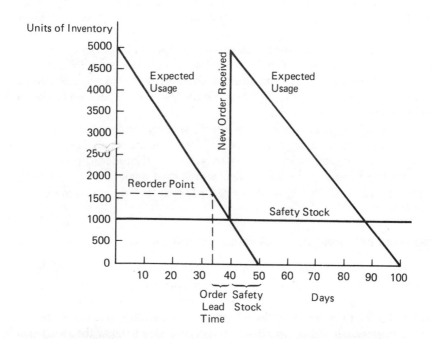

Then the cycle repeats itself. Remember, however, that Exhibit 16-2 diagrams normative behavior rather than actual experience.

OTHER ORDERING PROCEDURES

The economic order quantity lends itself well to an automatic ordering system. When stock reaches a certain low point, orders are automatically placed to replenish the stock. Such a procedure is easily programmable into a computer.

A variation of the automatic order system is the order cycling or cycle review method. Inventory items are classified into cycles. On a regular or periodic cycle, say, every 30 or 60 days, a review is made of the material on hand, and orders are placed accordingly. This method is more suitable for small firms who cannot afford sophisticated computer services.

The min-max method establishes a basic minimum and maximum quantity of inventory for each item. Minimum levels provide adequate protection against stockout. When the level reaches the minimum, a purchase order is placed to increase the level to the maximum. This method is more suitable for repetitious orders of stable stock rather than unusual unique items.

Some firms grade their inventory according to value. Such a plan is called the ABC plan. High-dollar items (Grade A) have low safety stock, detailed accounting records, and a frequent review of ordering needs. On the other hand, Grade C consists of low-priced items. A perpetual inventory system may not be used. Predetermined ordering points reduce the need for extensive review of items on hand. Safety stock tends to be high and physical control procedures less elaborate than Grade A. Grade B items fall between Grades A and C in theory and treatment.

The two-bin system is a method of establishing reorder points based on the physical depletion of stock in the first bin. Two bins are maintained; the first bin carries only enough stock to satisfy usage during the ordering period while the second bin contains the safety stock and normal amount used from order date to delivery date. Requisitions are placed when the first bin is empty.

OPTIMUM ORDERING OF PERISHABLE PRODUCTS

In retailing, the question often arises as to how many units of a perishable product should be ordered. Since the product cannot be carried in stock indefinitely, the goal is to minimize losses from spoilage without losing excessive potential sales. First, we must identify probabilities at various levels of demand (past experience should be helpful). It is also necessary to know the acquisition cost, salvage value, selling price, and cost of any illwill due to shortages. Of these illwill is the only difficult variable to measure.

Consider the following problem. We are trying to determine the optimum number of units to be ordered. Assume:

A = $5 per unit (cost is $6 a unit minus $1 salvage value).
B = $15 per unit computed:

Sales price	$18
Cost	5
Profit per unit	$13
Illwill if shortage	2
	$15

We calculate the critical probability (P) by the following formula:

$$P = \frac{A}{A + B} = \frac{5}{5 + 15} = .25$$

The probability distribution is as follows:

QUANTITY OF UNITS DEMANDED	PROBABILITY OF DEMAND	CUMULATIVE PROBABILITY
0	.1	1.0
1	.1	.9
2	.2	.8
3	.3	.6
4	.2	.3
5	.1	.1

The cumulative probability column tells us the probability of an additional unit being sold. For example, if we order one unit, it has a .90 chance of being sold, two units has a .80 chance of both being sold, and so on. We should increase the quantity ordered until the cumulative probability of selling one or more units in excess of quantity ordered is equal to .25, if possible, but not less than .25. This quantity is four units. If we try selling five units, the cumulative probability of selling all five units is .10, which is less than the critical probability of .25.

INVENTORY COST FLOW METHODS

We now discuss methods of recording inventory in the accounting records. There are two ways of establishing an inventory value at the end of an accounting period: (1) periodic and (2) perpetual. Both methods rely on taking a physical inventory, but the purpose of the physical inventory is different. Under the periodic method the dollar amount determined from extending the physical count of the inventory is used primarily to calculate an updated inventory figure for financial statement purposes. During interim accounting periods the firm does not know the cost of inventory on hand and must rely on an estimation method (e.g., gross profit or retail) if it wishes to prepare interim financial statements.

Detailed inventory records by stock items are maintained under the perpetual system. These records show at all times the balance on hand (in quantity and dollars). The balance is updated for each purchase and sale. The purpose of the physical inventory is to "correct" the accounting records. Obviously, a perpetual inventory system is far superior to the periodic method from the viewpoint of planning and control. Its advantages are that it:

1. Supplies a more reliable inventory figure for interim financial statements
2. Safeguards against errors, theft, and defalcations

3. Prevents over- or understocking of inventory
4. Aids in scheduling
5. Provides data for decision models
6. Facilitates material variance analysis (price and quantity)
7. Helps in budgeting and managing cash

Perpetual inventory systems are costly and therefore not suitable for firms marketing a high volume of low-priced items. The computer has made it possible for many firms which heretofore could not afford a perpetual inventory system to integrate inventory control with purchasing, production, and marketing. For example, major grocery chains have revolutionized their check-out procedures to:

1. Provide customers with sales slips itemizing goods purchased by type, quantity, and price
2. Recalculate the balance of items in stock
3. Reorder automatically at designated reorder points

If prices were constant, it would not be necessary to maintain a perpetual inventory in dollars, but when prices fluctuate we need some way of knowing the cost of items used in production or sold. There are four common ways of accounting for inventory cost.

1. Direct identification
2. First in/first out (FIFO)
3. Last in/first out (LIFO)
4. Average

None of these methods except direct identification has anything to do wth the actual physical movement of a particular inventory item.

Direct Identification

Under this method each item has a serial number or some means of physically identifying it. Direct identification is used for large expensive goods, such as diamonds, automobiles, airplanes, and so forth. When an item is sold, its cost (as identified by the serial number) is removed from the inventory account and transferred to cost of goods sold. Unsold items remain in inventory.

On the surface, direct identification sounds like the ideal method. It is not suitable for low-dollar items that are not easily identifiable or that may be too costly do do so, such as cans of peas in a grocery store. Moreover, it allows managers to manipulate income by selling those units that serve their goals.

For example, if managers wanted to increase profits this period, they could do so by selling low-cost units, whereas if they wanted to decrease profits they would concentrate on moving high-cost units.

First in/First out (FIFO)

We now illustrate the remaining three methods of accounting for inventory cost under a perpetual inventory system. Each method is adaptable to the periodic system too. Intermediate financial accounting textbooks can be consulted for an explanation of this and many other available inventory techniques that are beyond the scope of this book.

For each illustration you should trace through all calculations to be sure you thoroughly understand the procedures. They are all based on the following assumed data.

		NO. OF UNITS	PER UNIT COST	TOTAL
1/1	purchase	10	5.00	50.00
1/5	purchase	40	5.20	208.00
1/18	purchase	30	5.30	159.00
1/24	purchase	30	5.35	160.50
		110		
1/12	sales	5		
1/17	sales	20		
1/25	sales	40		
		65		

First in/first out assumes that the first item acquired is the first item sold, meaning that when a sale is made, the cost of the first item acquired is transferred to cost of goods sold. Note that inventory on hand at the end of the period consists of the latest buys; consequently in an inflationary economy, these buys will tend to be the highest-cost orders. Cost of goods sold reflects the lower-cost items.

A perpetual inventory record for one product looks like Exhibit 16-3. The ending inventory is 45 units valued at $240 ($79.50 + $160.50). Cost of goods sold is $337,50.

Last in/First Out (LIFO)

Last in/first out assumes that the last item acquired is the first item sold and transferred to cost of goods sold. Inventory reflects "old" buys at a lower price.

Exhibit 16-3
Perpetual Inventory Record—FIFO

		PURCHASES			COST OF SALES			INVENTORY BALANCE		
DATE	EXPLANATION	NO. OF UNITS	UNIT COST	TOTAL COSTS	NO. OF UNITS	UNIT COST	TOTAL COSTS	NO. OF UNITS	UNIT COST	TOTAL COSTS
1/1	P 10 units	10	$5.00	$50.00				10	$5.00	$50.00
1/5	P 40 units	40	5.20	208.00				10	5.00	50.00
								40	5.20	208.00
1/12	S 5 units				5	$5.00	$25.00	5	5.00	25.00
								40	5.20	208.00
1/17	S 20 units				5	5.00	25.00	25	5.20	130.00
					15	5.20	78.00			
1/18	P 30 units	30	5.30	159.00				25	5.20	130.00
								30	5.30	159.00
1/24	P 30 units	30	5.35	160.50				25	5.20	130.00
								30	5.30	159.00
								30	5.35	160.50
1/25	S 40 units				25	5.20	130.00	15	5.30	79.50
					15	5.30	79.50	30	5.35	160.50
				$577.50			$337.50			

High-cost items are in cost of goods sold. The inventory record is displayed as Exhibit 16-4.

The ending inventory is $234.00, and the cost of goods sold is $343.50.

Average

There are several ways of computing the average. We demonstrate with a moving average in Exhibit 16-5.

The average unit cost is recomputed after each purchase. When sales are made, the latest average unit cost is transferred to cost of goods sold. Ending inventory is $237.46 and cost of goods sold is $340.04. Note that the average method results in ending inventory and cost of goods sold partway between FIFO and LIFO. See Exhibit 16-6.

We purposely selected low numbers to make the arithmetic easy, but if you multiply the above figures by a million you can readily see that the dollar difference between inventory cost flow methods can be substantial. Also, if the time period is lengthened to reflect wider variations in material cost, the differences among the three methods are highlighted.

Exhibit 16-4
Perpetual Inventory Record—LIFO

DATE	EXPLANATION	PURCHASES NO. OF UNITS	UNIT COST	TOTAL COSTS	COST OF SALES NO. OF UNITS	UNIT COST	TOTAL COSTS	INVENTORY BALANCE NO. OF UNITS	UNIT COST	TOTAL COSTS
1/1	P 10 units	10	$5.00	$50.00				10	$5.00	$50.00
1/5	P 40 units	40	5.20	208.00				10	5.00	50.00
								40	5.20	208.00
1/12	S 5 units				5	$5.20	$26.00	10	5.00	50.00
								35	5.20	182.00
1/17	S 20 units				20	5.20	104.00	10	5.00	50.00
								15	5.20	78.00
1/18	P 30 units	30	5.30	159.00				10	5.00	50.00
								15	5.20	78.00
								30	5.30	159.00
1/24	P 30 units	30	5.35	160.50				10	5.00	50.00
								15	5.20	78.00
								30	5.30	159.00
								30	5.35	160.50
1/25	S 40 units				30	5.35	160.50	10	5.00	50.00
					10	5.30	53.00	15	5.20	78.00
								20	5.30	106.00
				$577.50			$343.50			

Exhibit 16-5
Perpetual Inventory Record—Moving Average

DATE	EXPLANATION	PURCHASES NO. OF UNITS	UNIT COST	TOTAL COSTS	COST OF SALES NO. OF UNITS	UNIT COST	TOTAL COSTS	INVENTORY BALANCE NO. OF UNITS	UNIT COST	TOTAL COSTS
1/1	P 10 units	10	$5.00	$50.00				10	$5.00	$50.00
1/5	P 40 units	40	5.20	208.00				50	5.160	258.00
1/12	S 5 units				5	$5.16	$25.80	45	5.160	232.20
1/17	S 20 units				20	5.16	103.20	25	5.160	129.00
1/18	P 30 units	30	5.30	159.00				55	5.236	288.00
1/24	P 30 units	30	5.35	160.50				85	5.276	448.50
1/25	S 40 units				40	5.276	211.04	45	5.276	237.46
				$577.50			$340.04			

Exhibit 16-6
Comparison of LIFO, FIFO, and Moving
Average

	ENDING INVENTORY	COST OF GOODS SOLD
LIFO	$234.00	$343.50
FIFO	$240.00	$337.50
Average	$237.46	$340.04

SELECTION OF METHODS

During periods of rising prices (inflation), LIFO results in a lower asset value on the balance sheet, a higher cost of goods sold on the income statement, and consequently a lower net profit figure. FIFO results in higher inventory, higher assets, higher retained earnings because of lower cost of goods sold, and higher profit. During periods of falling prices the opposite effects occur for each method.

Inventory valuation can have important implications for financial statements, inflation accounting, and tax management. We discuss each of these in later chapters.

During the last two decades there has been a swing from FIFO to LIFO. What are the advantages of LIFO? Advocates argue that:

1. Under LIFO the most recent costs are charged to cost of goods sold; hence, there is a better matching of costs with revenue.

2. In an inflationary economy LIFO results in lower profits and consequently lower cash outflow for income tax. The postponement of income tax improves cash flow and working capital. The deferred income tax can be invested in a profit-making activity.

3. LIFO virtually eliminates write-downs to lower of cost or market since the inventory is already carried on the books at a very low figure. The extent to which LIFO inventory is lower than market depends on factors such as the extent to which inflation affects the goods, lead time, and state of technology. Goods subject to rapid technological advances or style changes such as jewelry would not be valued on the books at old prices as would more stable products such as paper.

4. Since LIFO results in lower profits, any cash outflow measured by profits or retained earnings are likely to be lower. Cash dividends and cash bonuses to executives are examples.

On the other hand, those who dislike LIFO maintain that:

1. LIFO reduces profits and earnings per share, thus affecting the company's ability to raise capital.

2. The inventory on the balance sheet is understated, meaning that current assets, total assets, and total capital are also understated. All ratios computed on any of these figures are distorted. LIFO in essense creates a "secret" reserve.

3. LIFO does not completely match current cost with sales; hence it serves only as a partial hedge against inflation.

4. When layers of old costs are eliminated, LIFO can result in strange distortions of profit. For example, an item currently manufactured for $600 and sold for $1,000 results in a gross profit of $400. But if old inventory of $100 is liquidated, gross profit jumps to $900 a unit. Income taxes can be particularly severe when old inventory is sold because of strikes, shortage of material, product obsolescence, and the like.

5. LIFO allows "squirming" room for manipulation of income at year end because of buying practices. If a firm wants to increase its income in December it can postpone the purchase of inventory until January.

STANDARD COSTS

One way of circumventing the cost flow problem is through the use of a standard cost system. Recall that under standard costs direct material, direct labor, and manufacturing overhead are charged to inventory at standard. If there are no significant differences between actual and standard costs, variances can be written off on the income statement as period costs.

OTHER CONTROL PROCEDURES

Satisfactory control of inventories must extend far beyond cost control and the counting of physical inventory. It is essential that a firm establish good internal control procedures that minimize loss due to spoilage, theft, and obsolescence. Efficient purchasing, managing, and planning of inventory are dependent upon an accurate forecast of sales and production schedules. Controlling inventory is also accomplished through efficient scheduling of production. Some of these procedures include:

1. Separation of duties among individuals responsible for purchasing, receiving, inspecting, storing, and requisitioning materials, and paying invoices.
2. Inventory should be securely labeled and insured. Handling time should be kept at a minimum. Adequate bin records should be maintained.
3. Inventory should be periodically screened for obsolete items. Such items should be immediately disposed of in the most profitable manner.
4. Unused material should be immediately returned to stores and should not be allowed to accumulate on the factory floor.

5. Documentary evidence at various stages of operations is essential to monitor inventory cost and quantity.
6. Judgment plays an important role in managing inventory. Seasonal variations and other nonstatic data influencing order points must be considered.
7. Performance reporting is essential. A comparison of budgets with actual variances, explanation of variances, and corrective action reporting must be timely. A follow-up system is needed to ensure that unfavorable situations do not repeat. Many control reports should be on a management-by-exception basis. Excessive reporting should be avoided because it is costly and results in information overload.

SUMMARY

We discussed methods of controlling inventories and reviewed the placement of inventories on the financial statements and their effects on several financial ratios. What items and charges should be included as inventory were discussed and several inventory cost flow methods were illustrated.

The economic order quantity model is especially suitable for controlling excessive inventory build-up and its accompanying costs. Control over safety stock and reorder points are essential if a firm wishes to keep its inventory cost low. Keep in mind that for most manufacturing and retail establishments cost of goods sold is the largest cost charged against revenue on the income statement and must therefore be carefully controlled.

17. Taxes

What is the effect of income taxes on business decisions? The implications of
the Internal Revenue Code, which is extremely complex, are an integral part
of every business decision. Mastery of the details the tax code is a career in
itself; therefore, on completion of this chapter, you should not expect to be a
tax expert. Rather our goal is to make you sufficiently familiar with the tax
effects of various decisions that you seek tax counsel when needed, are able to
understand tax advice, and are sufficiently knowledgeable of the ramifications
of taxation to ask relevant questions.

AVOIDING AND POSTPONING TAXES

Avoiding payment of income tax, though very desirable, is many times not
possible, and the best that can be done is to postpone payment. Generally, the
longer the payment of income taxes can be deferred, the more beneficial to the
firm because the postponed amount can be invested in a profitable endeavor.
For example, if $100,000 in tax savings could be invested at 8% after tax, the
total earnings over five years would be $46,933 ($100,000 $\times$ 1.46933 =
146,933 $-$ 100,000). The factor of 1.46933 is taken from a future-value table
for n = 5 and i = 8%. Additional earnings of $46,933 would be considered a
material amount for most firms.

Again, the object is to minimize tax payments indefinitely or postpone the
payment of taxes as long as possible. We attempt to do this through legitimate
means, selecting alternatives that will best suit the circumstances. *Tax avoid-
ance,* as this is called, is legally acceptable, whereas *tax evasion,* the use of
illegal means of reducing taxes, obviously is not. Since we are not interested in
spending time in jail, we will not be discussing illegal methods of circumventing
taxes.

SELECTION OF FORM OF BUSINESS

Perhaps the first tax decision an individual must make upon establishing a business is to select the form of business he or she wishes to operate under. Of
course, there are many additional ramifications to this decision than taxes, such
as the limited liability offered stockholders in a corporation, but we limit our
discussion to the issue of taxes.

There are three basic forms of business:

1. Sole proprietorship
2. Partnership
3. Corporation

Each of these will be discussed in turn and illustrated by a comparison of the three.

Sole Proprietorship

The income (or loss) from a sole proprietorship is taxed solely on the proprietor's individual tax return (Form 1040). The proprietorship as such does not file a tax return and does not pay taxes; rather an income statement (Schedule C) is attached to the proprietor's 1040 and the business income is added to any other taxable income the owner has. Details of Schedule C closely parallel a published income statement. The full amount of profit is reported in the period earned, regardless when it is distributed to the proprietor.

Partnership

A partnership also does not pay taxes on partnership income, but it does file an information tax return. The purpose of the partnership return is to supply information, not to determine taxes due. One part of the return is basically an income statement, and another part provides details on the allocation of income or loss among partners. Each partner's portion of partnership income or loss is then reported on his or her individual tax return, Form 1040.

The income tends to maintain the same character as it did on the partnership's books and on the partnership information return. For example, dividend income or capital gains on the partnership's return are shown as dividend income or capital gains on the partner's individual tax return. This is important because these items receive favorable tax treatment. As with a proprietorship, partners report income and pay tax on it in the period earned, whether or not it is distributed to them. Drawings (asset distributions to partners) and salaries to partners are therefore irrelevant in determining the partner's share of partnership profit or loss reportable on their individual 1040s.

Corporations

A corporation files its own tax return and pays tax on its taxable earnings. The corporate tax rates (and individual tax rates) change periodically. The highest corporate rate has traditionally been about 50% of taxable income. In addition, the corporate tax rate is graduated according to level of income. In 1983 the rates were:

Taxable Income	Rate
0–$25,000	15%
$25,001–$50,000	18%
$50,001–$75,000	30%
$75,001–$100,000	40%
$100,000+	46%

These rates are likely to change in future years.

Under some circumstances it may be advantageous for tax purposes for a small corporation to be divided into more than one corporation. For example, a corporation reporting taxable earnings of $150,000 in 1983 would pay taxes of $48,750.

$25,000 × 15%	$3,750
$25,000 × 18%	4,500
$25,000 × 30%	7,500
$25,000 × 40%	10,000
$50,000 × 46%	23,000
$150,000	48,750

If the enterprise were divided into three separate corporations with each firm reporting income of $50,000, the tax for each corporation would be $8,250.

$25,000 × 15%	$3,750
$25,000 × 18%	4,500
	8,250

The taxes are $24,750 ($8,250 × 3) for the three corporations. The annual amount of tax savings as a result of the division is $24,000 ($48,750 − $24,750). The total reduction in taxes over the life of the business is the present value of the annual savings.

When corporate income is distributed to shareholders in the form of a dividend, the distribution is reported as dividend income on the shareholder's 1040 (assuming the shareholder is an individual instead of another corporation). Thus, corporate income is taxed twice, first at the corporate level and then again when distributed at the shareholder's level. Partial relief can be obtained a number of ways. First there is usually a dividend exclusion on the shareholder's return. The amount of the exclusion has fluctuated between $100 to $200 in recent years. If the exclusion is $200, the first $200 of dividend income is not taxable on the shareholder's 1040.

Second, if the shareholder works for the firm as an employee, reasonable salary may be deducted as an expense from the corporation's income, thus escaping corporate tax. Of course the salary is reported as income on the employee's 1040.

A third technique is for the shareholder to loan money to the corporation. Then the interest expense is deductible on the corporation's return but, like salary, interest income is taxable on the shareholder's return.

Finally, if dividends are not needed or desired by the shareholders the corporation can choose not to declare dividends. Other things being equal the value of the stock should increase. Through a variety of gift and estate planning techniques, the stock could be passed on to heirs at substantial tax savings. A word of caution is in order before this technique is used—bypassing dividends requires a sound business reason. Should such a reason be lacking, the Internal Revenue Service will levy a stiff excess retained earnings tax on accumulated profits.

Comparison of Three Forms of Business

We now compare the three forms of organization. Suppose a taxpayer's share of profit is $100,000. Our demonstration will use 1983 tax rates, but keep in mind that the rates change periodically for both individuals and corporations. In addition, the tax rate for an individual is dependent upon marital status and other taxable income. We assume a taxpayer who is single and whose sole taxable income is $100,000. For the corporation we assume that all earnings are distributed as dividends during the taxable year. Calculations are provided in Exhibit 17-1.

In this illustration the corporate form results in $12,825 additional tax. The amount of additional tax incurred by the three forms of business depends on several factors, the most important being the tax bracket of the shareholder and the amount of corporate profit.

What if the corporate earnings are not distributed as dividends? Then the short-range comparison is between $39,473 for the sole proprietorship or partnership and $25,750 for the corporation. Clearly, then the corporate form would result in the lowest taxes. Determination of tax savings for only one period is insufficient, since selection of a business form is a long-range decision and the savings are of a recurring nature. Keep in mind that over the long run, we must compute the tax savings utilizing present-value techniques.

Small corporations meeting certain criteria can elect to be treated as a partnership. This election (called Subchapter S corporation) allows an enterprise to operate legally as a corporation but be taxed as a partnership.

Exhibit 17-1
Comparison of Taxes Under
Three Forms of Business

		TAX
PROPRIETORSHIP OR PARTNERSHIP		$39,473
CORPORATION CORPORATE TAX	$25,750	
SHAREHOLDERS' TAX ($100,000 — 25,750 CORPORATE INCOME — $100 DIVIDEND EXCLUSION) TIMES TAX RATE	26,548	52,298
Difference		$12,825

ACCRUAL OR CASH BASIS ACCOUNTING

The second decision an individual must make when commencing a business is to decide whether the accounting records are to be kept on the accrual or cash basis. The accrual basis recognizes revenue when the firm has a legal right to the income and recognizes expense when a firm incurs a legal obligation. The cash basis recognizes income or expense when cash is exchanged. Generally, a taxpayer has more control over the timing of transactions with the cash basis. However, the Internal Revenue Service has decreed that where inventory is a material income-producing item, the accrual basis must be used; therefore, merchandising firms and manufacturing firms are usually required to use the accrual basis.

DEPRECIATION METHOD

Traditionally, selection of depreciation methods has made possible substantial tax savings. In recent years the Congress has established recovery periods to be used for tax purposes in lieu of one of the four generally accepted accounting methods. These recovery periods are similar to the accelerated depreciation methods (declining balance and sum of years digits) in that they result in more depreciation and consequently lower taxes during the early life of an asset than the straight-line depreciation method. The IRS's recovery periods and accelerated methods are in essence tax postponement techniques.

For example, suppose a corporation buys a new machine for $100,000 with an estimated life of eight years for the books and uses the IRS recovery life of five years for tax purposes. The first tax advantage the corporation might enjoy

Exhibit 17-2
Tax Savings from Depreciation

YEAR	APPLICABLE PERCENTAGE	DEPRECIATION	TAX RATE	TAX SAVINGS
1	15%	$15,000	46%	6,900
2	22%	22,000	46%	10,120
3	21%	21,000	46%	9,660
4	21%	21,000	46%	9,660
5	21%	21,000	46%	9,660
		$100,000		$46,000

is the investment credit, a direct reduction of taxes payable. The rules regarding investment credit (e.g., the percentage allowed, type of equipment, and life of the item) vary by year. We assume an investment tax credit rate of 10% of machine cost. This means that 10% or $10,000 is deductible directly from the corporate tax (not the taxable income) in the year of the machine acquisition. The method of accounting for the $10,000 on the accounting records is irrelevant insofar as calculation of taxes payable and cash outflow are concerned.

Depreciation expense and the amount of tax savings per the tax return are computed in Exhibit 17-2.

The tax saving each year for straight-line depreciation, assuming no salvage value and a tax rate of 46%, is $5,750.

$$\frac{\$100,000}{8} \times 46\% = \$5,750$$

If the firm could earn an 8% rate of return after tax, the total tax saving from the shorter IRS recovery periods is $6,727 (see Exhibit 17-3). The percentages allowed for the IRS recovery periods depends on the year the asset is put into service and the class of property.

Some firms may find it more attactive to lease property. The 1981 Economic Recovery Tax Act liberalized tax treatment of leveraged leases and sale and leaseback transactions. There is also special tax treatment for expenditures for energy savings and rehabilitation of low-income housing. Such special items are beyond the scope of this book.

RESEARCH AND EXPERIMENTAL EXPENDITURES

Some firms may want to expand their research and experimentation expenditures in order to take advantage of the more recent liberalized tax treatment,

Exhibit 17-3
Comparison of Tax Savings Between
IRS and Book Depreciation

| | TAX SAVINGS | | | | TOTAL |
YEAR	TAX RETURN	BOOKS	DIFFERENCE	FACTOR	EARNINGS
1	$ 6,900	$ 5,750	$1,150	.8509(a)	$ 979
2	10,120	5,750	4,370	.7138	3,119
3	9,660	5,750	3,910	.5869	2,295
4	9,660	5,750	3,910	.4693	1,835
5	9,660	5,750	3,910	.3605	1,410
6		5,750	(5,750)	.2597	(1,494)
7		5,750	(5,750)	.1664	(957)
8		5,750	(5,750)	.0800	(460)
	$46,000	$46,000	0		$6,727

(a) FV table, n = 8, i = 8%, factor 1.8509 − 1.0000

such as a new tax credit, allowed under certain circumstances. United States research and development expenditures made by multinational corporations are now fully deductible, whereas before they were allocated to worldwide income.

INVENTORY ACCOUNTING

Another tax postponement technique is the method of accounting for inventory costs. Of the three popular methods LIFO results in the lowest taxes payable because it results in the lowest income. Our brief review of the three methods can be supplemented with details from Chapter 16. LIFO assumes that the cost of the last item acquired is assigned to the first item sold. In an inflationary economy like that of the United States, recently acquired inventory costs more than older inventory. Therefore, under LIFO current costs are transferred to cost of goods sold, which results in less income and less tax.

FIFO, which is the opposite of LIFO, assumes that the oldest items acquired are the first items sold. Cost of goods sold is lower than under LIFO, and profits and taxes are higher. Under the average method, by which costs are transferred to cost of goods sold based on average cost, net income is about halfway between LIFO and FIFO.

We repeat: LIFO results in lower income and lower taxes and is thus a tax postponement technique. The general rule is that when inventories are a material income-producing item, the tax method of accounting for inventory must be the same as the cost flow method used in the accounting records; the firm cannot use LIFO for tax purposes and FIFO for book purposes.

CAPITAL GAINS AND LOSSES

Items qualifying as capital gains are awarded preferential tax treatment. Although the laws in this area are too numerous and complicated to discuss here, generally, you should have an understanding of what a capital gain is and its significance. Gains or losses from the disposition of most capital assets and investments (e.g., land, buildings, equipment, investment in stock) are capital gains or losses. Capital items are taxed at more favorable rates than ordinary income. If the capital gain is long term (the asset was held for more than six months) only 40% of the gain is taxable. Hence the maximum tax is 20% as compared to a 46% maximum rate on ordinary income for corporations and 20% versus 50% for individuals.

DIVIDEND INCOME CREDIT

Corporations are allowed a 85% credit from dividends received as a result of investment in another corporation's stock. This is an attempt to avoid triple taxing of income earned by a subsidiary:

1. As income on the subsidiary's corporate return
2. As dividends paid by the subsidiary to the parent
3. As dividends distributed by the parents to its shareholders

For example, if a parent corporation receives $10,000 dividend from another corporation, 85% can be excluded from the parent's income, thus only 15% or $1,500 is taxed on the parent's corporate return.

COMPENSATION

In the area of compensation several tax-saving devices are available. Incentive stock options result in no tax consequences to the firm or employee when the option is granted or when it is exercised. Stock options entitle employees to purchase shares of their employer's stock at a fixed price during a specific period of time. Should the market price of the stock increase the employee exercises the option. The gain from exercising the option (difference between market price and option price) is not taxed until the stock is disposed of and then at favorable capital gains rates.

Employers who meet certain criteria can take a tax credit up to $3,000 for wages paid to employees rceiving training under work incentive programs certified by the secretary of labor.

Employer's paid insurance and other fringe benefits may be desirable for both the employer and the employee because they are deductible on the corporation's tax return but not taxable as compensation on the employee's return.

Pension plans are another way in which the employer can receive an immediate deduction. Employees pay tax only when benefits are received after retirement when they are likely to be in lower tax brackets.

High tax bracket employees may benefit from deferred compensation plans. It is essential that employees study a deferred compensation plan thoroughly. The reduction in taxes from lower rates during retirement must be compared with the opportunity cost of investing the after-tax proceeds if the compensation were received immediately.

NET OPERATING LOSSES

Firms suffering net operating losses during the current year have the option of carrying the loss back a stated number of years or carrying it forward to future years. The effect of carrying it back is an immediate refund of taxes previously paid whereas a loss carry-forward reduces future years' taxes. Usually, it is preferable to carry a net operating loss back because immediate receipt of cash inflow is preferable to future reduction of cash outflow. The exception is when major tax credits are lost permanently from a loss carryback.

A loss carry-forward can be viewed as an asset and may be a positive feature in merger negotiations. At a 46% tax rate, a $100,000 loss carry-forward will result in a $46,000 reduction of future taxes. Of course use of a loss carry-forward is predicated on the firm's being profitable in future years.

TAX EXEMPT INCOME

Taxpayers in high tax brackets may find investing in municipal bonds attractive. Interest received from city, state and certain nonprofit organizations' securities is nontaxable. The interest yield is usually lower for tax exempt bonds than other bonds. To determine if tax exempt bonds are preferable to taxable securities it is necessary to compare after-tax income of the various alternatives.

Consider the situation shown in Exhibit 17-4 for a taxpayer in the 50% tax bracket. Clearly the municipal bonds are a better investment in the amount of $1,000 ($7,000 − $6,000).

USE OF DEBT

Use of debt in the capital structure rather than preferred or common stock usually results in lower taxes because interest is deductible in arriving at corporate taxable income whereas dividends are not. In the following example

Exhibit 17-4

Comparison of Taxes on

Taxable and Tax Exempt Bonds

	NONTAX-EXEMPT INDUSTRIAL BONDS 12% INTEREST	TAX-EXEMPT MUNICIPAL BONDS 7%
INVESTMENT IN BONDS	$100,000	$100,000
INTEREST BEFORE TAXES	$ 12,000	$7,000
INCOME TAX, 50%	6,000	0
NET INCOME AFTER TAXES	$ 6,000	$7,000

(Exhibit 17-5) we assume that the firm has a choice of obtaining capital by issuing 10% bonds or 10% preferred stock. Note that the interest expense is deducted toward taxable income, whereas preferred stock dividends are subtracted after taxable income is calculated. The firm has $230,000 ($270,000 − $40,000) more profit if it finances with bonds rather than preferred stock. Keep in mind that this is an annual savings that accrues to the common stockholders.

INSTALLMENT METHOD

Whenever possible, recognition of revenue should be deferred as long as possible. One way of doing this, called the installment method, allows profit to be

Exhibit 17-5

Comparison of Debt Versus Preferred Stock

	10% BONDS (IN 000)	10% PREFERRED STOCK (IN 000)
AMOUNT FINANCED	$5,000	$5,000
NET INCOME BEFORE INTEREST OR DIVIDENDS	$1,000	$1,000
INTEREST EXPENSE 10%	500	
TAXABLE INCOME	500	1,000
TAX EXPENSE 46%	230	460
INCOME AFTER TAX	270	540
DIVIDENDS	0	500
	$270	$40

recognized for tax purposes when the cash is received rather than when the sale is consummated. Incidentally, under generally accepted accounting principles, the installment method is usually not acceptable for book purposes. Exhibit 17-6 illustrates its tax advantage:

Exhibit 17-6
Comparison of Installment Method
With Recognition of Immediate Revenue

	REGULAR BASIS	INSTALLMENT BASIS
INSTALLMENT SALES	$500,000	
COST OF SALES	$300,000	
ACCOUNTING INCOME	$200,000	
GROSS PROFIT $\frac{\$200,000}{\$500,000}$	40%	
CASH COLLECTED IN YEAR OF SALE		$100,000
TAXABLE INCOME ($100,000 × 40%)		$40,000

The remaining $160,000 profit is reportable on tax returns in future years as cash received. Remember, our general guideline: The longer you can postpone taxes, the more preferable it is.

CHANGES IN TAX RATES

Income tax rates have not been constant in recent years. When devising a tax strategy, the taxpayer must consider the effect of future changes in tax rates. Obviously if rates are expected to decrease we want to postpone recognition of revenue as long as possible in order that (1) the revenue be taxed at lower rates and (2) payment of taxes be deferred. What if tax rates are expected to increase? Now the decision is not so clear. Let us consider an example. Assume that the tax rate is expected to increase from 48 to 53%. Should the firm attempt to postpone recognition of $100,000 revenue from year 1 to year 2? The analysis is performed in Exhibit 17-7. A 5% tax rate increase is not sufficient to conclude that reporting the $100,000 should be postponed until year 2 because the earning power of the postponed tax is not sufficient to offset the tax rate increase.

Not all examples will lead to the same conclusion. Variables such as the amount of increase in the tax rate, the earning power of the postponed tax, and the number of years the income is deferred affect the result. Thus each problem

Exhibit 17-7

Effect of Change in Tax Rate — Revenue

	YEAR 1	YEAR 2
AMOUNT OF REVENUE	$100,000	$100,000
TAX RATE	48%	53%
TAX	$ 48,000	$53,000
INCOME AFTER TAXES	$ 52,000	$47,000
EARNINGS ON $48,000 ($100,000 — 52,000) DURING YEAR 1 AT 8% (NET OF TAXES)		3,840
INCOME AFTER TAXES		$50,840

must be studied individually. Also, be aware that the above example assumes that deferral of revenue recognition is legally possible and we considered only the cash outflow for taxes and not when the $100,000 is received. If the choice includes a cash receipt of $100,000, in year 1 as well as deferral of revenue for tax purposes to year 2, then the 8% earnings should be calculated on $100,000.

Analysis of expense deferred is just the opposite of revenue. If a taxpayer expects tax rates to decrease, clearly the deduction should be taken in the earliest year in order to (1) maximize the tax effect of the deduction and (2) reduce tax payments as soon as possible. But if tax rates are expected to increase, an analysis like the one illustrated above must be performed. Here is an example. Suppose tax rates are scheduled to increase from 46 to 48%. Interest is 8% after tax. Should a firm deduct $200,000 of expense in the current year if the expense could legitimately be postponed until next year? Exhibit 17-8 shows that it is preferable by an amount of $3,360 to deduct the $200,000 in year 1.

CHARITABLE CONTRIBUTIONS

If a taxpayer makes a charitable contribution, in lieu of giving cash it is advantageous to donate capital assets that have risen in value. The fair market value of the asset (rather than cost or other basis) is deductible on the tax return. The increase in value does not have to be reported as a capital gain. The donee also profits from receipt of property since the donation can be larger if the donor does not have to pay income tax on the unrealized gain.

Exhibit 17-8
Effect of Change in Tax Rate—Expenses

	YEAR 1	YEAR 2
Amount of expense	$200,000	$200,000
Tax rate	46%	48%
Tax savings	$ 92,000	$ 96,000
Earnings on $92,000 at 8% (after tax)	7,360	
Total savings	$ 99,360	$ 96,000
	96,000	
Difference	$ 3,360	

DEFERRED TAX ACCOUNTING

Before we leave the subject of taxes, you should have a general understanding of deferred income taxes, which normally appear as a credit in the liability section of a balance sheet. The deferred tax can also appear in the asset section, but since taxpayers tend to postpone taxes, it is more likely to have a credit balance. Income tax expense is generally the tax rate multiplied by the book income (adjusted for permanent differences), whereas income tax payable is the tax rate multiplied by taxable income as reported on the tax return. Any difference between these two amounts is deferred tax.

There are two kinds of differences between tax amounts as shown on the accounting records (books of account) and the tax return: permanent and timing.

Permanent Differences

A permanent difference is an item on the books of account that will never appear on the tax return or vice versa. Permanent differences do not result in deferred income taxes. We illustrate with a very simple example.

Interest from state bonds is nontaxable. Suppose a firm receives $1,000 interest income from California state bonds. On the official accounting records there is a $1,000 increase in cash and a $1,000 increase in interest income. Assuming there are no other differences between income recorded on the books and taxable income shown on the tax return, the book income would reflect $1,000 more income than the tax return. The $1,000 is a permanent difference in that it will never be taxable on the tax return. The easiest way of handling permanent differences is to remove their effect from book income before applying the tax rate. Note that we said remove the effect from book income for tax computational purpose and not remove the $1,000 from the published income statement. Then the income tax expense will equal income tax payable and there is no adjustment to a deferred tax account.

Timing Differences

Timing differences, which always result in an adjustment to a deferred tax account, are differences that are expected to reverse themselves in a future period. For example, an item may be recognized as revenue earlier on the books than on the tax return or vice versa. An expenditure may be recognized as an expense on the books sooner than on the tax return or vice versa.

We demonstrate the treatment of timing differences with the depreciation example discussed in Exhibit 17-3. This situation results in a timing difference because during the asset's early years more depreciation is deducted on the tax return than on the books. Exhibit 17-9, which assumes an income of $100,000 before depreciation and a 46% tax rate, shows the deferred tax by year as well as the cumulative amounts.

The depreciation according to the tax return is based on IRS recovery periods, whereas the book depreciation is calculated by straight line over a eight-year life ($100,000/8 = $12,500). In early years payment of income tax is less and is deferred until later periods. In the sixth year the situation reverses itself, that is, the charge to deferred income tax becomes a debit figure, and at the end of the eighth year the deferred income tax account will have a zero balance. Look at the t-account in Exhibit 17-10.

Exhibit 17-9
Example of Tax Timing Difference

	PER TAX RETURN			PER BOOKS	DEFERRED TAX	
	DEPRECIATION	TAXABLE INCOME	TAXES PAYABLE	TAXES EXPENSE*	CURRENT	CUMULATIVE
1	$15,000	$85,000	$39,100	$40,250	$(1150)	$(1150)
2	22,000	78,000	35,880	40,250	(4370)	(5520)
3	21,000	79,000	36,340	40,250	(3910)	(9430)
4	21,000	79,000	36,340	40,250	(3910)	(13,340)
5	21,000	79,000	36,340	40,250	(3910)	(17,250)
6		100,000	46,000	40,250	5750	(11,500)
7		100,000	46,000	40,250	5750	(5750)
8		100,000	46,000	40,250	5750	0
	$100,000	$700,000	$322,000	$322,000	0	0

*($100,000 − $12,500) × 46% = $40,250

Exhibit 17-10
Deferred Income Tax Account

DEFERRED INCOME TAX			
		$1150	YEAR 1
		4370	YEAR 2
		3910	YEAR 3
		3910	YEAR 4
		3910	YEAR 5
YEAR 6	$5750		
YEAR 7	5750		
YEAR 8	5750		
		0	

Classification of Deferred Tax

A deferred income tax debit balance is usually classified as a current asset on the balance sheet only if it is expected to reverse itself in the current period; otherwise it is considered a long-term asset. If the deferred income tax has a credit balance, the same rules apply—it is classified as a current liability only if it is expected to reverse itself during the current period. Unfortunately, in the United States many large corporations show gigantic long-term deferred tax credits on their balance sheet because they purchased higher-price depreciable assets than those being replaced. Short recovery periods applied to high-cost assets will cause the tax impact of depreciation charges of the new assets to be higher than the tax impact of old assets; thus the deferred tax is never completely reversed.

SUMMARY

We discussed various aspects of income taxes, such as how taxes play an important role in determining the legal form of business organizations. Most larger firms use the accrual basis of accounting but smaller firms should seriously consider the cash basis, which gives them more control over the timing of cash receipts and expenditures. Tax methods such as fast depreciation write-offs and inventory cost flow are important techniques for postponing cash outflow for taxes. Some devices permanently reduce taxes, such as long-term capital gains.

We note other important tax-saving devices. Employee fringe benefits, stock option plans, and deferred pension plans can be advantageous for both the firm and its employees. Net operating losses entitle a firm to a refund of prior years' income tax or a reduction of taxes payable in future periods. Bonds usually result in lower income tax to the issuing firm than preferred or common stock. Generally, taxpayers should postpone the recognition of revenue on the tax return as long as possible but report expenses as early as possible.

In summary, we have touched upon only a few of the most common methods of avoiding income taxes. As we mentioned earlier, you cannot expect to be a tax expert from studying a short chapter, but you should be sufficiently knowledgeable about tax implications to know when to seek the expertise of a tax consultant.

18. Coping with Inflation

Inflation is one of the most perplexing problems facing managers, and is especially crucial for long-range decisions because the return from invested capital must be at least equal to the inflation rate or the firm will suffer a loss of real income. For example, if a firm's return on capital assets is 10%, but the replacement cost of the assets is equal to an inflation rate of, say, 12%, the firm will suffer a "real" loss of 2%. Similarly, if the replacement cost increases to 14%, the firm will suffer a 4% loss.

INFLATION DEFINED

Inflation is a rise in prices, or if looked at from the opposite side, it is a decrease in purchasing power. If it costs $1.00 today to buy a loaf of bread which cost $.20 five years ago, inflation has occurred. You can see that the price rose by a factor of five—from $.20 to $1.00. We can also look at the situation from the viewpoint of purchasing power. The original $.20 would buy 1/5 of a loaf today (assuming we could find a baker who is willing to sell a partial loaf), or $1.00 would be required to buy a whole loaf.

If inflation were constant as to time and goods, we could simply apply a price index to the original cost of an asset. Similarly, we could index liabilities. Unfortunately, this is not the case. The inflation rate varies substantially by year; it varies still more by product. During the 1970s, a house in Orange County, California, increased in price a great deal more than the average rate of inflation in Orange County and in the United States. On the other hand, during the same decade microwave ovens and calculators decreased in price.

Technically, a decrease in value is a netting of the decrease in costs with inflation, something like this:

```
        Inflation
      ─────────────────────────────────►

25                      45                                      75
      ◄───────────────────────────────────────
         Decrease in costs
```

This diagram shows that inflation increased $20 (from $25 to $45) but the cost decreased a total of $50 (from $75 to $25), rather than $30. Looking at another diagram from the opposite point of view, we find the cost of the product increased a total of $50 ($80 — $30) or $20 ($80 — $60) more than the inflation component of the cost increase.

Inflation
——————————————————————→

30   60   80

——————————————————————————————→
          Increase in cost

Decision making is easier when we can separate the inflation component from the real increase or decrease in value. This can seldom be done exactly because we have no perfect measurement of the rate of inflation. About the best we can do is estimate the inflationary component by use of a published index, such as the GNP implicit price deflator or the consumer price index.

These indices are based on changes in the price of a select basket of goods over a period of time. There are several major difficulties with the use of any index. The basket of goods upon which the index is based may not be representative of a particular firm's products. In a rapidly changing technological economy, products composing the basket of goods change. This product change is more troublesome than it may initially appear. Try to think of a major product manufactured in the United States which has not changed during the last 30 years. Compilers of indices attempt to adjust for changes in product mix and technological changes, but many times the results are less than satisfactory.

FAIR VALUE MODELS

There are many ways of valuing assets to reflect inflation other than applying an index to historical cost. These methods are known as fair value models. The term *fair value* has become a generic term meaning some form of current value. Since as a manager you will have to adjust data for changes in price level when making decisions, you should be generally familiar with the more common fair value models. Concentrate on the concepts because the terms labeling them are not standardized.

Current Cost

Current cost is the amount needed to replace an asset. Some theorists use the terms *replacement cost* to describe the cost of replacing an item with one of similar utility and *reproduction cost* for replacement with an identical item. Such refinement, though unimportant in many cases, can be critical in others. For example, the replacement cost of a 1908 automobile would be low in comparison to its reproduction cost. The obvious arguments against both of these models are that we may not wish to replace the item and it is difficult to define similar utility.

Present Value

The present-value method discounts the future cash inflow by an appropriate interest rate in order to determine its value. Recall from our study of capital budgeting, we found that we cannot always identify the timing or amount of cash inflows or a suitable interest rate.

Net Realization Value

The net realization value is the selling price of an item less the cost of disposal. For some assets, market values may be substantially different than the asset's value to the firm. For example, a special-purpose machine might have high utility to a firm and low resale value. If an item is not held for resale, its market value may not be useful information. A variation of the above model is the liquidation value under forced or distressed conditions, such as bankruptcy.

Each of these general models can be further defined. Entire books have been written advocating variations of each of them. Much of the disagreement has centered around the treatment of depreciation, holding gains and losses, and purchasing power gains or losses. Are these appropriate income statement items or should they be handled through the balance sheet?

The relevancy of the data, the cost of obtaining data, and the availability of the data are troublesome issues for most firms when selecting a current-cost model. In addition, educating users as to the significance of the information can be an overwhelming task.

CONSTANT-DOLLAR ACCOUNTING

Adjusting historical cost for inflation by use of an index is called constant-dollar accounting because measurement is a constant unit. To understand inflation and constant-dollar accounting, you must understand the concept of monetary and nonmonetary items.

Monetary Accounts

Monetary accounts, already in current dollars, are items that do not change with the price level. For example, if you have $100 of cash now and you keep your $100 for five years, you will still have $100. The federal government does not say to you, "Inflation has increased 60%; therefore, if you send in your $100 we will give you $160 in order that you may have the same purchasing power as five years ago."

So again, monetary items are fixed in amount by contract or their very nature. Examples include cash, accounts receivable, notes payable, bonds payable, and mortgages payable.

Nonmonetary Accounts

Nonmonetary items change with the price level. They include inventories, investments in common stock, and plant, property, and equipment.

The difference between monetary assets and monetary liabilities is called net monetary assets if the monetary assets are larger than the monetary liabilities. If the converse is true, the result is net monetary liabilities.

Purchasing Power Gains or Losses

In inflationary times, holders of net monetary assets suffer a purchasing power loss, whereas holders of net monetary liabilities enjoy a purchasing power gain. Although there is not a one-to-one relationship between current accounts (current assets and current liabilities) with monetary accounts, there are sufficient similarities to state that in highly inflationary countries such as some South American countries, a high current ratio or favorable working capital position is undesirable because monetary assets (e.g., cash, receivables) lose purchasing power. This loss in purchasing power can be measured. Consider this balance sheet at the beginning of a period.

Balance Sheet
(Beginning of Period)

| Cash | $200 | Owners' equity | $200 |

Suppose inflation increases by 50% during the period. At the end of the period the balance sheet should reflect the following.

Balance Sheet
(End of Period)

| Cash | $300 | Owners' equity | $300 |

Since cash was retained, the firm lost $100 in purchasing power. In reality, the substance of the balance sheet is like this:

Balance Sheet
(End of Period)

Cash	$200	Owners' equity	$300
		Retained earnings	(100)
			$200

Although under generally accepted accounting theory, the accountant does not record the $100 loss in retained earnings, the firm has experienced a $100 purchasing power loss.

Now let us expand our illustration to an entire firm. Assume that the price level has increased 10% during the year and the indices are as follows:

End of year	110
Average for year	105
Beginning of year	100

The historical costs are taken from the financial statements. The calculation of the purchasing power gain is shown in Exhibit 18-1.

The first step in the calculation is to identify the monetary items on the beginning-of-the-year balance sheet (end of preceding period). These monetary items are netted into a single amount, which is restated in end-of-year's dollars using the index. To restate accounts the basic formula is

$$\frac{\text{Index at time of restatement}}{\text{Index at time of incurrence}}$$

Thus, the ending year's index is 110 (the numerator), and the beginning period's index is 100 (the denominator). Now we restate changes in all monetary accounts during the year. Finally, we compare the net monetary items restated to the end-of-the-year purchasing power with the actual net monetary items as stated on the end-of-the-year balance sheet. In this case the difference is a purchasing power gain. If the 12/31/X1 monetary items had been larger than the restated monetary items ($686,190), the result would have been a purchasing power loss.

If constant-dollar financial statements were prepared, the purchasing power gain of $86,190 would be added to the price level adjusted net profit or loss of the income statement.

What is the relevance of knowing the amount of purchasing power gain or loss for you as a manager? Monetary assets and monetary liabilities are con-

Exhibit 18-1

ABC COMPANY

Computation of Purchasing Power Gain or Loss—19X1

(End of Year Dollars)

	19X1 HISTORICAL	INDEX	RESTATED TO 12/31/X1 DOLLARS
NET MONETARY ITEMS 1/1/X1	$(800,000)	110/100	$(880,000)
SALES	3,000,000	110/105	3,142,850
	$2,200,000		$2,262,850
DEDUCT:			
PURCHASES	$1,600,000	110/105	$1,676,190
SELLING & ADMIN. EXP.	400,000	110/105	419,040
INCOME TAX	500,000	110/105	523,810
CASH DIVIDENDS (PAID 1/2/X1)	300,000	110/100	330,000
	$2,800,000		$2,949,040
NET MONETARY ITEMS HISTORICAL—12/31/X1	$(600,000)		
NET MONETARY ITEMS RESTATED—12/31/X1			$(686,190)
NET MONETARY ITEMS HISTORICAL—12/31/X1			(600,000)
PURCHASING POWER GAIN ON NET MONETARY ITEMS			$ 86,190

(a) Assumed incurred evenly throughout year.

(b) Assumed paid January 2, 19X1.

( ) Denotes liabilities.

trollable. Managers do have influence over them. By carefully planning the level of these items, you can control the amount of the purchasing power gain or loss.

Obviously, holding excess cash is an undesirable business practice. Not only is there an opportunity cost to holding cash (loss of earnings that the invested cash could have generated) but also holding cash generates a purchasing power loss.

Since most liabilities are monetary, it is usually undesirable to prepay them. Early payment of a noninterest-bearing liability would be a poor practice. Suppose you have a $1,000,000 balance in accounts payable, and no purchase discount is available. It is preferable to pay the $1,000,000 when due (in 30 days) than to pay immediately because in 30 days you will be paying them with cheaper dollars. If inflation is 1% a month, the amount of savings is $10,000 (1% × $1,000,000). Most of us would agree that $10,000 is a nice piece of change. In addition, the $1,000,000 could be invested in short-term high-yield liquid securities.

METHODS OF COPING WITH INFLATION

Now we discuss some other ways of controlling inflation.

Inventory Cost Flow Methods

Since the matching of the most current costs against revenue is implicit in the LIFO inventory method, many theorists argue that it should be used to account for inventory. Consider the following comparison of gross profit based on FIFO versus LIFO inventory methods.

FIFO Inventory Method
Partial Income Statement

Sales (1000 units @ $10)	$10,000
Cost of goods sold (1000 units @ $3.50)	3,500
Gross profit	$ 6,500

LIFO Inventory Method
Partial Income Statement

Sales (1000 units @ $10)	$10,000
Cost of goods sold (1000 units @ $5.00)	5,000
Gross profit	$ 5,000

LIFO results in $1,500 less profit than FIFO ($6,500 − $5,000) because more expensive inventory is transferred to cost of goods sold. Recall in the last chapter we stated that LIFO also results in less immediate cash outflow for income taxes because the taxes on the $1,500 are deferred to a future period.

Still, some would say that the above calculation does not reflect the true picture. They argue that we should be using replacement cost. Here is a partial income statement reflecting an assumed replacement cost as cost of goods sold.

Replacement Cost Inventory Method
Partial Income Statement

Sales (1000 units @ $10)	$10,000
Cost of goods sold (1000 units @ $5.80)	5,800
Gross profit	$ 4,200

Since the cost of replacing the inventory is assumed to be $5.80 per unit, the real profit is $4,200 rather than a higher amount computed with one of the generally accepted accounting theory's cost flow methods. Unfortunately, this model's primary limitation is that we do not always know the replacement cost of inventory with a high degree of precision. In addition, replacement cost is not acceptable for published financial statements or income tax purposes. Still, there is nothing to stop you as a manager from making replacement cost calculations so you are cognizant of a more "realistic" profit for cash flow and inventory decisions.

Depreciation Methods

We talked previously about the desirability of using accelerated depreciation methods to postpone payment of income taxes. Accelerated depreciation coupled with the shortest possible depreciation life is also effective in matching current costs with revenue. Many European governments have allowed lives of equipment that are arbitrarily shorter than the equipment's actual eonomic lives in computing depreciation. In the United States, the Reagan administration has also authorized shorter depreciation periods. These cost recovery periods are applicable for income tax only and not acceptable per se for measuring depreciation write-offs for profit and loss statements.

Keep in mind that depreciation is not cash. A common misconception is that depreciation creates a cash inflow. This is not true. Depreciation expense is one of the few expenses on the income statement that has not been paid out in cash and is therefore added to net income during conversion from an accrual basis to a cash flow income statement.

Remember that accelerated depreciation results in lower profits during the early life of an asset but more cash resources are available to the firm because of the savings in cash outflow from deferring tax payments. Still, the advantage is only temporary since lower depreciation expense results during the second half of an asset's life. The total amount written off through depreciation cannot exceed cost. Many firms are able to keep their depreciation write-off high indefinitely from frequent replacement of plant and equipment. The result is large amounts of deferred income tax liability on the balance sheet.

Dividend Policy

Net profit is frequently a guide to dividend policy. When profits are low, dividends tend to be lower than when profits are high. There are many factors to consider in formulating a dividend policy, such as stockholders' desires. A firm might have sufficient earnings to pay dividends, but it may be short on cash or it might wish to retain the earnings for future expansion. There are strong doubts whether net income as reported on the income statement is a valid basis for dividends. How many firms found to their horror in 1980 after computing constant-dollar financial statements and other current-cost information required by the new Financial Accounting Standard no. 33 that they had been paying dividends out of past years' earnings or worst yet—paid in capital. In addition, many firms found that they had not adequately planned for plant and equipment replacement. High interest rates coupled with tight capital markets made expansion unfeasible, if not impossible, during this time period. Sometimes, inflation can make a company appear more prosperous than it really is. One solution to the dividend problem is to restate the financial statements in constant dollars or some other current-value model before establishing the amount of the dividend.

Evaluating Capital Investment Proposals

The effects of inflation should also be considered in evaluating capital investment proposals. The projected cash flow must be an inflated cash flow. Note that inflation is compounded just as the time value of money; therefore, the same time value tables can be used to calculate inflated dollars. Once cash flow is presented in expected cash inflow, it must be brought back to present value. The present-value factor is a total of the expected earning power and the inflation rate. An elementary example, Exhibit 18-2, should make this clear. The analysis leads to the conclusion that the equipment should be purchased since it has a positive net present value.

REAL INCOME

Real income is the amount of profit left after removing the effects of inflation. We said earlier that the inflation component should be separated from total

Exhibit 18-2
Evaluation of Capital Asset Proposal

YEAR	NET CASH FLOW WITHOUT INFLATION	NET CASH FLOW WITH 10% INFLATION	TAX EFFECT 40% RATE	NET AFTER TAX CASH FLOW	PV FACTOR*	PRESENT VALUE
1	$15,000	$16,500	$6,600	$9,900	.8696	$8,609
2	10,000	12,100	4,840	7,260	.7561	5,489
3	12,000	15,972	6,388	9,584	.6575	6,301
						$20,399
COST OF EQUIPMENT AT PRESENT VALUE						20,000
NET PRESENT VALUE						399

*15% (10% INFLATION AND 5% RETURN)

profit in order to measure the amount of real profit. Frequently, home owners rejoice when they sell their homes at a profit, but when the inflationary factor is removed the real profit is usually substantially less than the reported profit. Many times there is a real loss on the transaction after income taxes are paid.

Consider the following situation. On January 1, 19X5 Mary purchases a house for $75,000. She sells it five years later for $125,000 or a book profit of $50,000 ($125,000 − $75,000). During the period, assume that the price index increased from 125 to 183. What is Mary's real profit?

Selling price	$125,000
Cost ($75,000 × $^{183}/_{125}$)	109,800
Real profit before taxes	$ 15,200

Assume the capital gains tax is 20%. Mary's real gain after taxes is now $5,200. Obviously, $5,200 is a lot less than the book profit of $50,000. The $5,200 is computed as follows:

Real profit	$15,200
Income tax ($50,000 × 20%)	10,000*
Real profit after income taxes	$ 5,200

PRICE LEVEL DECISIONS

Management must be imaginative and flexible when dealing with changes in purchasing power. If costs increase faster than revenue, the selling price may have to be increased. If this is not possible, shifts in mix of product line may be necessary.

A highly leveraged company can usually cope with rising prices easier than a less leveraged company because most liabilities are monetary and will be paid off with cheaper dollars. High-leverage firms can be risky, though, because in loss years the interest still has to be paid. The firm's earnings must exceed the interest over the long run, and the firm must consider how the principal is to be repaid or refinanced at maturity.

Multinational corporations may find it profitable to hold cash and cash claims in relatively strong currency and liabilities in a weak currency. Hedging, that is, buying future contracts, is another way of avoiding declines in currency value.

Some firms find including an inflationary clause in their contracts helpful.

---

*Sometimes income taxes can be deferred on the sale of a residence, or the profit is permanently exempt from taxes. These specialized tax laws are beyond the scope of this book.

Unions have latched onto this practice as a means of protecting the earning power of their members.

CONSTANT-DOLLAR FINANCIAL STATEMENTS

Before leaving this chapter, we illustrate constant-dollar financial statements. Prior to 1979 the Financial Accounting Standards Board recommended that the GNP implicit price deflator be used to adjust historical-based financial statements. Then FASB no. 33, published in 1979, required approximately the 1,000 largest firms in the United States to supplement historical financial statements with selected price-level adjusted figures. The index suggested, the consumer's price index, has approximately doubled during the 10 years from 1967 to 1977 with this trend continuing into the 1980s.

The quarrel over how inflation should be handled in published financial statements has been a long and bitter one, not only in the United States but throughout the world. FASB no. 33 is not meant to be the "final word" on this subject. When sufficient experience has been obtained, the Financial Accounting Standards Board plans to reassess its reporting requirements.

A short summary of FASB no. 33 follows. FASB no. 33 allows a complete restatement of financial statements to year-end constant dollars or a partial restatement to average-for-the-year constant dollars. Since a complete restatement provides substantially more information for managers to base financial decisions on, we illustrate this method first.

The first step in a complete restatement is to classify the accounts of the financial statements as monetary or nonmonetary. All monetary items are already at current value, so they can be retained unchanged. Nonmonetary items have to be restated. The conversion fraction consists of the current index as the numerator and the index as of the transaction period as the denominator. Exhibits 18-3 and 18-4 demonstrate the process of converting a historical-cost balance sheet and income statement to constant dollars, respectively.

The FASB does not require a complete restatement of financial statements. If a firm so elects it can limit its disclosure to:

1. Income from continuing operations on a constant-dollar basis[a]
2. The purchasing power gain or loss on net monetary items
3. Current cost of inventory and property, plant, and equipment at end of year[b]
4. Income from continuing operations on a current-cost basis[a]
5. Increases or decreases in current-cost amounts of inventory and property, plant, and equipment, net of inflation[b]

---

[a] Accounts restated are limited to cost of goods sold and depreciation expense.
[b] Accounts restated are limited to inventories and plant, property and equipment.

Exhibit 18-3
ABC COMPANY
Balance Sheet
Constant Dollars
As of December 31, 19X1
(in OOO)

ASSETS	HISTORICAL DOLLARS	INDEX	CONSTANT DOLLARS
CASH	$ 100	110/110 (a)	$ 100
ACCOUNTS RECEIVABLE	400	110/110 (a)	400
INVENTORIES		110/80	
	500	110/105 (b)	622
LAND	1,000	110/60 (c)	1,833
BUILDINGS	2,000	110/60 (c)	3,667
ACCUMULATED DEPRECIATION	(600)	110/60 (c)	(1,100)
EQUIPMENT	800	110/70 (c)	1,257
ACCUMULATED DEPRECIATION	(700)	110/70 (c)	(1,100)
INTANGIBLES	50	110/90 (c)	61
TOTAL ASSETS	$3,550		$5,740
EQUITIES			
ACCOUNTS PAYABLE	$300	110/110 (a)	$300
ACCRUED LIABILITIES	100	110/110 (a)	100
MORTGAGE PAYABLE	1,500	110/110 (a)	1,500
TOTAL LIABILITIES			
COMMON STOCK	500	110/55 (d)	1,000
RETAINED EARNINGS 1/1/X1	750		
NET RROFIT FOR PERIOD	700	(e)	2,840
DIVIDENDS	(300)		
TOTAL EQUITIES	$3,550		$5,740

See Exhibit 18-4 for explanation of footnotes.

Additional disclosure of selected information is required for five years.

As for current cost, managers can generally determine which fair value model they consider most relevant to their firm. For constant-dollar calculations, information must be reported in average-for-the-year dollars instead of year-end dollars. This means in essence that the average consumer price index is used in lieu of the end-of-the-period index.

The accounting profession is still studying how to best report foreign financial statements in U.S. dollars to reflect the proper exchange rate and inflation. Clearly, the current foreign currency exchange rates alone do not adequately adjust for inflation. Multinational corporations with divisions or headquarters

Exhibit 18-4
ABC COMPANY
Profit and Loss Statement
Constant Dollars
For the Year Ended December 31, 19X1
in (OOO)

	HISTORICAL DOLLARS	INDEX	CONSTANT DOLLARS
SALES	$3,000	110/105(f)	$3,143
COST OF GOODS SOLD			
BEG. INVENTORY	$ 300	110/80 (b)	$413
PURCHASES	1,600	110/105(f)	1,676
END. INVENTORY	(500)	110/80 (b) 110/105	(622)
COST OF GOODS SOLD	$1,400		$1,467
GROSS PROFIT	$1,600		$1,676
DEPRECIATION EXPENSE	100	110/60 (c) 110/70 (c)	170
SELLING & ADMINISTRATIVE EXPENSE	300	110/105(f)	314
NET PROFIT	$1,200		$1,192
INCOME TAX	500	110/105(f)	524
PROFIT AFTER TAX	$ 700		$668
PURCHASING POWER GAIN		(g)	86
			$754

(a) Monetary items.
(b) Assume LIFO inventory. Denominator of indices are for the year inventory layers were purchased.

$300,000 \times {}^{110}\!/_{80}$ $412,400

$200,000 \times {}^{110}\!/_{105}$ 209,523

$622,023

(c) Denominator is year of purchase. Accumulated depreciation and depreciation expense follow the index for asset depreciated.
(d) Date of issuance.
(e) Amount to balance the statement.
(f) Average index during 19X4.
(g) From Exhibit 18-1, computation of purchasing power gain.

in highly inflationary countries face special reporting, measuring, and controlling problems, complexities that are beyond the scope of this book.

SUMMARY

In this chapter we acquainted you with many of the ramifications of inflation. We discussed the meaning of inflation, purchasing power gains and losses, and the advantages and disadvantages of various fair value models capable of serving as substitutes for constant dollars.

The mechanics of converting financial statements into constant dollars were demonstrated and the disclosure requirements of FASB no. 33 listed. Keep in mind that this very controversial standard is not a cure-all for dealing with inflation; rather its purpose is to provide readers of financial statements with selected constant-dollar and current-value information.

We discussed various ways of coping with inflation such as LIFO and accelerated depreciation methods. Inflation is a critical factor to consider in establishing dividend policy and asset replacement decisions. It is also an integral part of capital acquisition decisions.

The causes of inflation have long been debated. So have the means of coping with it. It is safe to say that the best way of accounting for and coping with inflation is to have zero inflation. Then our historical accounting model would remain relevant.

19. Behavioral Aspects of Managerial Accounting

Now we turn our attention to how human behavior affects managerial accounting and, conversely, how managerial accounting affects human behavior. Our primary focus is on the budgeting process because it is crucial that managerial accountants understand how budgets affect behavior and what employees do to circumvent them. Particular attention is given to the role of slack and its impact on budgets. It is important to understand that firms as well as employees are evaluated. Let us start out by reviewing the environment of the firm.

ENVIRONMENT OF THE FIRM

We have in Exhibit 19-1 a model of a complex organization. This exhibit is a continuous feedback model in which the elements have an impact on each other. The budget is the vehicle by which changes are made in planning, controlling, and motivation. For evaluation purposes actual performance is compared with projected; variances are analyzed; corrective procedures are instituted, and, if deemed necessary, objectives are revised. Budgeting reflects the firm's objectives, performance, and measurement and evaluation procedures. Errors made scanning the environment, appraising of resources, and identifying a strategic fit of the one with the other can be handled through budgetary slack.

If all publics agreed on the proper role of business, how much simpler the budgeting process would be. Alas, this is Utopia. Just as every other sector of society is plagued with the conflicting expectations of various groups, so too is business, maybe more so. The objective of the business organization may be the rendering of goods and service in the most efficient manner possible to assure its own continuity and growth. Its employees (especially its managers) are working toward more personal goals of career advancement, reward, longevity of employment, and self-actualization.

Owners and creditors are interested in profits, if not in a maximization of profits than at least in a satisfactory return on investment. The external environment includes the macrosociety of government and society in general, both of which differ in their expectations of business. The local community is likely to be more interested in an environment conducive to a desired standard of living, whereas consumers are seeking a high-quality, low-price product or service that is reasonably available upon demand according to individual whims.

Exhibit 19-1.
A Framework for Evaluation of Corporate Performance

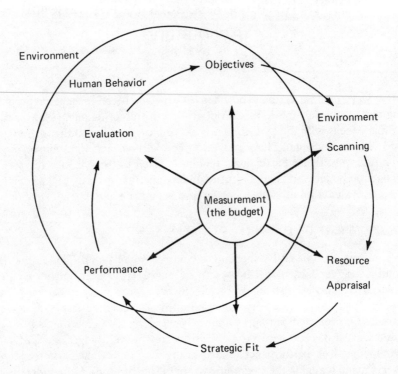

Government, be it state, federal, or local, looks to business to promote rather than hamper the general welfare of its citizens. Finally, for society in general business serves as a stabilizing force of efficiency, mirroring the values and beliefs society holds dear. With so many differing demands many of which are highly controversial and conflictive in nature, it is little wonder that business sees itself as operating in a turbulent environment. How can it possibly hope to play the role dictated by each of its publics? How can it know which strategy to select to achieve its many goals? There is no one specific princple or guide-line to know what business strategy ought to be, nor is there a foolproof way of knowing if the best strategy has been formulated.

BUDGETING

The two major functions of management—planning and control—are insepa-rable in the budgeting process. Both functions are necessary to obtain the firm's objectives. If human behavior is not considered, top managers are free to utilize the most sophisticated, scientific techniques feasible to establish the optimal amount of resources needed to operate efficiently and effectively.

Planning is future oriented and forms the foundation of control. Control is established through an analysis of the variance, that is, the difference between budgeted cost (plans) and actual costs. This analysis is extremely important because it either suggests corrective action, a revision of objectives, or a modification of plans. Frequently, the planning and control functions result in rewards for superior performance and punishment for the less "competent."

Human behavior complicates the planning and controlling functions. It affects all aspects of the budgeting process and cannot be ignored. It is the pivot around which the entire budgeting process revolves, a relationship depicted in Exhibit 19-2.

Exhibit 19-2.
A Budgeting Model

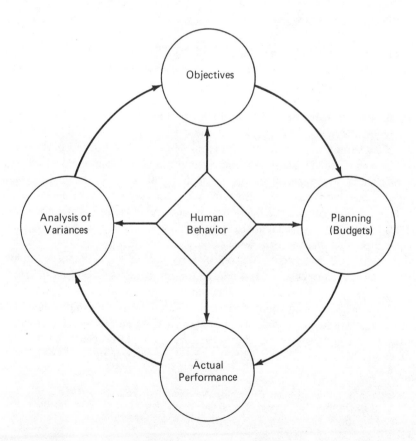

Budgets that are unacceptable to subordinates can cause morale to deteriorate, resulting in decreased productivity and lower profits. Human beings establish private goals out of a strong motivation toward personal fulfillment. When personal goals are incompatible with the objectives of management, conflict and anxiety tend to result.

HUMAN NEEDS

Maslow* was one of the first psychologists to popularize the idea that human beings have needs that require satisfying if they are to be productive. He categorized needs into a hierarchy. From highest to lowest they are:

Self-actualization
Esteem
Love
Safety
Physiological well-being

McGregor† expanded this concept with his Theory X and Theory Y: People are not necessarily lazy, inefficient, unmotivated, and likely to avoid work whenever possible. Furthermore, employees are not primarily motivated by monetary rewards. Given the proper environment, according to McGregor, employees will seek challenges and their own rewards.

Hence, the managerial accountant and management in general should have a basic awareness of what motivates employees. The best budgets in the world and the most efficient cost-reporting system are of no avail unless employees utilize them. Management brings the goals of the firm and the goals of individuals together. When they are compatible we have goal congruence. Managers seek goal congruence by motivating individuals to internalize the firm's goals as their own personal goals. Individuals will then aspire to achieve these goals, believing that they will satisfy their needs. Still, it is important to realize that management has very little control over much of what influences employees' aspirations, especially those related to their personal lives. The internalization process can be seen in the diagram in Exhibit 19-3.

The managerial accountant is concerned with the extent to which individuals internalize the budget, standards, and other controls. Past experience with controls is a significant factor. For example, if employees have been badly "burned" by budgets, they are likely to be skeptical of them.

---

*Maslow, A. H., *Motivation and Personality*. New York: Harper and Row, 1954.
†McGregor, Douglas, *The Human Side of Enterprise*. New York: McGraw-Hill Book Company, 1960.

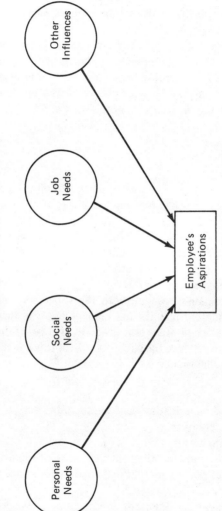

Exhibit 19-3.
Variables Affecting Employee's Aspirations

As mentioned previously, an important element is how closely individual needs tie in with the goals of the firm. Employees, consciously or unconsciously, assign priorities to needs they are trying to satisfy. These may be their own needs or those of the firm's. Some employees suffer intense anxiety if they cannot meet both expectations. For example, an employee who must travel frequently to meet the firm's goals may become anxious about prolonged absence from his or her family.

Another important element is the amount of satisfaction a person acquires from any given action. If an employee who must travel on company business generally feels an intense sense of achievement from accomplishing assigned work, he or she is more likely to internalize the firm's goals. This sense of achievement is based on what the employee expects to achieve under certain conditions.

PARTICIPATION

The research literature in the area of participation is extremely vast. We can touch upon only a few of the important findings of interest to managers and to the managerial accountant.

First of all, participation in drafting the budget must be real rather than psuedoparticipation. The latter occurs when the employee goes through the motions but has very little input into the final decisions. It pretends to be participation but really is a form of deceit.

Under a participatory system, both the supervisor and subordinate work together in formulating policies and plans. Of course they do not necessarily have to agree with each other and probably will not. Still, it is essential that the superior try to convince the subordinate of the wisdom of the final decision; otherwise goal incongruence is likely to result. The value of participation lies in:

1. Improved communication between superiors and subordinates
2. An atmosphere of trust
3. Greater team spirit
4. Subordinates understanding the objectives of the firm
5. Subordinates perceiving that expected performance is reasonable

Management style is important in determining the level of participation. Highly authoritative managers with passive subordinates can be an effective combination. Similarly, democratic managers work well with subordinates who put a premium on participation. The four combinations are diagrammed as Exhibit 19-4.

Obviously, the effectiveness of management style is dependent upon tasks and cultural environment. There is no one style appropriate to all situations. If

Exhibit 19-4.
Results of Managers and Employees' Styles

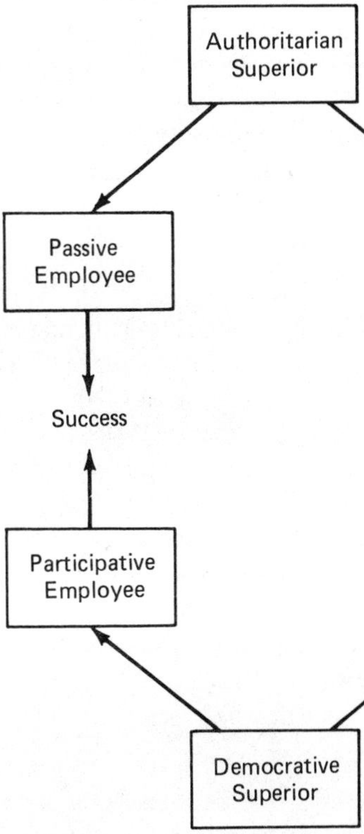

lower-level employees have been conditioned to accept orders, a participative style will not work. Similarly, if higher management is not willing to compromise and accept subordinates' input, a participative style will not work. But if employees demand to be heard, the group may band together in rejecting the organization's goals. Such action is more likely to be destructive than constructive.

CONTROLLABILITY

A basic principal of management states that managers should only be held responsible for activities they can control. The question often arises whether allocated cost should be included in performance reports. So long as the reports explicitly show the controllable part and the managers are held responsible for that part only, little harm will result. Including uncontrollable costs has the advantage of keeping managers aware that these costs exist and prepares them for broader managerial responsibilities in the future.

Several behavioral problems can surface here. One is that managers become so involved in their own areas of accountability that communication and coordination suffer to the detriment of the firm's goals. Similarly, managers may attempt to keep failures out of their reports or shift the blame or responsibility to another individual. For example, an unfavorable variance may be assigned to others. "Passing the buck" is seldom an effective way of controlling performance.

MANAGEMENT BY EXCEPTION

The management-by-exception principle states that only major material items should be reported. While the principle has the advantage of removing routine expected behavior from reports, all too often most of the items reported are unfavorable. This is demoralizing to managers. Obviously, no reporting and comprehensive reporting are both undesirable alternatives. If only failures and extraordinary successes are brought to the attention of top management, it is difficult for the consistently successful manager to gain recognition. Upper managers may suffer from insufficient information and subordinates may view the system as punitive. Therefore, the managerial accountant's job is to design reports and explain the purposes of reports to aid managers in decision making. The principles of report preparation will be covered in Chapter 20.

PRESSURE

Tight budgets can cause excess pressure. A tight budget is one where budgeted figures are projected at some minimum figure for costs and/or maximum amount for revenue; consequently, unfavorable variances are expected most of the time. The tight budget is supposed to include no slack, whereas in a loose budget there is room for expansion or contraction. Loose budgets should be met a large percentage of the time, and are more likely to show favorable variances.

If standards and budgets are set too high, the results are likely to be undesirable. Loose standards are also usually not effective. Standards should be tight but attainable; that is, they should be set above the mean level. Subordinates must be in agreement with the reasonableness of the standards, and managers must set standards at a level that motivates employees.

If meeting standards or budgets means failure or success for managers or workers, the budget may be looked upon as something to be feared. Employees may ignore the standards, suffer anxiety, or become disgruntled. In extreme situations mass rebellion will take place. It is more likely, however, that employees will distort their reports or put slack in their budgets.

SLACK

Slack is the something extra put in the budget beyond what should be there. Often called padding, fat, cushion, or water, it is the amount beyond the minimum amount necessary to operate efficiently and effectively. Slack is likely to appear in actual costs: Because superiors tend to cut budgets when funds are not expended, subordinates are encouraged to spend the slack.

All levels of management participate in the creation of slack because every level including the president needs "squirming room." Thus, much slack is intentional and arises out of the bargaining process. Contrary to popular conception, it occurs in bad times as well as good.

It would be relatively easy to condemn the incorporation of slack into budgets as totally undesirable and detrimental to profit maximization. But upon a closer analysis, padding has positive value. It is questionable whether the budgeting process as it is practised in firms today could even continue to exist without slack unless drastic changes were made in business philosophy and the business environment. This is especially true when budgets are inflexible, stifle change and innovation, restrict managerial initiative, induce unrealistic pressure, and encourage management by rules.

Is it completely undesirable when budgets are tight and encourage inflexible behavior? Many would say "no." Much depends upon the individuals involved. As long as the company's goals are being attained—whether they be a reasonable profit or some other goal—rigidity may serve as the ideal means to corporate ends.

Advantages of Slack

The advantages of slack are several:

1. Slack serves as a means of securing and allocating resources; hence, it establishes an environment wherein managers can bargain for power. Managers can best achieve their own personal goals and the firm's goals in a slack environment because slack provides the means by which managers can reconcile their goals with those of the firm.

2. Slack provides room for decision making. Decision making is not only one of the functions of managers, but it creates tremendous positive psychological power. Rigidity, on the other hand, produces tension and red tape to the extent that it can stifle the creative and imaginative ability of individuals.

3. Slack serves as a hedge against errors in estimates and uncertainty. Since no person can predict the future with certainty, it is unfair to hold employees responsible for all variances, especially if they are the result of forecast errors or events that could not be reasonably foreseen.

4. A budgeting cushion provides a pool of emergency resources for the company to draw upon in poor times and a means of stabilizing performance

despite fluctuations in the firm's environment. Through it figures can be manipulated to show a yearly profit, growth, and a balanced budget.

5. Slack allows managers considerable freedom to control their salaries, bonuses, promotions, and so forth, especially when compensation and career advancement are related to performance. Through it managers attain power, enlarge the size of their staffs, and increase control over the allocation of resources.

6. Slack allows managers room for counterbiasing. Otherwise, the only way they can influence or contribute to the budgetary process is through reshifting proposed dollars—increasing one department's funds by reducing another's, for instance. This "robbing Peter to pay Paul" approach is likely to be more unpopular with all parties concerned than a direct reduction of the proposed costs.

Disadvantages of Slack

On the negative side:

1. Slack may cause corporate profits to be less than optimum: sales tend to be understated and costs overstated.

2. Budgeted figures may not be the best motivator to improve performance.

3. The person less able to manage efficiently may acquire power through the "squeaky wheel gets the grease" response. If slack is practised it is imperative that everyone involved in budgeting (the budgetees) incorporate slack to the same degree, or major distortions will occur.

4. Slack defeats the fundamental purpose of budgeting—to plan and control. The more slack, the less valid are the forecasts and the variances generated.

There is a fine line between sophisticated management which can utilize slack to its advantage, and incompetency. Under present business practices, slack appears to be essential for everyone in the company. The lower managers must pad to protect themselves in terms of self-esteem, compensation, career advancement, and pressure from superiors. Middle to top managers also face pressure from executives above them. Even the president must report his or her accomplishments to the Board of Directors and the stockholders.

Counterbiasing

Any notion that slack is an elementary problem to be disposed of through such simple techniques as counterbiasing is naive. Rather the concept of slack is extremely complicated. A large number of factors determine the magnitude of slack, many of which are listed in Exhibit 19-5.

The unanswered question is how much slack is incorporated into budgets by managers to deal with uncertainty, differences in perceived roles, or goal incon-

Exhibit 19-5
VARIABLES AFFECTING BUDGETARY SLACK

Performance of Peers
1. Past performance
2. Expected future performance

Leadership
1. Style
2. Relationship with superior
3. Extent leader is aware of slack
4. Extent leader condones/condemns slack
5. Extent leader places "ceilings" on slack
6. Extent leader counterbiases

Environment
1. Static versus turbulence
2. Pressure groups—interested parties (publics)
3. Risk
4. Organizational structure

Control Techniques
1. Justification of budget
2. Explanation of variance
3. Examination of incurred costs
4. Explanation of incurred costs

Other
1. Resolution of management conflicts
2. Planning and control incompatibility
3. Frequency of budgeting revisions
4. Functional and dysfunctional aspects
5. Income smoothing
6. Loose versus tight budgeting
7. Attitude toward budgets
8. Incongruence with personal goals
9. Types of budgetary forms used

Past Performance of Budgetee
1. Favor–unfavorable variance
2. Past actual costs
3. Past budgeted dollars
4. Past slack in budget

Rewards and Punishments
1. Available to:
   a. Budgetee
   b. Peers
   c. Subordinates
   d. Superiors
2. Promotion and career development
3. Amount of
4. Frequency of

Personality Traits of Budgetee
1. Insecure versus secure
2. Power oriented
3. Cooperative

Decision Making
1. Cognitive style of decision maker
2. Budget that serves to justify decisions
3. Budget that serves to dictate behavior

gruency and to appease the firm's various publics (especially those who apply the most pressure). An additional complexity is that pressure groups tend to shift with time, which makes it difficult to weigh the impact of each in the next budgeting period. Hence, a generous amount of slack serves as a means of coping with uncertainty.

Detection of Slack

If all costs were purely fixed (that is, did not change with output) or purely variable (changed in direct proportion to output), slack would be easier to identify. Unfortunately, this is not the case. Few costs are entirely fixed or variable; most are semivariable. The longer the time period, the more likely the costs are semivariable; in the long run all costs are variable. Since budgets conventionally utilize several periods of historical costs, budgetees are usually dealing with semivariable costs.

The difficulty of detecting slack is compounded by the fact that management may deliberately even-out reporting income by decisions on accounting principles. While the accounting profession has established some rather rigid guidelines to prevent this practice, there is still considerable leeway for distortion. For many transactions (e.g., depreciation, inventory) managers can choose one of several generally accepted accounting principles to record the item, each of which would generate substantially different results.

In a well-managed company, detection of overspending should not be impossible, especially by the superior immediately in charge since he or she should have first-hand knowledge of the activities in his or her area. But this statement assumes that the supervisor is interested in detecting slack and is not a party to it, which is many times an unrealistic assumption. The problem of detection is compounded when several levels of managers band together to cover up slack. Although top management is at a disadvantage, there are various tactics that can uncover excess spending.

1. One is reviewing monthly variance reports for a reduction in favorable variances near year-end since a common method of padding is the spending of budget money about the time managers feel reasonably comfortable that nothing unforeseen will occur. This practice causes managers to purchase essential items during the early part of the year and those that are less essential later in the year.

An analysis of costs incurred, that is, establishing the purpose of the acquired item or service, could shed some light on the extent this padding technique is being practised. The analysis might require, at least to a certain extent, a departure from the management-by-exception principle.

2. Another practice of the budgetee is the opposite of the above—an early

overrun of the budget to provide substantiation for additional funds either in the current period or the next budgetary period. The early overrun is in essence a means of putting slack into incurred costs.

One must be careful when assessing the reasonableness of costs. Many costs incurred during good years (which could be classified as slack) are probably necessary, even though they could easily be postponed during one or two bad years. But if a company deletes them over the long run, the impact could be disastrous. Examples include failure to buy furniture prolonged postponement of remodeling, delaying the repair of equipment, bypassing bonuses, decreasing advertising, and cutting down on training, development, and recruitment. It is important to analyze a company's costs over the long and the short run before deciding if expenditures are really essential.

3. A third practice is expending funds for "frills" evenly throughout the year in the belief that if the firm's economy gets tight, the manager can easily eliminate the frills and still meet the budget. This approach depends on a sizeable amount of slack in the budget.

The use of accounting data as the basis for projections has made it relatively easy for managers to incorporate slack. There is a built-in assumption that the future will mirror the past and that past performance was optimal. Neither of these assumptions is true. In addition, historical data are seldom refined enough to detect learning. Yet, learning curves do exist, especially during the initial period of manufacturing a new product.

Even though managers have sought out various new techniques to solve the problem of slack, none has been successful in eliminating it. The computer has made possible more sophisticated estimating techniques, such as flexible budgeting, but it has also made detection of slack more difficult.

Flexible Budgeting

Flexible budgeting was once hailed as the solution to the budgeting problem, but it has not been implemented as widely as one would suppose. Difficulties include such elements as how to select the most appropriate volume base or measure of output and the breaking down of expenses into their variable, semi-variable, and fixed components. In addition, it is costly to operate and must be constantly updated. The output is so voluminous that there is a danger of managers' suffering from information overload.

Zero Base Budgeting

One way of relieving slack is through zero base budgeting, which basically advocates that managers start from zero for building up anticipated revenue or cost figures rather than relying on previous budgets, actual costs, or some other existing basis. All projects must be substantiated and ranked according to priority. If hard times hit, the firm can cut costs by eliminating the projects at the low end of the ranking scale.

Zero base budgeting has not proved to be free of behaviorally based abuses, however. Managers soon learn to rank "desirable" projects high, those they wish to be rid of are assigned low priority. Pad still exists in a disguised form, and the game becomes one of being able to substantiate the ranking as well as the amount. Some managers attempt to dictate ranking but this violates the nature of zero base budgeting and employee participation. An additional problem is that projecting costs from point zero has complicated the negotiation of resources rather than simplified it. The result is increased friction among managers.

The Budgeting Process

One thing inherently wrong with the budgeting process as it exists in the business world today is that favorable variances are accorded high praise, whereas unfavorable variances cause management concern, create pressure, and lead to investigations. Yet a consistently favorable variance is likely to be the result of padding in the original estimate rather than superior managerial ability.

Some idealists see the absence of any variance as the perfect state. This point is debatable because forecasters soon learn that if they want to be rewarded for meeting the budget, they must pad a reasonable amount to cover unforeseen circumstances: If the padding is needed, no variance appears; if unneeded, it is spent later to avoid any sizable residual variance. To say that the absence of variances whether favorable or unfavorable is planning realistically and effectively is naive; rather, it indicates that someone is using the budget to control behavior. In the final analysis the extent to which slack is a problem depends on the amount of reliance that is placed on budgets for decision making and on the ability of managers to effectively counterbias the original budgets without destroying the morale of subordinates.

INCENTIVES

A great deal of research has been performed on factors that affect subordinates' acceptance of controls. A positive, supportive attitude by top management is essential. If top managers ignore budgets and other controls, so will subordinates. Rewards motivate employees far more than punishment. Of course, individual employees must perceive the rewards as desirable since what is desirable to one may not be desirable to another. What incentives influence employee behavior? Generally, increased monetary rewards improve performance until a satisfactory level of earnings is reached. An employee, on the other hand, may feel disgruntled if a colleague of lesser or equal ability receives more compensation.

It is important that employees feel that they belong to the group, that their accomplishments are meaningful and recognized as such, and that their work contributes to the firm's goals. Constructive criticism, praise, and participation in decision making can be very effective in providing employees with a sense of importance. There is a maximum point beyond which people will not respond to increased incentives and may begin to interpret them as pressure.

Goals should be attainable. Goals set too high will frustrate employees, whereas goals set too low will fail to motivate them. Unless employees perceive the goals as fair, they will not feel committed to them. Participation in setting goals is usually effective. Finally, employees must be held responsible for achievement of their goals. A responsibility accounting system gathers and disseminates information by responsible individuals, thereby increasing the intrinsic reward of success.

MANAGERIAL ACCOUNTANT'S ROLE

How does the managerial accountant resolve behavioral issues? We should keep in mind that much of the work of a budget staff is incompatible with a warm relationship with line employees. The budget team is responsible for criticizing budget proposals, investigating variances, enforcing compliance with prescribed procedures, and informing top management accordingly. There is little wonder that line managers often criticize the budget team as insensitive to their problems. Additionally, line personnel may not have the accounting expertise to understand or interpret what they perceive as accounting jargon; hence line managers are on the defensive and likely to behave with a certain amount of hostility.

Accountants must, nevertheless, attempt to build effective relationships. An attitude of helpfulness that extends to providing sufficient technical help during the budgetary process will lessen the number of defects discovered during the review process. Accountants must establish an atmosphere of trust by convincing line managers that accountants are there to facilitate the budgeting process. They must provide information helpful to solving problems and making decisions. To a large extent, cooperation from line managers depends on their perception of whether accountants furnish information useful for achieving the line managers' goals. A considerable amount of conflict is likely to be present, but as a minimum, accountants should be aware of behavioral problems with line personnel and take steps to minimize their impact.

Accountants should also be aware that their position makes them vulnerable to attack. Just as a tax preparer may feel the wrath of a disgruntled taxpayer for taxes owed because a fight with the Internal Revenue Service may prove too risky or ineffective, so too accountants can become the scapegoat for unhappy managers. Upper managers also make accountants into villains to relieve themselves of the need to justify the demands they make of subordinates.

SUMMARY

Budgeting is a means of planning and controlling a firm's operations. Both activities are heavily affected by human behavior. Goal incongruence results when employees' needs deviate too far from the firm's goals. Such a situation can result in lower morale, productivity, and profits.

We discussed the elements of good budgeting. Participative budgeting is desirable only when the leadership styles of superiors and the expectations of subordinates are complementary.

Managers should be held responsible only for activities they can control. Reporting is often done on an exception basis. If employees suffer from extreme budgetary pressure, they are likely to insert slack in their budgets. Substantial attention was given to slack including its advantages, disadvantages, and methods of reducing its amount.

20. Communication and the Value of Information

Our final chapter is devoted to communication and the value of information. During the first half of the chapter we discuss elements of good reporting. Timeliness is so critical that important information should initially be communicated orally. Oral reports should be followed up with written reports. The latter should contain no "surprises." The second half of the chaper is concerned with decision making under conditions of uncertainty and the value of perfect information.

COMMUNICATION SYSTEM

Let us start out by reviewing a basic communication system. A communication system is a control system in which feedback is an important element. The complexity of a communication system is depicted in Exhibit 20-1.

The source of data is an economic event, such as a threatened labor strike. Because the managerial accountant compiles for management reports of the potential cost of the strike, he or she is in effect a transmitter of information. The channel of communication is an accounting report. Management is the receiver of the information. To the extent that management perceives and interprets the report differently than the managerial accountant intended, there is noise in the system. The action that management takes, say, a 10% raise to union employees, is a decision that is communicated to the transmitter. This feedback activates a new economic event of increased labor cost, and now the cycle starts over again.

A communication system is reliable if it produces consistent output. Reliable systems have a high probability that the recipient will interpret the data the same way as the transmitter intended. A system has noise if the input signal causes two or more output signals. One signal may be the way the transmitter intended and another might be how the receiver interprets the data. Noise affects the reliability of information sent because it is not clear how the output would be interpreted.

Some communication theorists differentiate between the words *data* and *information*. *Data* are unprocessed numbers or facts, whereas *information* is data made relevant for decision. The number 62 is data but $62 written on a check is information to the holder of the instrument. We will avoid such niceties and use the two words interchangeably.

Exhibit 20-1.
Communication Model

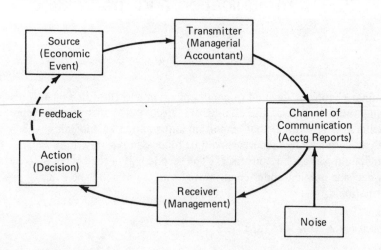

TYPES OF BUSINESS REPORTS

Business reports are of two types: (1) information and (2) analytic. Information reports present facts without evaluation, comments, or recommendations. Many computer reports are of this nature. Information reports tend to be routine and repetitious. Examples are labor distribution and material usage reports.

The analytical report, on the other hand, presents interpretation, appraisal, evaluation, or recomendations along with the data it delivers. It may be periodic or special purpose. A monthly reporting of variances (including an explanation and recommendations for corrective action) is an example of the periodic report, whereas a report concerning the detemination and evaluation of an usually high amount of scrap is more likely to be a special-purpose report.

Both information and analytical reports require that the data be presented to aid rather than hinder the recipient. Reports must be understandable. Good writing ability on the part of the report preparer can do a great deal toward report clarity. Appearance is also an important aspect of communication.

The managerial accountant is likely to be bombarded with requests for information, especially if unlimited data processing services are available. The tendency to fulfill all requests should be avoided. Furnishing data is so expensive that an extensive effort should be expended to determine if the benefits derived from the data exceed the cost. Information requests should be prefaced by the following steps.

1. *Attainment of goals.* Who is going to make the decision? When? How frequently? The decision maker needs to know how his or her decision contributes to the attainment of goals and how it affects other areas of the organization.

2. *Identification of critical factors affecting the decision.* Some of these are quantifiable; others are not. For those that can be quantified, it is necessary to know the best way of compiling the data. When, where, and by whom are the data needed? What form should the data take, and what will be the cost?

DATA SHEET

All major routine reports should have a data sheet supporting them. This is especially true of computer printouts. It is not at all unusual for a large corporation to generate between 3,000 and 5,000 computer reports a month. A data sheet is just one of the few controls over excessive reporting. Some of the items on the data sheet should be:

1. Report number
2. Job number (if computerized)
3. Requester
4. Recipients (number of copies)
5. Source of information
6. Employee(s) responsible for source of information
7. Tie-in with other reports (for example, payroll and labor distribution reports are generated from common base)
8. Explanation of columnar headings
9. Explanation of subtotals and totals
10. Date of report
11. Period covered by report
12. Date report is distributed

The data sheets should be filed (a loose-leaf binder will suffice), and unless a report is confidential, they should be accessible to all employees. These data sheets provide users, potential users, and outsiders (e.g., auditors) knowledge as to the contents of existing reports, what data are already available, and whom to consult if additional data are needed. Because generating new reports is very expensive, decision makers should scan existing reports to see if they contain the desired information before requesting new ones. Many times a small modification or addition can render an existing report suitable for another use. A conference with a system designer can be helpful in exploring new possibilities. For internal control purposes, access to programming and system files should be limited to authorized personnel only and should not be part of the data sheet.

CHARACTERISTICS OF A GOOD COMMUNICATION SYSTEM

Now let us look at some of the characteristics of a good information system and of good reporting, both oral and written.

Relevance

Reports must be relevant to the needs of the decision maker and must identify areas requiring his or her attention. This also means that data must be presented in the style of the decision maker. Fitted to the recipient and to the organization chart, reports should pinpoint responsibility and highlight problems. Some managers want lots of data; others desire very little. The type of information required varies with the level of the manager. Top executives are interested in summary reports (often on an exception basis) that are helpful in strategic planning and overall decision making. Reported data tend to be highly aggregated, focus on deviations from plans, and provide feedback on achievement of goals and objectives. Middle managers desire summary reports, too, but more frequently. Their reports include weekly or monthly revenue and expense reports. Lower-level managers need frequent detailed reports, even as frequently as by the hour. For example, a plant foreman may desire a daily scrap report by operation and product; middle management may want to know monthly scrap cost by product; and top management may only be interested in annual scrap cost.

Reports should be tailored to the expertise of managers. A personnel manager needs reports on manpower distribution, training, welfare, safety, and compensation. A purchasing manager is more interested in data for vendor selection, ordering, transporting, receiving, and inspection. Still, if we limit the contents and distribution of reports too severely, managers will operate in a vacuum, which decreases cooperation and the cross-fertilization of ideas. The point that defines enough but not too much data is elusive. Periodically all reports should be evaluated for usefulness, and distribution should be reviewed to eliminate unused and "nice to have" copies.

Timeliness

Generally, the more timely the data, the more relevant. Old data seldom have much bearing on current decisions; therefore reports must be received before decisions are made. To ensure timeliness, data must be captured as close to its source as possible. Another dimension of timeliness is the period of time covered by the report. An annual report can hardly be very helpful in correcting a problem that occurred in the first month of the year. Unfortunately too often a firm has established a regular reporting schedule—the report covers a fixed period of time and is due by a fixed date. While some routine and consistency is desirable, special problems or unusual circumstances should be reported immediately.

Perhaps the most frequent complaint levied against information departments is that decision makers cannot obtain the information they need, and when they do, it is obsolete. Report preparers need to be cognizant that their primary function is a service role and that they exist to meet the needs of decision makers.

Accuracy

Reports should be accurate within reason. Material errors in data cause material errors in decisions. Errors can be intentional or unintentional. The latter can be prevented by avoiding human intervention as much as possible, for example, by using a real-time computer system. Intentional "errors" result when employees are trying to circumvent a reporting system. Too much emphasis on accuracy causes employees to intentionally falsify records, especially if these reports are used for evaluation purposes. Communicators tend to withhold information if it is damaging to their positions. Subordinates frequently hold back bad news, or if withholding is not possible, the data are modified to make the news more palatable. Human beings tend to provide readers with what they think the readers want to hear.

The more levels of command a report passes through, the higher the chance of report distortion. By the time it reaches top management, it may be almost useless or even damaging. Holding back or distorting data can have several important repercussions. Obviously, an important one is that the recipients receive erroneous figures which result in one of two situations, both undesirable. Decisions are based on erroneous data or decision makers must rely on the informal grapevine to know the facts. Grapevines are notoriously inaccurate. Additionally, superiors are not always tuned in to grapevines, especially when the gossip affects their jurisdictions.

There is no one way of stopping distorted information. Periodic audits are sometimes helpful. Managers must be careful that their attitude and behavior do not influence subordinates to distort or withhold information.

A word of caution concerning accuracy—do not expect data to be error-proof or precise. Such perfection is obtainable only at high cost.

Completeness

Completeness in this context simply means that decision makers receive whatever data is crucial to their decisions. Reports that fail to fulfill the purposes of their recipients are inadequate. Report preparers should take the "you-attitude" whenever possible; that is, in order to determine how much information to provide, they should empathetically imagine themselves in the decision maker's place.

Individuals tend to make decisions based on relatively few variables, 5 or 6, perhaps. To furnish data for 100 variables would probably result in information overload. Still, structuring reports too tightly can cause considerable additional effort to be expended in tracking down supplementary information. Many times a broad-base information system can supply much of the information needed for a number of decision makers.

Conciseness

The criterion of conciseness avoids information overload and aids clarity and understanding. Reports should convey essential data only and not excessive detail. If reports are too concise, the principle of completeness is violated. As mentioned previously top management in particular requires concise data. One way of accomplishing this is to use report formats other than columnar listing. Visual aids can also be very effective. Modern computer drafting devices can print visual presentations with a minimum of effort. Examples include bar, pie, and line charts.

Bar Charts. Horizontal bars extend to the right from the y axis. Each bar represents some quantity, volume, degree, and so on. The bar chart in Exhibit 20-2 shows the number of students receiving various grades in an university

Exhibit 20-2.
Bar Chart of Students Grades

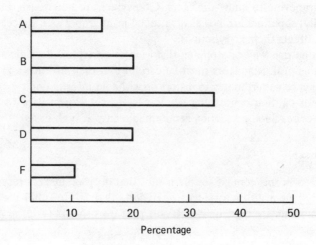

Percentage

Exhibit 20-3.
Pie Chart of Students Grades

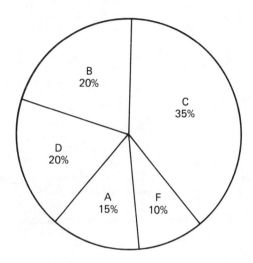

accounting course. A variation has the bars running vertically rather than horizontally.

Pie Chart.   The pie chart consists of a circle cut into wedges. The data in Exhibit 20-2 are redrafted as Exhibit 20-3.

Line or Curve Charts.   These are used to show the relationship of one kind of information to another. They are especially helpful in relating time to a variable. For example, if we wanted to know the trend in grades we could grasp it quicky from Exhibit 20-4.

Use of color may be helpful in highlighting data and stimulating interest. Too many and overlapping lines quickly create confusion. Adding lines for grades D and F to Exhibit 20-4 would cause the presentation to be unwieldly and less clear.

Flexibility

A too-rigid reporting system handicaps decision makers in adapting to changing conditions and needs. Many people, fearing the unknown, find it difficult to adjust to new report contents, formats, and styles. Involving persons affected by the change encourages cooperation.

Exhibit 20-4.
Line Chart of Students Grads

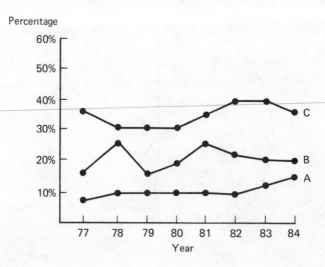

Cost-benefit

The benefits of a good communications system must exceed the cost. One way of meeting this criterion is to utilize or expand the current reporting system. How many times have you seen 10 different inputs for 10 different outputs, when a little modification of the system might have resulted in 1 input and 1 output sufficient to solve all 10 problems? The goal is to keep the number of reports at a minimum and avoid duplication of effort. To the extent possible, activities should be kept simple, standardized, and routine. Information should be stored in such a way that it is conveniently available to managers.

We conclude this section by making a comment about a phenomenon for which we coined the word "reportitis." Reportitis defines the state of confusion, panic, and anxiety employees suffer during established report preparation periods, such as the end of the month or year. Perhaps some of it is caused by an abhorrence of report preparation similar to the examination anxiety of university students. Some of it may be due to employees' inflating the importance of their jobs. Some may be caused by superiors' pressuring subordinates under deadlines.

One way to avoid these panics is to encourage employees to submit reports as early as possible because many people procrastinate in performing undesirable tasks as long as possible. Another alternative is to do a better job of matching the person with the job. An insecure individual who cannot cope with strict

Exhibit 20-5
Probabilities of Demand

	TOTAL TIMES	%
50 HOT DOGS	10	.20
1000 HOT DOGS	20	.40
1500 HOT DOGS	15	.30
2000 HOT DOGS	5	.10
	50	1.00%

deadlines is hardly suitable for a position as an analytic cost accountant, however technically competent.

ECONOMICS OF INFORMATION

Now we turn our attention to the economics of information. Perfect information is seldom possible in the real world; therefore managers must make decisions under conditions of uncertainty, which they do through the use of probabilities. Consider the example of a concession stand.

Suppose on Sundays we operate a concession stand at the local race track selling hot dogs. Suppose that all unsold hot dogs and buns cannot be returned to the vendors or frozen, so they are a complete loss, given, perhaps, to charity. The question is, How many hot dogs should be ordered to maximize profits?

From prior experience we find the following data given in Exhibit 20-5. Assume the meat and buns cost $.70 for each hot dog and the selling price per hot dog is $2.00. We can now compute a pay-off table, Exhibit 20-6.

The pay-off is computed by the following formula:

Items sold × selling price per unit = Total revenue
Items stocked × cost per unit = Total cost
Pay-off

Hence, pay-off is the gross profit at various levels of operation.

Looking at the pay-off table we might be tempted to conclude that we should try stocking and selling 2,000 hot dogs, the level where profit is highest. Remember that the probability of selling 2,000 hot dogs is only 10%. Therefore, we have to weight the pay-offs by the probability of their occurrence. This calculation, called expected value, is shown in Exhibit 20-7. The expected value table shows that we should purchase 1,500 items. Please do not think that on any particular Sunday our profit from selling hot dogs is necessarily $1,150. Actually if we sold 1,500 hot dogs, the profit is $1,950 as shown on the pay-off

Exhibit 20-6
Pay-off Table

	NUMBER OF ITEMS STOCKED			
SALES DEMAND	500	1000	1500	2000
500	$650[a]	$ 300[b]	$(50)	$(400)
1000	650	1300	950	600
1500	650	1300	1950	1600
2000	650	1300	1950	2600

a 500($2) — 500($.70) = $650
b 500($2) — 1000($.70) — $300

table, Exhibit 20-6. The $1,150 means that over the long run our profits will average $1,150 per Sunday if we stock 1,500 units. During the short run we can experience substantial deviations from this figure.

Of course probabilities change over time, so decison makers must update their decision models to reflect the new probabilities. One rather complicated technique for doing this, called Bayesian process, can be used to update the probabilities. Please consult a mathematics book for details.

There are other ways of utilizing the above data to make decisions. One of these is the maximax rule. Here we seek the maximum profit regardless of risk. Selling 2,000 unts is the most profitable. The profit is $2,600 per Exhibit 20-6. Stocking 2,000 items is also the most risky in the short run because if demand were only 500 units we would suffer a loss of $400 (Exhibit 20-6). The maximax rule is unconservative and focuses on the largest possible gain.

Another decision rule is the maximin rule. This rule maximizes the minimum profits of the various alternatves. We select the state with the largest minimum profit—the 500 unit level (Exhibit 20-6). Profit is a constant $650 regardless of demand. Note, however, that we suffer an opportunity loss if

Exhibit 20-7
Expected Value by Demand Levels

DEMAND					EXPECTED VALUE
500	.20($650)	+ .40($650)	+ .30($650)	+ .10($650)	$ 650
1000	.20($300)	+ .40($1300)	+ .30($1300)	+ .10($1300)	$1100
1500	.20(−$50)	+ .40($950)	+ .30($1950)	+ .10($1950)	$1150
2000	.20(−$400)	+ .40($600)	+ .30($1600)	+ .10($2600)	$ 900

For each level of demand we compute an expected value by summing the products of (1) the probabilities by (2) the pay-offs from Exhibit 20-6.

Exhibit 20-8
Regret Table

SALES DEMAND	NUMBER OF UNITS			
	500	1000	1500	2000
500	$ 0	$350	$700	$1050
1000	650	0	350	700
1500	1300	650	0	350
2000	1950[a]	1300[b]	650[c]	0[d]

a $2600 — $650, Exhibit 20-6
b $2600 — $1300, Exhibit 20-6
c $2600 — $1950, Exhibit 20-6
d $2600 — $2600, Exhibit 20-6

demand exceeds 500 hot dogs. We can compute the opportunity loss at each level of operation by means of a regret table.

Regret Table

Our regret table looks like Exhibit 20-8. In this example, we determine the minimum regret by reference to the pay-off table, Exhibit 20-6. We subtract each pay-off in the row from the highest pay-off in the row. Again, the idea behind this calculation is to determine what the opportunity loss is for each alternative. For example, if on any Sunday we ordered 1,500 units and could have sold 2,000 units, we have suffered an opportunity loss of $650.

Value of Perfect Information

Is there any way of improving our decision? If we could obtain perfect information, we could select the optimum order point. For example, if we knew that customers' demand is for 2,000 hot dogs, we could order ingredients for this number.

Mathematically the value of perfect information is the probability of each demand multiplied by the maximum profit (from the pay-off table) for that demand. In our illustration this is $1,495.

$$.20(\$650) + .40(\$1,300) + .30(\$1,950) + .10(\$2,600) = \$1,495$$

in other words if we had perfect information, we would make an average profit of $1,495 over the long run in lieu of $1,150. Hence, perfect information reduces risk.

We can compute the maximum dollar amount that we would be willing to pay for perfect information. Obviously, there is no way of knowing exactly how many attendees will demand hot dogs on any particular day but we can pay for information that would help us estimate the demand. For example, we might be willing to pay for data such as the capability of the race cars or the expertise of the drivers, and so on. We hope such data will give us some notion of the crowd to expect and consequently the number of hot dogs that will be demanded. The maximum we would pay for perfect information is $345.

Expected value of perfect information, computed above	$1495
Expected value of pay-off (1,500 units, Exhibit 20-7)	1150
	$345

Risk

An important element in any decision is the propensity for risk taking. Some people enjoy risk; others do not. Consider the following pay-off table and expected value for two potential investments.

Alternative 1	
$200 × .55	$110
($200) × .45	(90)
Expected value	$20
Alternative 2	
$1,000,000 × .60	$600,000
($1,000,000) × .40	(400,000)
Expected value	$200,000

Both investment opportunities result in positive expected values with the expected value for alternative 2 being substantially higher than alternative 1. Still, most of us would probably select alternative 1 because whereas most of us cannot afford or are not willing to risk losing $1,000,000, the loss of $200 may be tolerable.

SUMMARY

In this chapter our focus was on communication. A reporting system is a communication system with feedback serving as a major control element. The managerial accountant is responsible for providing financial information to users for decision making. The cost of reporting must be controlled as it can quickly become excessive. The more knowledge the managerial accountant has concerning the communication process and the decision making process, the easier and less costly it is to furnish users with the optimal amount of information.

Essential features of a good reporting system are:

1. Revelence
2. Timeliness
3. Accuracy
4. Completeness
5. Conciseness
6. Flexibility

Reports can never provide all the information needed for decision making. We live in a world of uncertainty; therefore, the decision maker must rely on a decision model. A frequently used one is the expected value of information model, but it needs to be adjusted to the decision maker's propensity for risk-taking. The value of perfect information lets us know how much cost to incur to obtain additional information.

Obviously, in this chapter, we have only touched upon the more important aspects of the theory of information economics and communication. This has been our goal throughout each chapter. A person could easily spend a lifetime studying managerial accounting and control. We hope we have stimulated your interest and given you the tools to search for decision models beyond the limited theory presented in this book.

Index